Noble Friendship

Other books by Khantipālo include

Tolerance: A Study from Buddhist Sources
Buddhism Explained
Pointing to Dhamma
Banner of the Arhants
Calm and Insight
Buddha, my Refuge
Jewels Within the Heart (Dhammapada)

KHANTIPALO
(LAURENCE MILLS)

NOBLE FRIENDSHIP

TRAVELS OF A BUDDHIST MONK

WINDHORSE PUBLICATIONS

Published by Windhorse Publications
11 Park Road
Birmingham
B13 8AB

Cover design Vincent Stokes

The cover shows the author in 1961, and stone dwellings clinging
to a hillside in Dunkar, Spiti Valley, Northern India; lower
photograph courtesy of the Royal Geographical Society, London

Printed by Biddles Ltd, Guildford, Surrey

British Library Cataloguing in Publication Data:
A catalogue record for this book is available from the British Library

ISBN 1 899579 46 X

Contents

ILLUSTRATION CREDITS

About the Author

The son of a shopkeeper and a school teacher, Khantipālo was born Laurence Mills in North London in 1932. During the Second World War his family was evacuated to Thetford in Norfolk, where he attended Thetford Grammar School. A high point in his school career was a year of Indian and Chinese history. Following a diploma course in horticulture, he was called up for two years of National Service in the deserts of the Suez Canal Zone. While in the army, he read his first book on Buddhism and immediately became a Buddhist.

Khantipālo then returned to the UK – and horticultural work – for a few years, but during a Buddhist retreat he decided to take ordination as a Buddhist monk (bhikkhu). His teacher for the novice ordination was Ven. Dr Saddhātissa Mahā Thera. Following ordination, Khantipālo spent three years in India. He then lived in Thailand for eleven years, studying in Bangkok with Ven. Phra Sāsana Sobhana and meditating in forest monasteries with Phra Acharn Mahā Boowa and others. In 1973 he accompanied a senior Thai monk – Phra Pariyattikavee – to Australia, where they established Wat Buddharangsee in Sydney. Wat Buddha Dhamma was founded in 1978 at Wisemans Ferry, where Khantipālo stayed on as a teacher for fourteen years. Towards the end of this time he became a student of Chogyal Namkhai Norbu, a famous Dzogchen master. Khantipālo disrobed and left Wat Buddha Dhamma in 1991.

Khantipālo is now married and is the co-founder of Bodhi Citta Buddhist Centre, a non-sectarian place of practice in northern Queensland, Australia.

To Sangharakshita,
a Noble Friend indeed,
I dedicate this small work.

Foreword

Kalimpong is a small, cosmopolitan town in the foothills of the Eastern Himalayas. It commands a fine view of Mount Kanchenjunga, the third highest mountain in the world, as well as of the passes leading into Tibet. I lived there for fourteen years, from 1950 to 1964. During that period I had many visitors, especially after the establishment of the Triyāna Vardhana Vihāra, or Monastery Where the Three Yānas Flourish, in 1956. Some of the visitors came from India itself, others from the Buddhist countries of South-east Asia, and some even from the West.

Among those who came from the West was Sāmanera Sujīva, a tall, angular young Englishman who had been ordained as a novice a year or more earlier in London. He did not come direct from London. He came from Bodh Gaya, where he had been staying at the Thai monastery, and he came accompanied by the Thai monk Vivekānanda and the two of them stayed with me at the Vihara for a few days. This was in 1960, towards the end of the hot season. Thereafter he spent altogether a year with me, either at the vihara, or on preaching tour in Central and Western India among the followers of the late Dr B.R. Ambedkar, many of whom had converted to Buddhism.

In this way I got to know him quite well and came to appreciate his sincerity, his desire to learn, and his willingness to be of service. This was especially the case during his two long stays with me in Kalimpong, the first from November 1961 to March 1962, after he had spent six months with my old friend Buddharakkhita in Bangalore, where he received the bhikkhu ordination and was given the name Khantipālo. His second stay took place from June 1962 until December 1962, it having been preceded by his three months of travel in Nepal.

I am delighted that my old friend and travelling companion has now written an account of the two years he spent in India all those years ago and that this has included an account of his time at the Triyāna Vardhana Vihāra and our work among the followers of Dr Ambedkar in Nagpur, Bombay, Poona, and Ahmedabad. The experience of reading *Noble Friendship*, and seeing our life together through his eyes, has been a fascinating one, especially as he remembers scenes and incidents I have since forgotten. I am particularly pleased that he has written about our training course for New Buddhists in Poona, about our meetings with Yogi Chen, and about the bodhi tree sapling we planted in the grounds of the Triyāna Vardhana Vihāra.

Thirty years later that sapling is now a flourishing tree. Our friendship, too, has continued to grow, even though it has been kept alive mainly through correspondence, and I rejoice that it has eventually born fruit in the form of Khantipālo's timely and very welcome book. May it be a source of inspiration and encouragement to all who cherish the ideal of friendship!

Urgyen Sangharakshita

Madhyamaloka
Birmingham
14 January 2002

PREFACE

Although for a long time I had been contemplating a record of my life, an interesting and unusual one certainly, and had made ten years ago a series of tapes with my memories of it and these had even been transcribed as a sort of Notes on a Life, yet nothing more had happened, partly due to lack of time, partly to other projects seeming more important.

This book owes its beginnings to Dharmachari Buddhadasa who at present lives in Melbourne. During a telephone conversation he suggested to me that my life in India with Sangharakshita would make very interesting reading. A seed had been sown by him and it seemed that the factors for its growth into a beautiful tree were all propitious. As I prefer quiet when writing and as the mornings here before six o'clock have only the small noises of tropical insects together with local 'mountain sound', I thought that these small hours would be best. Their quietness and the seeming approval of the local guardians has made the writing – mine is all in longhand – both possible and enjoyable. I have not tried to include in this book all my experience of India but rather to prune the material and focus attention upon the most significant of my teachers whom I met there, and for whom I felt the deepest connection, Sangharakshita. The title of this book and its dedication, together with all the work on it, is an offering to him for his kindness and noble friendship to a young and uncertain monk all those years ago.

Khantipālo (Laurence Mills)

Bodhi Citta Buddhist Centre
Cairns, Queensland
Australia

Chapter One

LONDON TO INDIA

Awakened Heart, till it is found
For Refuge to Three Jewels I go.
Awakening may I attain
For benefit of beings all.

Bodhicitta verse from the Tibetan

On a cold, wet, and windy day in March 1960 the plane took off from Heathrow. Buffeted by violent air and rain, it soared upwards towards the lowering dark grey clouds. London receded, then vanished, and soon through the window only a formless grey could be seen, with runnels of rainwater obscuring even this view. Slowly, slowly the light grew stronger, the dense oppressive clouds lightened, and the rain lessened as the Vickers Viscount, with its load of perhaps forty human lives, struggled upwards. Suddenly the aircraft was lit by the dazzling light of the sun, which is always shining in splendour, even when blanketed by heavy cloud. As we gained increasing height my old life fell away.... It was a moment like a rebirth, a reincarnation....

Among the passengers I was the only one wearing the robes of a Buddhist monk. I had been wearing them for about a year, an exotic sight in London in the late 1950s. (It was also a dress I had discovered to be quite unsuited to my native British climate – even when boosted with various woolly layers underneath.) The whole story of how I came to be part of the budding monastic Buddhist community would be the subject for a longer book than this, but one early pointer I recall is that I was uninterested in almost every subject at the various schools I attended – except for one year of Indian and Chinese history taught by the excellent Mr Charles Taylor at Thetford Grammar School. This subject, however, awakened my mind – perhaps touching, who knows, some buried strata from long-gone lives.

When school had passed and my chosen education in horticulture was also finished, the Army, not knowing quite what to do with me, sent me off, in their compassion, to further studies in the Suez Canal Zone. I was doing my compulsory national service and I did not fit very comfortably into the army's categories. I possessed the educational qualifications which should have fitted me for an officer's insignia, but I had written on my call-up papers (in the 'any other remarks' section) 'I shall not kill a human being.' This conviction sprang not so much from any religious background, for I was barely Christian and had not yet read a Buddhist book, still less come into contact with a living Buddhist, but rather from an idealistic socialism and a strong aversion to any sort of violence.

But by the time I emerged from National Service in September 1956, I was a Buddhist. Reading Christmas Humphreys' book *Buddhism* was the immediate cause of this, but fundamental to my search for 'something' was keen dissatisfaction with the direction my life was taking – and my yearning to see some meaning in it. My experience of the sufferings of the native peoples living in the Zone had also moved me deeply, and a failed love affair provided the personal suffering for me to seek further. This potent combination made me a Buddhist.

I read Humphreys' book (about 240 pages) in one day of an exceedingly idle army life, and even though it is, as I now know, wrong in many places, there was enough of the medicine of Dharma in it – the teaching of the Buddha – to right my mind. I felt as though I had 'come home', discovered what made sense of my life, and returned to something very familiar, a teaching or law that I had never really left. Until that moment though, in the 'education centre' of two tents strung together surrounded by the sands of Suez, I had not found the formulation of it. Thanks to Christmas Humphreys and his Penguin Books publisher I had found the missing piece of the puzzle and all the other pieces fell into place.

Looking back to that momentous occasion with the benefit of hindsight, I suppose I became a Buddhist for many reasons, some of which were more important then, while my appreciation of others has deepened over time. These reasons, though rooted in the causes mentioned above, are mostly concerned with the attractions of the Dharma.

First, there was my attraction to the historical Buddha as a person, arising mostly from the Pāli Canon, especially his emphasis on non-violence and cultivating compassion. I found the Path, the Noble Eightfold Path, a practical, straightforward, and down-to-earth map for living life – though one that involved searching investigation in order to uncover its deepest aspects.

Also I at last had a satisfying explanation for the inequalities of human beings, indeed all beings. Beings, I discovered, were 'owners of their karma, heirs to their karma, born of their karma, related to their karma, abide supported by their karma; whatever karma they will do, good or evil, of that they will be the heirs.'[1]

I know I welcomed the absence of a creator God. After seeing the poverty of the Suez Canal Zone I had had a little awakening. These poor people prayed to an omnipotent God – the Christian one or the Muslim – but mostly all they 'possessed' was disease, a short life, and much suffering, while the British sold off their churches as bingo halls and possessed, in a worldly sense, a great deal. Was God, I wondered, sleeping or dead, or just a capricious tyrant? The Buddha's message, however, needs no such figure: all arises and passes away due to causes and conditions; among them, of course, karma.

Buddhism emphasized the practice of meditation. Even though this was far down the list of my initial reasons for embracing the Dharma – as I had no experience of it – yet somehow I saw that this practice would lead me to understand myself and the world more deeply.

Last but not least was the fact that the Dharma was logical – but went also beyond logic. It was refreshing to discover a profound teaching which, amazingly, was not couched in obscure language. This clarity of expression promised insights in the realm beyond words.

It is not surprising, therefore, that my first great choice after the army relinquished its hold on me was to join the Buddhist Society in London. In fact I joined on my way from the demobilization camp in south London, still clad in regulation uniform, to my home in the north. Perhaps I was their only member who joined in khaki after clomping up the stairs to their abode in Gordon Square in my army boots?

The Buddhist Society, of which Christmas Humphreys was the founding president, was at that time the only organized manifestation of the Buddha's teachings in London,[2] indeed the only spark of the Dharma in the whole of the country. The Buddhist Society, though it was founded as long ago as 1924, had remained quite a small body. From our perspective, beginning a new century, to look back a mere fifty years and realize that there was then an almost total lack of study and practice of the Dharma, reveals the Dharma's miraculous growth in the present time. That is not to say, of course, that the mere increase in Buddhist groups, or even of temples and centres, signifies a greater acceptance of the Dharma's message – that can come about only by profoundly understanding the process of Going for Refuge, a subject which cannot be elaborated on here.[3] The expansion of centres, teachers, and books on Buddhism has been so great that it is perhaps necessary to draw a sketchy picture of what I found fifty years ago.

The Buddhist Society ran classes on the basics of Buddhism, meditation, and, for those thought to be highly advanced, classes on Zen. And so my practice of Buddhism started. I attended one of these classes on a weekday evening, one which focused upon meditation practice. Though I persisted with my attendance, I sensed that the leader of this class, a sweet-tempered lady by the name of Carlo Robbins, often did not know the answers to the vital questions that were asked.

I also attended the occasional public lectures at the Society by Dr Edward Conze. Upon entering the lecture hall one would see him sitting in his chair waiting to begin the lecture. He did not chat to people and, as the look on his face was rather severe, some in his audience may have been intimidated. I saw a rather small man with a sharp, strong-featured face and piercing eyes. Even the look of him told me that he was not a person who would tolerate fools gladly. When he spoke his enunciation was precise but with a very slight German tinge. Though sometimes he used notes, a lot of what he said appeared to be extemporary. Punctuating his learned discourse would be a few humorous remarks of a dry and acid variety which I appreciated.

However, I quickly recognized that this humour had made him a good many enemies – for he was quite merciless when it came to criticizing the wrong views of others and generally demonstrating the inadequacies of their grasp of the Dharma. His criticism was not mere spleen but represented an authoritative statement, couched often in bitingly humorous language. He was then one of the very few Buddhists in Britain who knew what he was talking about, for he had read the texts: Pāli, Sanskrit, and Tibetan (but not Chinese), and his interests ranged far beyond sectarian boundaries. Even then, he had translated the vast corpus of Perfection of Wisdom sūtras which I read, fascinated but puzzled, in typescript form. He had also endeavoured to practise meditation during the early part of the Second World War, but lacking teachers had had to feel his own way forward. There was no doubt that he had *seen* something, for his answers to questions were spontaneous and enjoyably unexpected. I entertained feelings of profound respect for him, tinged with a certain apprehension of his spontaneity. I guess that others in the Buddhist Society, notably Christmas Humphreys, found him an uncomfortable companion simply because he had mastered his subject, while they spoke as amateurs.

At the end of a lecture he would glance at the audience, sometimes even glare, as if to dare anyone to ask a question. If one was bold enough to question him – and I do not remember that I was – the question had best be clear and well phrased, for the results of a muddled question would not be pleasant for the enquirer. It seems he had some expectation that enquiries should either be made on a level of Dharma knowledge comparable to his own or not at all. Unsurprisingly, there were few questions! He could fry anyone who tried smuggling non-Buddhist ideas (such as God or the Great Self) into the Dharma. He himself, though, would occasionally slip into his discourse references to astrology, in which he believed strongly, and was indeed quite expert. It was worth going a long way to hear him speak.

But few people involved at that time had real knowledge of what they were trying to practise. One of the principal events of the Buddhist year being Wesak or Awakening Day, celebrating the Buddha's enlightenment at Bodh Gaya, the Buddhist Society had a public meeting in Caxton Hall in central London. Various dignitaries spoke – there was not much chanting or other traditional practices in those days – and one year I recollect an older member of the Society recited the *Heart of Perfect Wisdom Sūtra* in Dr Conze's translation, though retaining the Sanskrit for the mantra at the end. Even though I knew very little about Pāli and Sanskrit then, I did know that *'gate'* in that mantra was pronounced as two syllables – *'ga-te'* – and to hear it spoken as though homophonous with the English 'gate' aroused in me a mixture of amusement at the mistake and sympathy for the speaker's gaffe.

Besides these regular and occasional events there was the Summer School run by the Buddhist Society, which I attended two or three times. Again, in those days not much emphasis was put on practice, much more upon lectures; so much so that one ended the Summer School with what I described to friends as 'mental indigestion'. Generally the limitations which I have noted here sprang from a lack of qualified teachers: there just were not experienced and committed Buddhists available.

The next Buddhist centre to be born in London was the London Buddhist Vihara in Knightsbridge. In those days in Britain, not much happened in the small Buddhist world. No famous teachers arrived, no new retreat centres opened. When I heard therefore that three Sinhalese Buddhist monks had arrived and would be teaching the Dharma in English, my curiosity was aroused. Until then I had only seen photographs of monks, notably Ven. U Thittila in Humphreys' book. How would the real thing look and act? I went to find out.

My first pilgrimage to their abode was quite dramatic. I cycled from my home in Enfield Wash to Knightsbridge, perhaps twelve or fifteen miles each way, and at Manor House, as it was getting dark, my wheels became trapped in the tramlines and a large trolleybus immediately behind me nearly cut off my life. Apart from the shock at falling off the bike, however, I was not injured and pursued my vigorous way to Knightsbridge. There the monks were somewhat amused at the cyclist who asked if his bike could be carried up their steps and stored in their hallway. As for the Dharma they spoke, it being undoubtedly less dramatic than the journey to see them had been, I remember not a word. However, I do recall their kindness and concern for a cyclist who had come so far to see them and, though their Dharma left little impression, I was pleased to have seen them. Perhaps again, it stirred memories of some other time? It was at this vihara that, eventually, the monk who was to be my teacher for novice ordination came to reside, Ven. Dr H. Saddhātissa Mahāthera. But I shall say more about that ordination in Chapter Six.

The third centre for Buddhism to be set up was the vihara established by the English Sangha Trust at Alexandra Road in the lower parts of Hampstead. I went to stay there halfway through my student gardenership at the Royal Botanic Gardens, Kew. This involved some more long cycle rides, roughly ten miles to Kew and another ten back, every day. Why did I go there? I suppose it was because the Buddhist Society offered no community and little emphasis on practice, and the London Buddhist Vihara I found too culturally different, catering as it did mostly for Buddhists from what was called Ceylon in those days. That left me only the Hampstead Vihara. My novice ordination took place about a year after I arrived there. From then on I lived in that rackety old house – the main line into and out of Euston ran at the end of the small back garden and the house jumped and rattled as expresses and local trains, many of them still steam, roared past.

The establishment of this vihara was inspired by an English monk who trained briefly in Thailand and then, much too soon as it turned out, returned to Britain to teach. His ordination name was Kapila-vaddho, though officially he was still William Purfurst. A complex character, the positive side of which – his energy and forcefully-presented Dharma talks – inspired many people to practise the Dharma. Some admired him for his austerities (cotton robes and bare feet in an English winter) though personally I found such extremes repelled me. On the negative side there was more than a touch of the showman about him and there was no doubt that he *wanted* disciples to ordain so that he could be their teacher. His career as a monk ended in a grand display of delusion, in fact of megalomania, when he announced at a large gathering that he had attained to Arhantship and would disrobe and disappear. Notwithstanding this, I admired his explanations of Dharma and the evident devotion of at least half of him to the monastic life in a sangha. He inspired the formation of the English Sangha Trust, while at least three other men were sufficiently impressed by him to become monks, though of these disciples only Paññāvaddho remains, still a respected monk in north-east Thailand.

After Kapilavaddho's 'disappearance' this budding sangha was guided by Paññāvaddho, and it was with him that I discussed my own leaving home. I shall always be grateful for the gentleness and under-standing he showed me while I was a novice for a year under his guidance. I was also grateful to the English Sangha Trust for their support of me for that year. They generously provided all the four necessities of a monk – that is, robes, food (two meals a day), shelter, and medicines. As a novice monk I paid for nothing and only carried money for such things as bus and train tickets. I contributed nothing materially nor did I teach the Dharma, so their generosity was greatly appreciated for the amount of time it gave me for study and practice. While such generosity towards monks is usually found in Asian Buddhist countries it was quite another thing for the small and strug-gling Sangha Trust in London.

After a year in the Hampstead house, a year left to my own studies and meditations, I gradually formed the wish to see the land where the Dharma first arose, and perhaps find some guidance from teachers there. The English Sangha Trust rose generously to assist me once again and kindly gave me a one-way ticket to Calcutta, as well as £25 – quite a lot of money in those days, some of which remained after three years in India. And so I found myself on that Vickers Viscount – headed for India.

Chapter Two

First Impressions of India

If for practice one finds a friend,
Prudent, well-behaved and wise,
Mindful, joyful, live with him
All troubles overcoming.

Dhammapada 328

Emerging from the plane onto the tarmac at Dum-Dum Airport much resembled jumping into a bowl of warm soup, the Calcutta air was so humid. We wended our way through some shabby huts and sheds, mostly grey in colour, and so passed desultorily through Indian customs and immigration. Leaving the last airport building I got a taxi to the distant Maha Bodhi Society's headquarters in College Square. That journey, a slow one through dense masses of humanity, wandering cattle, crazily packed buses, and clanging trams, showed me what a different world I had come into with people, people, people, all swimming in the Calcutta soup.

I had arranged to stay with the Thai monks at their new temple in Bodh Gaya, but first I went to Benares and met my namesake – both of us novices and both named Jīvaka. I had corresponded with him from Britain and told him when I would arrive. He met me on Benares (Varanasi) station and together we went to Sarnath where he was staying. He was Irish and a medical doctor who had become interested in the fantasies woven by Lobsang Rampa. Eventually he moved to India and obtained novice ordination from the Sinhalese monks at Sarnath. Though it was interesting to meet another Westerner in Buddhist robes, I found his company difficult. He was unable to discuss any matter for more than five minutes without a display of

negative criticism. Everybody and everything came in for his disap-
probation. I was also curious about the scar tissue that could so clearly
be seen upon his chest, but as I did not become very close to him during
our meetings I refrained from asking him about it. I sensed that here
was a deeply troubled man whom no words would pacify. How
troubled he was became clearer a little later on.

After a brief stay in Sarnath I took a train back to Gaya, which I had
passed on the outward journey, and there made my way to the place
of the Great Awakening. While I was there one expedition I made was
to meet the group of monks studying at Nava Nālandā Mahā Vihāra –
the Great Monastery of New Nālandā. This was a Buddhist-oriented
research institute for postgraduate students erected by the Indian
government near to the ruins of the famous Buddhist university of
Nālandā.[4] The monks who studied there came from many countries to
obtain Western-style degrees in Pāli Buddhism. One of them, a Thai
named Vivekānanda, was very friendly and we talked a great deal
about all manner of Buddhist matters. He had travelled quite widely
in India and met most of the monk-teachers then active there. One
teacher he told me about intrigued me. He said that outside Kalimpong
in the Himalayan foothills lived an English monk called Sangharakshita. He told me that Sangharakshita was learned; he used the
word *pandita* (pundit), signifying in Thai a person who has not only
studied but also acts and speaks accordingly. Very few Buddhists in
India could be so described in those days. Moreover, Vivekānanda
continued approvingly, he knows Mahāyāna Buddhism.[5] A word of
explanation here. Most Thai monks, having been brought up on a diet
of Theravāda Buddhism, the Pāli commentaries of which declare that
it is the true and undistorted teachings of Śākyamuni Buddha himself,
regarded Mahāyāna at best as a later overgrowth of Dharma but more
likely a total distortion of it. Usually they had read no Mahāyāna
scriptures (*sūtra*) or treatises (*śāstra*), so their condemnation was both
dogmatic and ignorant. On my part, though I had occasionally attended Dr Conze's lectures in which he referred a little to Mahāyāna,
I had no contact with the living tradition. During my time at the
Hampstead Vihara where I had read Buddhist books indiscriminately,
a few Mahāyāna works – such as were then available – were devoured.
Now I might have the chance to meet a living master of both Buddhist
traditions!

Vivekānanda also told me of his visit to Sangharakshita's mountain
abode, a small monastery in the Himalayan foothills where it was quiet

and suited to both study and practice. 'Very tranquil' was his description. Most Thai monks in India at that time were only there to get
Western-style degrees and had no connection with Indian Buddhism,
such as it was then. Vivekānanda was different – illustrated by the fact
that he appreciated the efforts made by Sangharakshita to re-establish
the Dharma in the land of its birth, especially by his annual journeys
to teach in western India. All this sounded to me more and more
attractive, almost too good to be true: a learned monk who knew both
Theravāda and Mahāyāna, who could explain the Dharma in my own
language, and lived in a secluded mountain retreat, venturing down
to the Indian plains every year to teach.... The more he told me of this
teacher, the more I wished to meet him.

At that time the hot season was, it seemed, getting hotter by the hour
and to escape from its rigours (temperatures of over 38°c were quite
common in the afternoons) a group of monks planned to go to the
wetter and cooler state of Assam for a month or so during their
vacation time. Vivekānanda was to be among them, while an Assamese
Thai monk, Sīlabongsha, would be their leader, and others in the party
would be another Thai and a Burmese. I was invited to join this
international group and was all the keener as Vivekānanda remarked:
'After our Assamese visit we might well go to Kalimpong and there
meet Sangharakshita.'

There then followed the long train journey – in three different trains
spread over as many days – from the Buddhist heartland of Bihar
eastwards to distant Assam. Then there were the joyful receptions
accorded to Sīlabongsha by his friends, relatives, and pupils in the
many Thai villages that we visited. The hospitality and generosity
shown to us by all the Thai villagers opened my eyes to traditional
dāna, generous giving, an aspect of Buddhist practice which up to that
time I had hardly experienced. In our turn, the party of visitors also
practised the generosity of teaching Dharma to our kind hosts. I may
even have stuttered a few words myself, though my understanding of
Dharma could best be described as 'patchy', where it existed at all.

On our return towards the Indian plains, we interrupted our journey. Alighting from our train one wet night we went to visit Tibetan
monk refugees housed by the Indian government in Buxaduar, a camp
built by the British as a prison for Indian nationalists in the foothills
near the Bhutanese border. They were there, of course, because the
Chinese occupation of their country begun in 1950 had turned very
nasty: the persecution of Tibetan Buddhists, notably their teachers and

practitioners, had begun in 1959, together with the razing of monasteries and hermitages, the seizure and destruction of artistic treasures, and sinicization of the unwilling Tibetan population to the point of genocide. Monks, nuns, and lay practitioners – those who were fortunate – fled to India, Sikkim, and Nepal, to try to reconstruct their shattered communities and their interrupted practices. Buxaduar, near the Bhutanese border, was just one of the receiving camps for these refugees, a camp specially set aside for the accommodation of lamas[6] and ordinary monks.

Our small party reached this camp by some sort of Indian official lorry on the day before the birthday of His Holiness the Dalai Lama was celebrated. He was not present, being perhaps then engaged in establishing the place for a Tibetan government-in-exile at the opposite end of India. It was my first introduction to Tibetan monastics, hundreds of maroon-robed figures, with impressive chanting and rituals, together with an irrepressible energy and joy, amazing to experience in refugees who had suffered so much. After meeting many lamas and sitting through long ceremonies of offerings we were invited to partake of especially delicious Tibetan breads and buttered tea. I was very touched by this generosity, made all the more poignant by the poverty of this monastic community. Our orange-robed party of monks was welcomed with much warmth and happiness by Tibetans who in many cases had only the reddish robes in which they had escaped and who at that time depended on the rice and lentils supplied by the Indian government. For them, we would have been their first visible evidence that other Buddhists existed, that traditions of Dharma still flourished in distant lands in contrast to the Dharma's condition in their own. We were given *khata* – white offering scarves – and shown the Dalai Lama's empty throne with his picture, where we reverently deposited them. Only one small cloud marred the brilliance of this occasion: by the time that pujas and offerings had been accomplished, it was already afternoon, the time when strict Theravāda monks no longer partook of food. Our kind Tibetan hosts pressed us to have some of the bread and tea, but my colleagues did not feel that they could accept this food as noontime had passed. However, I decided, somewhat to their displeasure, that it was far from courteous to refuse this generosity. This is how I know that the bread was so especially delicious! The Tibetan buttered tea was also good and I acquired a liking for it at that time.

We spent only one night at Buxaduar before boarding another west-bound express out of Assam. At Siliguri, the junction for Darjeeling in the narrow neck of India north of what in those days was East Pakistan, our party split up, with Vivekānanda and myself catching the 'toy train', while the others returned to Nālandā.

The 'toy train' which ran between Siliguri and Darjeeling was a major engineering triumph, climbing from plains not much above sea-level to 7,000 feet. Its 18-inch gauge track wound round the tightest bends, frequently crossing the road with no gates or other signals, zig-zagged up cliffs and in places looped over itself. It was not the fastest way to get to Darjeeling, for it took five hours while a jeep might cut that time almost in half; but it was enjoyable. The wheezing little high-pressure steam locomotives, made in Scotland in the 1890s, valiantly pulled three or four short coaches up the very steep grades. We caught one of these trains in the early morning, which chugged across the plain to the foothills at a modest 25 m.p.h., and then got into the serious business of tackling the hills. When the road crossed the rails – dozens of times in the course of the journey – the engine would shriek once or twice, a signal we hoped would be heard by the intrepid Nepali jeep and truck drivers. At around 4,000 feet, signs of Buddhism appeared in the shape of stupas and prayer flags. My heart, oppressed by the plains, lightened upon seeing even this slender evidence of the Dharma. The highest point on the line was Ghoom, a town often swirling in mist, after which the train descended about a thousand feet to Darjeeling.

There we caught a small bus to Kalimpong, descending most of those thousands of feet into the Tista valley, and then climbed up a few thousands to Kalimpong, a warmer place than Darjeeling in winter. By the time we arrived in Kalimpong it was already afternoon and we searched for a taxi to take us out to Sangharakshita's vihara. Though the distance could be walked easily, unless one was sure of the way the small hill roads could be confusing.

We arrived with our small luggage, alms bowls, and a few robes, and set off down the path from the road towards the small bungalow below us. As we turned the corner onto its veranda we saw a monk in dark orange robes standing there, smiling as we approached. I noticed that he had a certain poise, a certain authority, combined with obvious pleasure at our arrival. He appeared to be about ten years older than I was, shorter in stature and slender in build. His movements were graceful and his greeting of Vivekānanda warm-hearted. While these two monks exchanged respectful bows with hands together at the heart, as a newly-ordained novice it was my duty to pay respect to Sangharakshita more formally, which I did with three prostrations 'with the five members' (forehead, two hands, two knees) on the ground. While I went through this traditional greeting, Sangharakshita blessed me with usual Pāli words, '*Sukhī hontu* – May you be happy!' I presented him with a *khata* – a Tibetan offering scarf – and he then invited us to sit with him on the veranda while he enquired how we were and how our journey had been.[7] This is what the Pāli suttas call 'courteous and amiable talk', and while this was going on Sangharakshita asked his cook to serve us with tea. We talked with him for a long time on the state of Buddhism in Britain and what was happening in the world of the Dharma generally. I liked his easy and relaxed manner for, though obviously a teacher, he did not stand upon ceremony.

I liked, too, the place in which he lived, a small bungalow set on an immense, mostly terraced, hillside overlooking a deep valley and facing another huge hill and further rolling ridges. It is difficult to call these foothills 'mountains' because occasionally from Kalimpong a glimpse of the real thing, towering rock, snow and all, could be had, yet to speak of 'hills' of five or more thousand feet seems inappropriate. As it was situated high on one of these hillsides, the view from its windows was truly splendid, in fact its view seemed to me to symbolize the panoramic vision of the Dharma implied by its name. Sangharakshita had asked Chattrul Rimpoche if he would be able to establish a monastery and had been told that he would soon do so. Moreover, Rimpoche confirmed, it should be called Triyāna Vardhana Vihāra: the 'Abode Where the Three Vehicles Flourish'.

Until then, as a novice monk, I had lived only in places where one vehicle was esteemed. For example, the teachings at Alexandra Road were drawn mainly from the Theravāda body of texts in the Pāli language, and certainly no alternatives to this were known in the Thai Temple at Bodh Gaya, which will be described below. This means that the teachers in those places adhered to one tradition or vehicle of Dharma teachings and more or less ignored the others. Kapilavaddho in London had drawn his teachings exclusively from the Pāli tradition, presenting it with a Thai flavour, while Paññāvaddho was more liberal and did explore other traditions to some extent. Sangharakshita, by contrast, included all Buddhist vehicles in his study, practice, and teaching, for he had studied deeply the Theravāda (representing the

so-called small vehicle, Hīnayāna), investigated the subtleties of the
Mahāyāna (great vehicle) – though the range of translations available
in those days was very limited – and practised the Adamantine Vehicle,
the Vajrayāna, with the help of Tibetan teachers. 'Triyāna Vardhana'
therefore expressed a devotion to and practice of all currents of the
Buddhist tradition. As I thought about this, I perceived that close
adherence to one tradition would be more comfortable and less chal-
lenging, while to undertake study and practice of all three would
require courage and involve a renunciation of all sectarian attitudes,
obviously something which Sangharakshita rejoiced in.

One conversation that I had with Sangharakshita concerned Jīvaka,
the Irish novice monk. I was curious about this unhappy person and
asked Sangharakshita if he knew anything about him. He told me that
Jīvaka had been advised, through correspondence with that fake
Tibetan lama, Lobsang Rampa, to go to India and find a Buddhist
teacher there. The monks from Ceylon who lived at Sarnath were quite
happy to ordain him, but when Jīvaka stayed for a time with Sangharakshita the latter questioned him about his past life. Jīvaka by then
was seeking to become a fully ordained monk, but it is not customary
to give such ordination to people unknown to the monks, so it fell to
Sangharakshita to make enquiries. Jīvaka told him that he had been
born as a girl but as she grew up she experienced strong desires to be
a man. Qualifying as one of the first woman doctors in Ireland, she
became aware of the possibility of a sex-change operation and later
submitted herself to extensive and frequent surgery to change herself
into a man. In fact she was one of the first to undergo this tremendous
change of body. The manhood that she achieved was not very convincing. I had already seen the scars left by the removal of breasts, while
her periods could only be suppressed and her voice deepened by
regular doses of medicine. Though a man in some outward appearance, it was still the body of a woman that Jīvaka had, and consequently, Sangharakshita explained to me, she or he could not be
ordained as a monk – who must have the body of a complete man. I
reflected that Jīvaka must indeed have a great burden of suffering: he
had changed his body but not his mind. He had gone to extraordinary
lengths to rid himself of the marks of a woman while the mind, which
cannot be changed so easily, was still filled with conflicts, as had been
evident during my meetings with him.

While Vivekānanda and I stayed a few days at his vihara, Sangharakshita encouraged me – though I felt that my knowledge was

insufficient – to write some articles on Dharma for publication in the *Maha Bodhi Journal*, the premier English-language Buddhist journal in India at that time. He had been the editor of this monthly magazine for some years and naturally endeavoured to find suitable material to fill its pages. The fact that I contributed a number of articles to the *Maha Bodhi* was certainly due to him, the first of them appearing in the November 1960 issue with the title 'Some Light Upon Tibetan Buddhism', by Sāmanera Sujīva, one of my two novice names. When I read now what I wrote so long ago it is astonishing that there are so few errors. The substance of the article surely was derived from what I had learned in conversation with Sangharakshita, while I am sure that he suggested corrections for the finished draft. He was dedicated to the reawakening of the Buddha-Dharma in India and keen to motivate others in this immense task. His own life then involved a great deal of Dharma writing, some of it for the *Maha Bodhi*, so when he came upon a potential writer, as I was then, he encouraged me to make use of this talent. Some of my other articles will be mentioned in the following pages.

Our stay with Sangharakshita, of only a few days, gave me time to produce this article, to talk extensively with him on a wide variety of Buddhist topics, and to admire his knowledge, wisdom, and generosity. Though Vivekānanda and I had soon to depart, he to Nālandā and completion of his studies, I to the Thai temple at Bodh Gaya, I for one looked forward to returning to the Abode Where the Three Vehicles Flourish. I found much there which was admirable, while there was little that did not satisfy me. My dissatisfaction, such as it was, was illustrated by Sangharakshita's informal way of communicating the Dharma; I would have welcomed a programme of study classes, but such things were trifles. I reflected that nowhere in saṁsāra will everything be perfect – all one's desires will never be met in any one situation. Sangharakshita invited me to stay longer with him, though he warned me that the monsoon season in Kalimpong looked very different from the fair skies, sun, and moderate temperatures that we had enjoyed during our visit. In all, I regretted leaving Sangharakshita, but I had promised the abbot of Wat Thai at Bodh Gaya that I would stay there for the coming Rains Retreat.

Chapter Three

MY FIRST RAINS RETREAT AND BODH GAYA

Seated serene at the sacred Bodhi's root,
Over-mastered Māra and his armoured host,
Attained to Sambodhi with wisdom that is infinite,
Highest in the universe, that Buddha I revere.

A translation of traditional Sri Lanka Pāli verses

After returning to the plains from Assam and Kalimpong, I stayed for the first of my three Indian Rains in Wat Thai. 'Rains', with a capital initial, indicates the three months when Buddhist monks and nuns must stay in one residence and may not travel except for certain pressing reasons. It coincides, more or less, with the monsoon season in India, Sri Lanka, and the South-east Asian countries.

The Thai temple at Bodh Gaya, or Wat Thai as it was usually known, was still in the process of construction while I was there. The Indian government had donated to the Buddhists of Thailand a parcel of land. The Thai government prepared the architectural plans in Bangkok in Thai style and contracted with a brahmin from Gaya, a Mr Bhattacārya, to construct the complex. There were to be two wings, in one of which monks would stay, in the other nuns and lay-people on pilgrimage. Only these two wings had been constructed at the time of my sojourn there. The main temple, the body – so to speak – of this complex, had not been started, nor was it completed for some years after I left. Five Thai monks, including an abbot, were in residence. Each had a room, and there was a spare one which they gave to me – with its own shower and toilet, ceiling fan, and simple furniture.[8] A Thai layman looked after the monks, accompanying them on journeys and cooking their meals every day. As the architecture was Thai, so was the food, with supplies of such things as dried fish and fish sauce coming regularly from Thailand. These Thai monks, though they were in India, showed little adaptation to their new surroundings, such as by becoming vegetarian. Sangharakshita was strictly vegetarian – and so was I when not in residence at Wat Thai.

This place was in fact a little bit of Thailand, and what went on beyond its high fences was of little concern to those monks. They thought of Thai people visiting: certainly never of making much contact with the local Bihari villagers. The highly divergent standards of living would have been embarrassing in any case. Thai monks were comfortably provided for, while in the space of the room that each one occupied a whole family would live in nearby villages. Those people existed on meagre rice and chillies – and if they were lucky some pulses and greens – while the meals at Wat Thai were rich by comparison. *Piṇḍapāta* – going out early morning with one's alms bowl, a practice that all the Thai monks had done in their own country – was unthinkable at Bodh Gaya. They might get food but would they be able to eat it? I tried *piṇḍapāta* one day and certainly obtained some food, but they could not eat it when I offered to share it. I did not repeat this experiment as I could see that it would cause too much disharmony in the small world of Wat Thai. Besides, I felt a bit uncomfortable living in such 'luxury', then to go out to beg alms from those who scrabbled a bare existence from the exhausted Bihari soil.

This seems to be the appropriate place to write a few words on Buddhist and Hindu attitudes to food. Higher-caste Hindus have, with a few exceptions, maintained the importance of vegetarianism, especially in relation to religious practice. Thus if one travels in monk's robes on buses and trains through India, sooner or later the question is bound to arise: 'Are you a vegetarian?' If one answers in the affirmative one's stock is bound to rise in the eyes of questioners. Thai monks could not reply affirmatively to this question, nor could Tibetans. It seemed to me that it was important in India to declare that one was not a meat-eater, though I had private reservations about dogmatically declaring myself totally and at all times vegetarian. Partly this was because I had respect for the Asian cultures of my teachers: Sinhalese, Tibetan, Thai, and Chinese. A certain degree of adaptability is required to stay in Buddhist cultures, and besides this, a monk should be one 'of few wishes', making no special demands on generous supporters. I remember Westerners who on becoming monks tried to maintain their lay vegetarian habits, often, it seemed, placing their food preferences and sometimes neuroses before the practice of Dharma. This is certainly putting the cart before the horse. I have lived for years on vegetarian food quite happily but I would never declare myself only a vegetarian, still less would I say that other Buddhists must be vegetarians.

The Buddhist world is divided between the followers of the Three Vehicles, and in each of them there is a distinct attitude to the eating of meat and fish. In the countries of south and South-east Asia where Theravāda is dominant, monks are supposed to be supported by the food that donors place in their alms bowls. Monks have no choice: they eat whatever they receive. This ancient tradition of the almsround has come down from the Buddha's day and is still widely practised. No monk is allowed to ask for special food unless he is sick. The Vinaya, the monastic code of discipline, states that monks may accept meat or fish as long as they are sure – they neither see, hear, nor suspect – that it has been killed specially for them. There are a number of places in the Pāli suttas, the Buddha's teachings in the Theravāda tradition, where it seems that he occasionally ate meat. Of course, lay-people in this tradition who have the purchasing power of money (which monks are not supposed to have) can choose to be vegetarians, or not, as they please. There is no idea, generally, among lay-people that eating non-vegetable produce is breaking the first precept.

Mahāyāna attitudes are also governed by scripture and long-established practice. Among scriptures, in this case, is the *Laṅkāvatāra Sūtra*, particularly chapter 8. This sets out to undermine the Theravāda/ Hīnayāna position and establish that what the Buddha taught was really strict vegetarianism based on compassion for the sufferings of living beings. This tradition continues in China, Taiwan, Korea, Japan, and Vietnam, where all Buddhist monks and nuns are vegetarian (their food is usually cooked in their own temples' kitchens) and where devoted lay-people follow their practice or at least adopt a vegetable diet on special days.

The Vajrayāna is a different kind of response from Hindu society, a society very much governed by strict caste laws decreeing that brahmins and other 'high' castes must use no flesh, fish, or alcohol. The Buddhist tantras, which are the scriptural element of this tradition, advise people (already practising the other Vehicles) to go beyond their limitations. For example, fixed rules are needed to give the new practitioner the direction of Dharma, but even they must not become a repressive code which may never be transgressed. In Tantric Buddhism meat is eaten to make a close connection with beings out of compassion for them; alcohol is drunk with awareness of one's energy and one's limitations.

Though I went on almsround only once, almost every day while I was Bodh Gaya I walked in the early morning to the ancient Maha Bodhi Temple. I cannot easily describe the emotions I experienced there. Bodh Gaya, even after twenty-five centuries, with the last seven or eight of them seeing the temple abandoned and ruinous, has an amazing sense of presence, a power and majesty which also contains compassion. It is hard to say whether this was 'my' emotional reaction or whether, quite apart from my experience, others felt the same. It seems, from the testimonies of pilgrims and visitors, that the latter is more likely to be the truth.

The great tower of the ancient Gupta-period temple, rather mysteriously situated in its hollow, gradually impresses those who approach it. As I drew near for the first time my general impression was of rather battered old age, an impression confirmed as I circumambulated the temple and noticed its shabbiness – with many of the images in its outside niches headless or otherwise damaged. Even in that condition, which was due to various British officials including an army general in the 1880s, it was extraordinarily impressive. Perhaps Buddhists should dedicate some merit out of gratitude to General Cunningham and Mr J. D. Beglar whenever they visit this temple of the Great Awakening, for without their inspired efforts, we would today have nothing but a heap of bricks. That they did this with public moneys caused them to be criticized in the Westminster Parliament for restoring 'a seat of idolatry'. On the whole they did a fine job with the resources then available. They could hardly envisage that Buddhists from all over the world would soon visit the restored temple and would later build around it temples from their own countries' traditions. Still less could they foresee that in India, where the word 'Buddha' had been a faint echo for centuries, there would arise new followers of the Awakened One who would journey there and make offerings of flowers, incense, and lights.

General Cunningham also planted the present bodhi tree, a distant descendant of the tree under which Śākyamuni found Awakening. When that event of cosmic significance occurred, of course, the bodhi tree was just another large tree in the extensive forest of those times.

The first temple of which we have record centres around the bodhi tree. It was perhaps erected in the emperor Aśoka's days or even before that.[9] A sculpture from Bharhut shows the open arcading of this temple with the tree's boughs growing through the arches. From the sculpture it seems to have been a very pleasing and naturally harmonious temple. Some 700 years later the present temple was erected, though it is really more a stupa, since most of it is solid brickwork with comparatively little room inside the mass. By the time it was constructed, Buddha images, quite absent at the time of the first temple's erection, had replaced the bodhi tree as the centre of people's devotions. Today, the shrine-room with its magnificent Buddha is the central focus, with the bodhi tree rather peripheral on the outside of the temple's mass.

Early mornings and evenings were the times to visit the Maha Bodhi during the summer. When the sun was high, but specially in the afternoon, not only was there the sun's blazing rays but also the blast of the burning *luh*, a furnace-wind from the west. Even the ceiling fans of Wat Thai made little difference, for the interiors of the rooms were like ovens and the fans merely shifted around air well over 38°C, a doubtful comfort indeed.

During this time of intense heat, I remember that one morning quite early the friendly contractor for the building of Wat Thai, Mr Bhattacārya, came with a large vessel of cool palm juice, the sap tapped from certain palm trees which is mildly sweet and pleasantly refreshing. If left only a short while in that heat it becomes a quite potent alcoholic drink. He offered this juice to the Thai monks, who all refused it politely, I assumed because it was an Indian custom to drink it, rather than Thai. As he had brought it specially for the monks I thought this was a shame, so I accepted his invitation readily. The day was very hot, the palm juice cool and refreshing, so when he offered a second large glass I did not refuse it. After I had drunk this as well, peculiar sensations began to manifest, such as distortion in the distance of my hands away from the rest of the body. Though there was no indication of alcohol in the taste of this drink, clearly some was present. A third glass might have made standing and walking difficult! I am sure that the kind donor had no intention of causing the monks to get drunk and so breach their precepts, but clearly the sugars in this juice rapidly change to alcohol though without its flavour. Perhaps my experience explains the strange story of Sāgata,[10] a monk of many powers who was so fêted that he fell down dead drunk in the street.

Before the Rains had formally commenced I was offered the higher ordination by the abbot of Wat Thai, that is to become a monk (*bhikkhu*) rather than remain as a novice (*sāmanera*). However, I had doubts whether I would be able to keep all the precepts of a monk, 227 of them, with numerous other regulations, and so declined at that time to undertake them. The abbot probably found this surprising, as Thai men ordain for the Rains and then return to the lay life, quite without such qualms. For me, though, ordination as a monk would be a step into the kind of commitment for which I was not yet prepared. Another man, however, was prepared for this 'Rains ordination', having arrived with all his family at Bodh Gaya some time before Rains entry.

This candidate for the customary period in robes was no other than Field Marshal Phibun Songgram, the former dictator of Thailand, who had been ousted by a coup not long before. The *coup d'état* had been in Thai style, quite bloodless, with the ousted dictator allowed to flee the country with family and a certain amount of possessions accompanying him. As a dictator who had been for years in control of the Thai government he was no doubt responsible for the commission of much unskilful karma – such things as the imprisonment of opposition figures and the 'disappearance' of some of them. He was *de facto* ruler of the country as the king's power was limited, so although nominally Buddhist he had to take measures that were opposed to the Dharma in order to maintain his position. In order, he hoped, to make it more likely that his future life or lives would not be miserable due to the fruiting of this evil karma, Phibun Songgram had undertaken to have Wat Thai built with government money, though it was not completed until years after he was forced to relinquish his grip on power. It had been his plan that worthy Thai monks would live at Bodh Gaya for a year or two before returning to Thailand. The abbot of Wat Thai must have communicated the ex-dictator's wish to be ordained for three months to the new masters in Bangkok. Presumably they replied that his wish could be accommodated. His ordination for three months was another attempt to make merits or good karma, to offset the wrongs he had already done. However, he took his practice of the monk's life in quite a relaxed way as though the mere donning of robes and shaving of the head, mixed in with a few rules and a bit of chanting, would be strenuous enough.

I found him agreeable to talk to, though of course I did not touch on Thai politics, where his real interests lay. A small dapper man with a rather stern expression which relaxed easily into a smile, he seemed quite at home in robes – temporarily. He was respectful to the abbot and other monks and agreeable with me, but underneath this I sensed a man used to power, and who expected obedience. As a wealthy refugee, his family now represented the limits of his rule, formerly so extensive. His family stayed in the lay wing of the residence and produced quantities of food. On the chosen day he was duly ordained by Thai monks who must have assembled at Wat Thai from various educational establishments in India for this purpose. (Monk ordination in the Middle Land, the area in which the Buddha lived and taught, required no fewer than ten monks, while Wat Thai had only five.) I did not witness this ceremony, as I had chosen to remain a novice. However, his presence at the temple meant that all of us were fed devotedly twice a day upon rich Thai food.

It happened one day that the former dictator (resplendent in monk's robes and with a newly shaven head) and I were talking about Dharma in English, his knowledge of my language being at that time much better than mine of his, when he made a remark to the effect: 'Rebirth, of course, is just an ancient superstition.' Considering that, as dictator, he had been accompanied by a couple of 'heavies' wherever he went, and that they or others commanded by him had killed quite a number of opponents, I was not surprised at his reluctance to believe in future lives. Still, I could not let him get away with such a wrong view while he wore Buddhist robes, so I asked him, 'Well, do you believe in the possibility of a human being Waking up completely?' In his present condition he could hardly deny this possibility and so answered, 'Yes, it is possible.' At that, I pounced upon him, saying, 'In that case, you will have to accomplish it in this very life, won't you?' The conversation, not surprisingly, ended at this point as he was visibly annoyed. Had I not had the protection of the robes and had he still unlimited power I do not doubt that this disrespect would have signalled serious trouble in my life.

Perhaps worth recording here was another event that occurred during this Rains. One day, when I was in my room, a young Thai monk, giggling with embarrassment, asked me to come with him and meet a visitor. The temple quarters had a sort of sitting-room area where monks could talk to guests seated in the comfort of teak armchairs carved in Thailand. When we reached this large open space, an Indian was standing there talking to another embarrassed monk. Our visitor had long carefully combed hair, an intelligent face, and no clothes at all. His sole 'covering' was a thin silver chain around his waist. Thais are particularly sensitive about adult nudity, though quite relaxed when it comes to naked children. Certainly they do not associate nudity with religious practice, for even their depictions of the old pre-Buddhist *reusi* (rishi or sage)[11] are adequately clothed. It was not surprising, then, that the Thai monks did not know how to cope with this visitor, hence my invitation to speak with him. Besides the unusual challenge that he posed to the Thais, they spoke only a fragmented English, while he spoke it well but, of course, no Thai. When we had all introduced ourselves and had sat down (much to the relief of the Thai monks who were wearing at least two robes) and tea had been served, he informed us how he had studied at university, become disillusioned with worldly life and then renounced everything. I remember him saying, 'I renounced everything, even clothes,' with a meaningful look at us well-robed ones. He might well have cast his eyes wider at the rest of our surroundings which spoke of a well-settled and generously supported monastic life – although he looked far from starvation himself, having in fact a particularly good physique – one, I could not help reflecting, that village ladies would find very attractive. He had only one cloth with him which he wore, he informed us, when he travelled on crowded buses and trains. I cannot now recall the rest of our conversation, which was friendly and relaxed, but I thought that this unexpected intrusion of an Indian ascetic into the Thai temple was rather a good thing for the Thais and for myself. They were amused and somewhat dismayed, while I regarded the ascetic's courteous challenge as good source of reflection: bhikkhus (monks) once wandered freely as he did, but most of them in the present time inhabit well-appointed temples. What price renunciation?

India does pose some unexpected questions for Buddhist monks, though what I am about to relate did not happen to me. I learned of this from other Thai monks studying in Indian universities. Occasionally it happened, they told me, that an Indian married woman who had been unable to conceive a child would approach a monk and ask him to 'help' her. The Indian rationale behind this is that as monks are celibate their sexual energy must be super-powerful! Of course it was not only Buddhist monks who were invited to help; any likely ascetic might be approached. Thais, when they told me of this, laughed with incredulity that such a situation could occur, for in their own culture monks are placed in a category transcending sex. Whether our Indian visitor ever received invitations of this kind I do not know. Bodh Gaya, once the place of the Buddha's Awakening, had many possibilities.

For example, one day I was invited to meet the disciples of Gandhi who inhabited the Sarvodaya Ashram, situated behind the Tibetan temple. I was courteously received and offered tea, followed by a long conversation in which one of the ashram inhabitants tried to convince me how unnecessary it was to wear robes or to have any sense of being distinctively a Buddhist. At this point in our conversation he brought out the frequent Hindu view, 'Buddhism is just a part of Hinduism,' a contention that naturally I did not agree with. Taking little notice of my objections, he continued his onslaught by declaring that puja – that is, devotional chanting with offerings – was unnecessary. In fact, my would-be teacher said all these things were a waste of time and energy, thoroughly out of date, as well as being out of touch with the people. Monks, he continued, should do good to the people, as was the declared intention of his ashram. I perceived that this line of argument actually would lead to the diminution of the Buddha-Dharma so that it could be easily swallowed by Hinduism. No sangha would mean no committed practitioners in whom the Dharma would live and who would be living examples to inspire others. No proclamation of the Buddha's distinctive Dharma would lead likewise to its death, and therefore augment the sufferings of this world. No puja? If the Buddha and his wonderful Awakening were not to be praised, who would be worthy to be honoured at all? Though the cups of tea were nice I came away from the ashram feeling that I had been invited for not completely honourable reasons. Perhaps the presence of a Westerner in Buddhist robes was perceived as a threat? It also occurred to me that Mahatma Gandhi's proclaimed principles of *ahiṁsā* (non-harming) had not been observed very well by his followers on this occasion.

Evening walks to the great Maha Bodhi would reveal how the place came alive after the *luh* had abated, or after the rain had finished. One could see such a variety of Buddhists practising many different forms of devotion. Most striking, and in those days most numerous, were the newly-arrived Tibetan refugees, many of them with nothing apart from the clothes they stood up in, doing prostrations and lighting lamps. There was no doubt about their devotion; even though they had lost everything – family, home, and possessions, and of course their own country – they had something in their hearts which no oppression could take away: devotion to the Three Jewels. You could see them prostrating around the ancient *pradakṣiṇa* path of the temple, 'measuring their length': from a standing position in which the hands were held at head, throat, and heart (representing body, voice, and mind), while a mantra was recited and visualization done of the Three Jewels and one's spiritual teachers, they bowed down the body (visualizing that all sentient beings are likewise paying their respects), and slid into a prone position with the hand holding the rosary out in front. Leaving the rosary there they got up with hands together, advanced to the place where the rosary lay and bowed down again. Strenuous devotions for hot Bodh Gaya! But then some Tibetans had covered hundreds of miles like this from their villages to the holy city of Lhasa, so that this mode of circumambulation posed few problems apart from the fact that one would get very hot, sweaty, and dirty. Though Tibetan monks could be seen undertaking this, it would have been unthinkable for those dressed in neat Thai robes to express themselves in this way. In fact, I found that devotions at the Thai temple were rather sterile. Twice a day we assembled at the temporary shrine (the real temple had not then been built) and chanted a set pattern of Pāli passages and verses which rarely aroused the heart. Formality reigned there, devotion died. This was evidently not the case with the Tibetans, who possessed many formulations of Buddhist practice that involved the mind through visualization, voice through mantras, and body through these long prostrations. Other Tibetans had well-polished boards which they placed in front of the Maha Bodhi Temple and prostrated themselves, sometimes for hours at a time, accomplishing during a day a few hundred more prostrations, bringing the total nearer to the desired 100,000. I was not sure then whether this would take one further upon the Path to Awakening, but certainly it would deepen one's devotion.

Bodh Gaya, though an endlessly fascinating place where our great 'teacher of devas and humanity'[12] awakened, was also very much a part of the round of birth and death. This meant, of course, that all was not perfect there (at least, not to those with ordinary eyes). There was, for example, the intrusion of a *Shiva-linga* right in front of the main Buddha image in the Maha Bodhi Temple. That phallic worship should occur (brahmins came to make offerings every day) in the heart of Buddhism's holiest shrine, says much for both the power of craving and for Hindu determination to insinuate itself and try to absorb every other religious teaching. Some waxed indignant that Hindus had managed to insert this stone in the floor of the Maha Bodhi's shrine-room. I thought it strange and inappropriate, but came after a time to regard it with amusement. Whether it is still there I am unable to say, though it would not have been easy to remove it because of Hindu pressure. The broken images around the temple were another indication of the power of impermanence and, in some cases, of hatred. While impermanence can never be stopped, the Tibetans soon intervened to repair the sacred images of Buddhas and Bodhisattvas. Tibetans were appalled by the notion that ancient broken things must remain so and may not be repaired, a doctrine inherited from the British by the Indian archaeological authorities. And though one might glory in the ancientness, architecture, and spiritual aura of this place, directly outside the temple one was confronted with hordes of beggars – and with village poverty generally. At that time, Buddhists on their 'island' of Bodh Gaya did next to nothing about the state of Indian society around them, though there was a dire need for schools, medicines, and all sorts of facilities taken for granted in the homelands of those Buddhists. This situation has now been amended somewhat, and the barriers to social and spiritual contact have been removed. This was not the case when I lived in Wat Thai, for while I was there I had the uncomfortable feeling of being an alien, a strange thing for a Buddhist, surely, in this most sacred Buddhist place!

Apart from the ancient and restored Maha Bodhi Temple and the monuments immediately surrounding it, there were no *Indian* Buddhist temples, monasteries, or stupas, a fact which emphasized how dead the Buddha's doctrines were almost everywhere in India. This was further emphasized by an excellent new museum containing many images and other artefacts from the ancient Buddhist past. Apart from this, one could say that only the Birla Dharmasāla, a rest-house for pilgrims built in the old courtyard style by the Indian millionaire benefactor, showed that Buddhism must still be somewhat alive, even if only outside India.

The oldest building at Bodh Gaya in what could be called the 'Buddhist revival', was the Maha Bodhi Society's Pilgrims' Hall, mostly used by Sinhalese (Sri Lankans) during winter pilgrimages. A lone monk from that Isle of Dharma inhabited the premises. Next to it was a larger and much livelier institution: the Tibetan Gelug monastery and pilgrims' rest where perhaps as many as fifty monks resided. Due to the guidance of Dhardo Rimpoche, of whom more later, they had a proper course of study and practice, and while they ministered to pilgrims' needs, their establishment was really the only example of living Dharma in Bodh Gaya. They were there, not just waiting for pilgrims, but actively practising in the place where it was said that well-practised Dharma bore fruits one-hundred-thousandfold.

Other national temples existed but, like the Maha Bodhi Society's, had only one monk or nun in residence. For instance, a small Chinese temple had been established a few minutes' walk from the Maha Bodhi which was staffed by an ageing and solitary nun. The temple, though well-cared for, was small and perhaps reflected the troubled times of its home country, the upheavals of which affected the Dharma adversely.

The Burmese also had only managed to put up a rest-house with one monk in residence. While a useful facility for Burmese pilgrims, it in no way reflected the flourishing state of the Dharma in its homeland. Last of these national establishments, of course, and sponsored by the Royal Thai Government, was the incomplete Wat Thai where I stayed. Though much money was spent on its construction, the quality of practice among the monks there was not outstanding. Not that they violated any of the major Vinaya rules; they certainly did their duties and chanted twice a day, but that was all.

In all, general impressions of Wat Thai Buddhist life were not all that inspiring. Around six in the morning the monks gathered to chant the praises of the Three Jewels – Buddha, Dharma, and Sangha – with some reflections on impermanence, loving-kindness, and their dependence upon the four requisites: robes, almsfood, shelter, and medicines. This half hour of chanting was completed by the Dedication of Merits – all of this chanted in Pāli, a language related to Sanskrit, in which the Theravāda scriptures and commentaries had been preserved. When this had been learned by heart it was possible to go on thinking all manner of things quite unrelated to what the mouth was saying. Perhaps this was only my experience, though I suspect not. More immediacy in the chanting, which was repeated in a slightly different form at night, might have been present if they had chanted all this in their own language. I found the atmosphere of this ritual rather sterile.

A Thai breakfast of flavoursome soupy rice (usually not vegetarian) followed, prepared by the Thai man who served as the monks' steward. The monks had no duties during the morning and some, I suspect, retired to their rooms not to meditate or to study but to sleep. In fact, the striking thing was the absence of study and meditation at the Wat. Westerners usually assume that a monk's life is all about meditation, but as I discovered in Wat Thai, and later in Thailand, for about 95 per cent of the monks their monastic life was mostly about study and passing examinations. The small remainder, forest-dwelling monks, meditated. Lunch followed at eleven and was finished at noon in accordance with the Vinaya rules. Though vegetables would be local, other ingredients were flown in from Thailand. It seemed almost as if Thai monks at this temple had never left their home country. This was very odd, as it suggested that a very important element of Asian monastic life consisted of eating one's own national foods.

There is no doubt that some of the afternoon was taken up by a siesta, very necessary during the hot season, and monks emerged towards the end of the afternoon to drink black tea. As there was no meal in the evening, once the chanting concluded the monks talked among themselves and retired early to their rooms.

I do not remember having been taught any Dharma at Wat Thai, though one of the younger monks helped me to decipher the morning and evening chanting so that I could learn it. The abbot, a senior monk from Bangkok where he was in charge of a large city temple, was much attached to books. He was kind to me and tried to communicate with his patchy English and my even more patchy Thai. The abbot and other monks asked me to teach them English, and for a short while I interrupted the tedium of their lives with language classes. However, I was not pleased with their laziness in completing the simple exercises that I gave them, and their enthusiasm for English waned quickly.

During my Rains at Wat Thai I was left very much to my own devices. This had been the case at the Hampstead Vihara, but at least there was some emphasis there on meditation. At Wat Thai, though, there was nothing of this, all the more astonishing as the temple was only a few minutes' walk away from where the Buddha Śākyamuni was Awakened! I would later discover living traditions of Buddhist practice at Sangharakshita's mountain abode and a different approach to the Dharma with Buddharakkhita.

I found the Thai neglect of the principles of meditation and awareness quite bewildering. In my own room I meditated every day and tried to practise what I had learned from books, while for inspiration I had only that short walk to the bodhi tree and vajra seat. The gap between the ancient realization of Bodhi and the modern Thai monks was too obvious, too glaring in my eyes. But perhaps I was being too judgemental of these monks, I said to myself; perhaps also much is lost through language difficulties. However, it seemed to me that their role at Bodh Gaya was merely that of caretakers of their national temple and that what they really looked forward to was not Awakening but a return to their accepted place in Thai society.

In general, these foreign Buddhist establishments did nothing at all to propagate the Dharma. Even though, in those days, many Indian tourists and pilgrims visited Bodh Gaya, no effort at all was made to inform them about it. There was no Buddhist bookshop, nor any place where artefacts for Dharma practice could be obtained. In fact, it would have appeared to Indians then that in the very place where the Dharma was awakened to, its present manifestations were all foreign and of little concern to them. None of the monks residing there tried to teach the Dharma in Indian languages, even Hindi. For Indian visitors, then, Bodh Gaya was a trip to exotic lands where they could see strange customs and practices, none of which could benefit them in any way. Of course, on the positive side it could be said that at least the situation was a great improvement compared to the time when the first British officials, a hundred years earlier, identified the heap of rubble as Bodh Gaya. Roughly 2,500 years after the Buddha's Final Nirvāṇa there were some signs that the Dharma still lived – even in India, as we shall see later – but at Bodh Gaya these were as seeds which though still alive had not yet germinated, still less flowered and borne fruit.

Chapter Four

NEW BUDDHISTS

Eight-factored Noble Path for people everywhere,
For those seeking Freedom, the Way that is straight,
This Dhamma fine and subtle, making for peace,
Leading out of dukkha, that Dhamma I revere.

A verse in praise of the Dharma Jewel

Interested in seeing some of the more promising new seeds of Buddhism in India, I had asked Sangharakshita, before leaving Triyāna Vardhana Vihāra, if we could go together to western India, mostly Maharashtra, for his annual teaching tour. I had also asked him to spend a night or two at Wat Thai beforehand.

Sangharakshita has reminded me of an incident that occurred while we were there. To understand the significance of this we need to look at the recent history of Bodh Gaya beyond the few facts already mentioned. Some time in the fifteenth or sixteenth century, a swami-disciple of one of the gurus from the lineage of the great Hindu Vedantist teacher, Sankara, wandered into Bodh Gaya and found it utterly deserted and ruined. He was attracted to the place, settled near the ruinous Maha Bodhi Temple, and slowly collected disciples; at the same time, since there were no Buddhists to dispute it, he laid claim to the whole temple area. Such Buddha and Bodhisattva images as were removable he installed at his own centre, giving them Hindu names; others were honoured with puja in the brahminical manner among the ruins. Though occasional Buddhist pilgrims from Burma might object to this they were not powerful enough to combat the Mahant – the title literally means the Great One – as his well-landed and funded successors were called.

An example of misappropriation which still persisted, even at the time I am writing about, could be found in a building near the entrance to the Maha Bodhi Temple which plainly contained a fine set of the Five Tathāgatas, but was labelled by Hindu guides 'Five Pandava brothers' and duly worshipped.

When Anagārika Dharmapāla[13] had arrived in Bodh Gaya in the nineteenth century the situation was much worse. The brahmin *pujaris* (priests) from the Mahant's *math* or monastery dominated the newly restored temple. The Mahant of those days was determined to maintain his hold on the temple and repulsed the various peaceful Buddhist initiatives of Dharmapāla by force. This left Dharmapāla no alternative but to appeal to the courts. Long-running court battles ensued from which Buddhists gained little, while the Mahant was able to claim correctly that his predecessor found the holy place deserted. Moreover, he was manifestly in control at present and his lineage had managed the place for hundreds of years. His interest was not totally spiritual, since he derived considerable pecuniary benefits from the Hindu pilgrims who visited Bodh Gaya to make offerings for their ancestors.

It was because of this series of past conflicts between Dharmapāla and the Mahant that Sangharakshita one day suggested that we should call upon him and try to put Buddhist-Hindu relations upon a more friendly footing.

The math, which is situated on the road from the city of Gaya to Bodh Gaya, resembled a fortress more than a monastery. Entry was by way of an impressive gateway into which were let niches for various salvaged pieces of Buddhist statuary. As we entered the math's compound, a sandy courtyard surrounded by monastic buildings and containing a Hindu temple at its centre, I spotted a heap of fragmented carvings from the Maha Bodhi Temple and found one small Buddha quite unbroken. Carrying it with me, we approached the largest building and asked if we might see the Mahant. After a short time we were shown into his presence. Sangharakshita remembers that the Mahant was surprised to see us. Perhaps he suspected the motives for our visit, as he can hardly have had a very friendly view of Buddhists. However, our meeting went well enough, and when at the end of it I showed him the small stone Buddha and asked for his permission to take it he readily agreed. Shortly after this meeting we were joined by Vivekānanda and set off from Bodh Gaya, travelling by train from Gaya station.

'Going by train' has for Western ears a rather staid feel about it: you easily buy the tickets and then there is the orderly disembarking of passengers followed by the embarkation of others and of course, most people have a seat. Do not even dream this if travelling on Indian railways in second (which still existed in those days) or third class! The prelude to travel begins with purchase of the ticket, which may involve much time and several officials. The ticket secured, as the train appears one needs to position oneself near the edge of the platform – hundreds of others are, of course, trying to do the same thing. Then as the train slows down there is a sort of wave effect among the intending passengers who mark down the entrances to carriages or compartments. And if it is a train without barred windows some athletic fellows will already be hoisting themselves into the air in order to enter the train that way. Of course, this surge of activity to enter the train and secure seats or sleeping places conflicts with the desires of other passengers to alight, so that both doors and windows can be occupied by bodies attempting to go in two different directions at once. Interesting! Generally the whole exercise is an occasion for the practice of two of the Buddhist perfections, patience and effort, together with perhaps a certain amount of low cunning that does not really qualify as the perfection of wisdom. With luck you may secure seats or sleeping spaces. On express trains there was then a bookable third-class seat or sleeper where passengers slept on wooden benches, three high on each side of the compartment – these folded to form seats and luggage racks during the day – and passengers brought along their own bedding rolls. I believe it was in this fashion that we travelled on a night train from Gaya. This had the added attraction of getting into a compartment, the inhabitants of which were already asleep and had locked themselves in. Indian railway travel has, as you will know if you have experienced it, nothing staid about it – in fact anything could happen, and it often did.

How does one while away the long hours of travel? Maybe in the very early morning you have a chance to meditate. As the daylight grows, besides the scenery, which changes little on the north Indian plains, there is the distraction of disembarking for breakfast – the train stops for about twenty minutes for this pleasant excursion – and when one has settled in again after the meal break there might be some religious discussion. Sometimes this is of the fantastic and speculative variety in which all manner of assumptions may be made by the passenger with whom you are talking – such discussions are tiresome but the time does pass swiftly. On other occasions the discussion may be with a person or group of people who genuinely want to understand the Buddha-Dharma, in which case hours fly past most profitably.

I do not remember the destination of that trip, one among several dozen Indian train journeys I made during my three years in India, but at some point one of these trains finally set us down in Nagpur, the City of Nāgas (or dragons) right in the centre of India. We were met on the platform by Sri Kulkarni and a group of former Untouchable Mahars who had become Buddhists. Kulkarni and the Buddhists came from the opposite ends of India's social spectrum and it was very rare for an ex-brahmin and ex-Untouchables to unite upon any matter. In fact, their views would normally be quite opposed, the brahmins defending their social privileges against the lower castes generally, certainly against the outcaste communities, while the latter denounced the oppression by the brahmins and other high castes and endeavoured to scramble up the social ladder to gain a somewhat better life. In this case, Kulkarni was a very unusual brahmin who had become convinced of the value of the Buddha-Dharma, while the Mahar community as a whole had recently converted to this Dharma: as many as 10,000,000 'new' Buddhists. Of course, in an India where for hundreds of years Buddhism had been confined to border areas – the Himalayan foothills, the Assamese valley of the Brahmaputra River, and the far eastern plains of what is now Bangladesh – this sudden influx in Buddhist numbers changed many things beyond the numbers on the census records.

A large community suddenly no longer counted itself as 'Hindu'. Nevertheless, census-takers, who were often high-caste Hindus, marked these Buddhists, the majority of whom were illiterate, as: 'Religion: Hindu. Caste: Buddhist'. The ex-Mahars, however, reckoned themselves to be Buddhists due to the brave decision of their leader, Dr Bhimrao Ambedkar.[14] He became a Buddhist together with nearly 400,000 of his followers in an impressive ceremony held in Nagpur on 14 October 1956. Sangharakshita, though he was not present at that historically important event, had already established close connections with these people and their leader. When Dr Ambedkar died, not long after this ceremony, Sangharakshita was requested to tour the areas inhabited by the bereaved Buddhists and bring comfort to them. This he did with characteristic vigour, often addressing several large meetings each day and travelling extensively in Maharashtra to do so.

Now a Buddhist community, however impoverished, existed in the kind of numbers that make the headlines, certainly that make politicians sit up, in the land of the Buddha-Dharma's birth. For 800 years or so, due to the destruction of north Indian Buddhist educational and spiritual centres by invading Muslims, as well as the enmity of brahmins, Buddhism had all but ceased to exist in India – but now the Dharma was once again a power to reckon with.

Knowledgeable people in India generally consigned Buddhism to ancient history, an interesting movement of the past but no longer part of the living religious scene. High-caste Hindus were apt to hold forth on Buddhism as a past aspect of Hindu Sanātana Dharma,[15] something transcended, according to them, by the onward flow of Hindu manifestations. Buddhists, of course, could not agree with such an interpretation, nor with their oft-repeated catch-phrase that 'the Buddha was born a Hindu'. Sangharakshita counteracted such assumptions by pointing out that 'Hinduism', existing now in numerous forms, was not found in the Buddha's days, even the name being an anachronism for the Brahmin's Vedic Dharma. He would further emphasize that what we now label 'Buddhism', better called the Buddha-Dharma or Buddhasāsana,[16] was the outpouring in words, in practices, of Perfect Unsurpassed Awakening of the Buddha Śākyamuni.

This tendency to regard Buddhism as a historical phenomenon is also illustrated by the attitude of the Indian Archeological Service. It was willing to conserve Buddhist ruins as evidence of a *past* flowering of Indian culture, but should living Buddhists appear they were usually unwilling to allow them to use sacred sites for their puja and practice. This attitude consigned the threatening Buddha-Dharma, which announced that all people possessed the seed of Buddhahood and that the caste system was a mere convention invented by the brahmins, into the safe waste-basket of history. It could then be discussed as an interesting but dead movement having no use for the present time. Sangharakshita protested that such assertions, comfortable to high-caste Hindus, were distortions of the truth. Buddha-Dharma, he was never tired of emphasizing, transcended all boundaries of time so that its essential teachings were as true in the present as they were at the time when they were first expounded, 2,500 years ago.

These digressions seem rather to have left Sri Kulkarni and the followers of Dr Ambedkar standing on the platform of Nagpur railway station, but such background information is necessary to appreciate, even in part, the situation of the Buddha-Dharma in India. We stayed with the generous Kulkarni and travelled to the neighbourhoods of the newly-converted Buddhists. This activity did not prevent us from sitting together in the early morning and chanting our puja, though we could only occasionally do evening sits and puja together, depending on our schedule.

To really understand the importance of the conversion to these 'new Buddhists', we must look further into the caste system and how those at its lower end were oppressed. Ancient Hindu treatises laid down four main sections of society, which were supposed to include everyone: brahmins, warrior nobles, merchants, and workers.[17] Brahmins, who had constructed this system around their desire for prestige and power, naturally placed themselves first. Their assumption was not unchallenged: the Buddha firmly placed them second after the warrior nobles. Brahmins were supposed to be in charge of all matters religious, to lead lives of study and practice, and to attend to cattle, their source of wealth and numerous milk products. Warrior nobles' dharma,[18] here meaning caste duty, was in the brahmin conception of things to rule and to fight, a role explained clearly in the *Bhagavad Gītā*. Many, though not all, of India's royal dynasties came from warrior noble families. Still further down the scale were the merchants, whose 'dharma' was the accumulation of wealth. They were obviously, in this scheme of things, not much esteemed. It is interesting then to note that Indian merchants became the strongest supporters of the Buddha-Dharma and ensured, as they travelled with their merchandise, that Buddhist teachers and their teachings spread far and wide.[19] At the bottom of this system were mere workers, supposed to obey the commands of all the higher castes, provide the labour, and do the dirty work.

In fact, this rigid conception of society excluded large numbers of people. For instance, tribal people speaking languages unrelated to the Indo-European group were consigned to rubbish-dump or 'outcaste' status, hardly recognized in any way as human or having any connection with brahmin-controlled religion. Similarly, other groups that would not fit into the system found themselves regarded as outcastes. It seems very likely – a thesis developed by Dr Ambedkar – that after the collapse of Buddhism in India, many of its adherents were suppressed as outcastes or Untouchables since they would not accept the pretensions of the brahmins: it should be emphasized that the epithets 'outcaste', 'Untouchable', and their Indian equivalents were never accepted by these people themselves. In recent times they have often referred to themselves as Dalit, meaning 'the oppressed'.

Many barbarous rules made by the higher castes featured in a Dalit's life. They could not even pass in front of Hindu temples, much less enter them; they had to wear cast-off rags, never good clothes; they had the duty of clearing away dead animals as well as removing human excrement; in some places they were forced to wear clay pots round their necks so that their spittle would not reach the ground, while their footsteps were obliterated by a broom tied to their waists; their womenfolk were compelled to wear non-precious jewellery of iron or pottery; their children had to be given 'ugly' names, and finally they could not venture outdoors when shadows were long lest their shadow fall on a high-caste person and pollute him. This fear of ritual pollution, very characteristic of Caste Hindus, underlies all these suppressive rules. It is easy to understand that people who have been so treated for hundreds of years, with no chance for education or self-improvement, would feel that their lives were a hopeless round of degradation. Brahmins emphasized that they had been born into such 'low' births because of their sins – in other words, they were to be humble menials, do the dirty work, and say nothing. Some groups of outcastes were so polluting to the eyes of Hindus that they were not only untouchable but 'unseeable' as well. There was a bitter saying among outcaste groups deriding caste hypocrisy that goes as follows: male Untouchables are always untouchable but female Untouchables, untouchable by day, become touchable at night. Perhaps the most suppressive rule of them all forbade low-caste people and Untouchables to have any religious education or practice. Religion, largely controlled by the brahmins, involved the learning of Sanskrit, and as this was reckoned to be the 'root-language' spoken by the Hindu gods it was utterly forbidden for outcastes even to hear it, let alone learn it.

Women fared worse than men in this heap of misery. Though outcaste women could not be controlled as rigidly as those from high castes, still something of the rules laid down by brahmins was reflected in the treatment of women among the Untouchables. The general disabilities suffered by women under the caste system are well illustrated by a verse from the Hindu laws contained in the *Mānavadharma-śāstra* ('Laws of Manu'):

When young, in charge of her father,
When grown, in charge of her husband,
When old, in charge of her son,
A woman must never be without a master.

This oppressive regime, as well as the consequent need for clearly formulated points to educate the new Buddhists, lay behind the unsigned article appearing in the July 1961 issue of the *Maha Bodhi Journal*, entitled 'The Position of Women in Buddhism'. This article was a précis of a lecture Sangharakshita gave at eight different locations around Poona.[20] I had taken notes on the subject and later produced this summary with him in point form. It was not signed, as it was a composite work. This article, or rather list of points, opens with the statement, 'The Buddha's Dharma teaches equality amongst all humanity.' Point two continues, 'So amongst Buddhists, women and men are equal and opportunities must be the same for both sexes. Woman is *not* the slave of man.' This article then clarifies point by point such matters as women's participation in the Dharma, their knowledge of Buddhist sūtras, courtesy towards them, and concern for their complete education. Then comes the topic of marriage and how they must not be forced into it, or forced to marry an unwelcome suitor, nor is it necessary that their marriage partner comes from the same caste – since Buddhism does not recognize the caste system. After condemning the dowry system (still the focus of much suffering for Indian women) the article lists a woman's five obligations towards her husband, as well as his five towards her. These are taken from the thirty-first sutta of the Long Collection (*Dīgha-Nikāya*), which contains a summary of the Buddha's advice to lay-people. Points 15–17 concern children: how women have a duty to educate their children according to the Dharma, that girls are as welcome in Buddhist families as boys, and that women who cannot conceive children are not to be despised. Divorce and widowhood follow; the emphasis is in sharp contrast with Hindu ethics. Divorce in Buddhism where there are proper grounds for it has never been forbidden to women, while widows may remarry without stigma if a celibate life is not appealing. The last three points concern a woman's right in the Buddha-Dharma to train and qualify in and take up any position in government or private business; her property rights as a single or married woman; and the status equal to men that she may occupy in society, either still living the household life or as those who have left home to learn, practise, and teach the Dharma.

Altogether, these twenty-two points, which may not sound remarkable to Western ears used to liberal values, are truly revolutionary in an Indian context. I hope very much that this list has been translated into many Indian languages and is still available at the present time.

Sangharakshita and I went every day to different parts of town where the former Mahars were now Buddhists. Their areas of town were always marked by poverty – small unpaved lanes with crowded shacks of which only an occasional one was brick or two-storey. Even in those early days of their transition there was evidence of their change of heart inspired by Dr Ambedkar. The beginnings of schools and dispensaries for basic medicines could be seen with tiny Buddha-*vihars*, sometimes just a room set aside in a house, sometimes a small building housing a plaster Buddha image and a picture of Dr Ambedkar. These places were mostly too small for the sort of audiences attracted to Sangharakshita's discourses, so these had to be held in whatever open space there was. If large numbers of people were expected, a platform with microphone and loudspeakers would be set up. The platform had either Western-style chairs and table or large sitting cushions covered with new cloths backed by the Buddha image garlanded with marigolds and the framed picture of Dr Ambedkar, always garlanded as well. Frequent reference was made to this great man, and by general acclaim he was known reverently as Bodhisattva Dr Babasaheb Ambedkar. In truth, as he had rescued his people from a degrading life and set them on the path to Awakening, such devotion to their good over many years was the practice of a Bodhisattva.

Generally speaking, meetings started when everyone was ready, with no great emphasis on the clock. However, Sangharakshita, who occasionally would speak at two or three such gatherings, had some-times to prompt people to begin. Usually there would be a chairman to introduce Sangharakshita, and that completed his first action was to garland the Buddha image, as well as Dr Ambedkar's portrait. Then would follow the Refuges and Precepts in Pāli, and when these were finished Sangharakshita would deliver his talk. This was translated into Marathi by someone who was bilingual, not then so common among these people. His talks, usually very attentively listened to, were upon a variety of Buddhist subjects and were well matched to the local people's interests and comprehension. Sometimes they made reference to the Buddha's teachings on the evils of caste, but on other occasions they were focused on the need to conduct oneself as a Buddhist, as one who had gone for Refuge. The Three Refuges were frequently explained from various viewpoints, and as I listened to these talks, their infinite variety and the depths of Dharma revealed, I greatly admired Sangharakshita's ability to teach in ways so interest-ing to his audience. People were usually very quiet and most of them really tried hard to understand what was being explained. The whole atmosphere of the function was impressive, though without the heaviness of solemnity. Sometimes question time followed, at others there would be speakers who would elaborate in Marathi the message given by Sangharakshita, so that the people had two or more opportunities to grasp its meaning and how to practise it.

I remember in particular that, besides emphasizing a clear comprehension of karma as taught by the Buddha, Sangharakshita often spoke on such words as 'Bhagavan' and 'Dharma', words that were shared with other Indian religions. The first of these was applied in Hinduism to various manifestations of the Hindu pantheon as an honorific, thus Bhagavan Vishnu, for instance. As Buddhists usually referred to Śākyamuni as 'Bhagavan Buddha', the question arose as to what meaning this word had. Sangharakshita was at pains to point out that this in no way implied that the Buddha was a god; indeed he was born in a human manner and his body died after eighty vigorous years of life. He would also make clear that due to his perfect Awakening, the Buddha was also superhuman. But no Buddhist, he emphasized, would agree that Bhagavan Buddha was an emanation of Vishnu, as many Hindus averred.

The other word shared with all Indian religions, 'Dharma', had many meanings that were non-Buddhist, some even completely opposed to the Buddhist conception of Dharma. An instance of this that Sangharakshita frequently related was the common Hindu use of Dharma to mean 'caste duty', a fact mentioned above. Sangharakshita stressed the need to recognize the difference between these two meanings, the Hindu one being quite opposed to the Buddhist conception of a universally true Dharma applicable to everyone, whatever their status in society. He would say that even the gods had come to the Buddha to be instructed in Dharma, for it was a teaching or law that applied to them as well, hence little good could be expected of praying to the gods. To the listeners, these words and ideas were revolutionary, a gate to genuine liberation, so it was not too surprising to observe that the speaker of them was much revered.

Some invitations to Sangharakshita, in which I was usually included, were concerned with more 'concrete' matters. Abstract Dharma teachings are not easy for uneducated people to grasp. Many in this new Buddhist community thought of Buddhism in terms of ceremonies for birth, marriage, and death. The old ways of organizing these functions were generally stained with non-Buddhist ideas and new ways had to be devised that accorded with the Dharma. Sangharakshita was the authority on such matters and his recommendations were carefully followed. I remember going to a number of name-giving ceremonies for small children at which Sangharakshita not only explained how this was to be done but also bestowed upon the child, or children, names with Buddhist significance.

One place we visited in Nagpur lacked the usual crowds; it was what would be described in English terms as a park – without much grass, however, and with little effort at beautification. It was a large flat expanse of ground surrounded by suburbs, known as the Diksha Bhumi, 'Initiation Place'. This was where Dr Ambedkar had, with half a million of his followers, over two days, become Buddhists. I imagined all those people sitting on that expanse of ground and the momentous event of so many people chanting *Buddhaṁ saraṇaṁ gacchāmi, Dhammaṁ saraṇaṁ gacchāmi, Saṅghaṁ saraṇaṁ gacchāmi* (to the Buddha, Dharma, and Sangha I go for Refuge). The great man died shortly afterwards and Sangharakshita addressed a large condolence meeting in Kasturchand Park immediately after his death, followed by an extensive teaching tour to reassure the stricken Buddhists that all was not lost.

While Sangharakshita still lived in India his strong connection with the new Buddhists meant that he spent the hot season and the wet one in Kalimpong writing and meditating, but the cool season on the other side of India aiding this peaceful Buddhist revolution. His energy and devotion to this were most remarkable, for though India in those days had a scattering of Buddhist monks from different communities, none could match the determination of Sangharakshita that the new Buddhists should truly know what Buddha-Dharma was, in learning, practice, and realization.

Another fact should be recorded of my travels with Sangharakshita: he never lost his temper. India is a country where the least expected things happen, or perhaps that is the view of those like myself who were not born there. Whichever the case, the unexpected usually reveals what people have in their hearts, their normally hidden failings. Since events that do not go according to plan can often lead to disappointment, reactions to this are usually angry ones. However, not even once in all the time that I knew him did I ever see Sangharakshita angry. This is surely remarkable, especially in such trying conditions. I could not say the same for myself, for when I was young I was rather impetuous and could erupt into anger all too easily; still I could admire in another what I did not see in myself then. Sangharakshita was patient in the face of difficulties and certainly did not grumble about them. When he travelled his arrangements were well organized, though the odd bit of chaos could not be avoided. I noticed that he had a stoic acceptance of unexpected obstacles, with the ability to make light of them in a humorous way.

We pass on now – no doubt by another train – to Bombay, which we reached by the end of October. Here Sangharakshita had friends from many strata of society. Some of them were from a Parsi (Zoroastrian) background, a community which was generally wealthy; others came from high-caste Hindu roots but had shed most of their prejudices in the international business world of the city. They comprised a group of intelligent and cultured people who appreciated the Buddha's teachings certainly, but did not generally take the step of committing themselves to Buddhism. Many held back from this commitment for family reasons, fearing that relatives of older generations would blame them, while others feared they would become isolated from members of their caste. This was not an idle fear. There was the case of Sri Bhattacārya, though he lived in Gaya not in Bombay, a brahmin by birth and builder by trade who was contracted by the Thai government to build Wat Thai. He came to like the Thai monks so much that eventually he accompanied one of them to Thailand and was temporarily ordained. Now the good Bhattacārya, at whose house I stayed in Gaya – and ate there as his guest – had many daughters. Seven, I believe. As soon as the brahmin establishment heard of his trip abroad and of, horror of horrors, his ordination as a monk, they outcasted the whole family. This meant effectively: no brahmin husbands for those daughters, being sent to a kind of Coventry, no brahmin business, no brahmins to eat or drink tea with, no friendly greetings.... The power of caste, though loosening its grip in big cities, was still the force governing society in the smaller towns and villages where most people lived. It was not easy to change one's religious affiliation in these circumstances, and many who would otherwise have declared themselves Buddhists refrained from doing so. Of course, the new Buddhists, having occupied the lowest position in society, had nothing to lose and in fact everything to gain from their religious change.

While Sangharakshita and I were comfortably provided for by pro-Buddhist friends, those we went to teach lived quite other lives. Our Buddhist friends were quite happy that others, better off than they were, undertook to look after us. Many of them only just scraped by from day to day, never far from famine and debt, so it would have been a burden to support Sangharakshita and myself, even if the space could be found to accommodate us. Though grateful to our kind hosts, Sangharakshita did not acquiesce in their wrong views, such as the occasional appearance of that ingrained prejudice that 'Buddhism is only part of Hinduism, after all.'

In general, his approach to people's wrong views was not to contradict them outright, but rather to examine their ideas and make them think where they would lead. Sometimes in response to their views he asked them a question, on the principle perhaps that they should query their own statements. At other times he would divert attention from the expressed view, especially if this was voiced in a provocative manner, with an anecdote or story. Within it would be the key to unlocking the view, or at least a nudge in the right direction. Of course there were times when the view was set so solidly, so arrogantly, that nothing could be done – so it was ignored or passed over. Sangharakshita obviously considered it to be a waste of breath to argue with such people.

Sangharakshita's teachings to the Buddhists were much the same here as those he gave in Nagpur. He gave teachings originating in the Pāli Theravāda tradition on most occasions because this was the kind of basic teaching that was needed. These Buddhists had attended ceremonies during which they changed their religious affiliations and had glimpsed the robed figure of a monk or two, later listening to an outline of Buddha-Dharma from them. Even assuming they remembered some of this, their Buddhist knowledge was still very slight. For this reason, Sangharakshita's discourses dwelt upon foundational aspects and seldom explained aspects of the Mahāyāna. Moreover, he had to take care that the doctrine of karma and rebirth was properly understood so that it did not sound like the Hindu explanation offered to outcastes: you did evil things then, so now you have a low birth. As this had been rubbed into outcaste faces for centuries, it was essential that the Buddhist view was properly distinguished. Dr Ambedkar, in his book *The Buddha and His Dharma*, which became the 'bible' of the new Buddhists, was careful not to confuse his followers on this matter, and Sangharakshita had to spend quite a lot of time clarifying the karma and rebirth aspect. On other occasions he spent time emphasizing the moral values of the Five Precepts, especially their social importance, rather than individual advantage. The latter would receive more attention when he addressed an educated audience who perhaps could also find space and time in their lives to practise meditation and wisdom. But when he addressed Buddhists who lived in miserable cramped conditions – whole families packed into a small room or into some rickety shack – the social implications of the precepts and such methods of development as the Divine Abidings were generally what he emphasized.[21]

I remember, for instance, a visit to one of the *chawls*, concrete blocks of flats, each family having a room which opened on to a fairly wide veranda. Toilets were shared by many people. There was a meeting – perhaps it was to name a child – on one of these verandas with so many people packed onto it that I could not help wondering whether the construction would stand it. Fortunately, it did. I believe that at that time he spoke on the meaning and practice of the mantra *oṁ maṇi padme hūṁ*. Though I have forgotten the substance of this explanation, Sangharakshita's voice, as always, was persuasive and gentle, expressed the Dharma clearly, and was a joy to listen to. The fact that he would visit them and patiently explain the Dharma to them as no other person at that time would or could do, greatly endeared him to these Buddhists. Obviously, he was not after name and fame, as some of the political heirs of Dr Ambedkar certainly were, nor, like some of them, was he trying to squeeze money out of the former Mahars. The efforts he made for fellow Buddhists were purely to spread knowledge of the Dharma without regard to selfish considerations of his own comfort. People saw that he ate their food and expected no special treatment – not something which could be said of many Buddhist monks from outside India.

Digging away at these memories, I should like to contrast two meals to which Sangharakshita and I were invited. The first of these was in the house of wealthy people, Marwari merchants I think, though their names now escape me. It was the most magnificent pure vegetarian feast I have ever seen and tasted. Perhaps as many as fifty guests were present, but before the food could be consumed they listened to a feast for their ears and hearts from Sangharakshita. After his discourse, the guests – including ourselves – were invited to help themselves from an array of dishes laid out on tables stretching the whole side of one large room. The variety of the food was indescribable and the quality of it very rich. The experience of 'helping oneself' to food, while unremarkable to most people, felt a little strange to me. Though I had been a novice monk only for a year or so, I had by that time become accustomed to being offered food by Buddhist donors while I was seated. Now I was wandering around helping myself, as I noticed

Sangharakshita was doing, as though this was an everyday occurrence. On other occasions in this book I shall also remark upon Sangharakshita's ability to adapt to conditions which the strictest interpretation of the monastic discipline,[22] established 2,000 years before our time, would not allow. Rigid adherence to the letter of the law – a grasping at the lesser precepts without any consideration of the changes in this world – which characterized many Theravāda monks, could not be found in Sangharakshita. He led a pure and blameless life morally, but when it came to the precise details of, for instance, eating, he thought that concern with such unimportant matters led to an unadaptable rigidity and often to hypocrisy.

The other meal, the greatest contrast to the above, was in the Bombay slums, closely packed huts made of scraps of corrugated iron and cardboard intersected by winding lanes and pathways. Though people tried to keep their surroundings clean, their efforts were hampered by the pressure of people and lack of basic facilities. We were escorted to a small house – to Westerners this would count as a small room – into which we were invited, bending down to pass through the low doorway. The floor was of cow-dung plaster with a mat for us to sit upon. The food offered was the more precious since it represented many days of work on low wages. The Dharma talk which followed, inspired by the great generosity of the donors, was a moving account of well-practised Dharma. This picture of a meal in the Bombay slums has not left me after all these years.

During the visit, Sangharakshita and I went on an excursion, with a few Buddhist friends, to visit the Kanheri Caves outside Bombay. We reached them by crowded electric commuter train, so crowded that large numbers of passengers travelled on the outside of the carriages, there being no room inside. Arriving at our destination, the small town of Borivli, we alighted and walked a mile or so to the caves. From the word 'caves' one might picture natural erosions of rock by wind or water often decorated by strange formations and mysterious irregularities. Kanheri (and other Buddhist caves) were nothing like these. For them to come into existence a mountain of unfractured rock, not too hard but resistant to erosion, would be required. Next, wealthy donors who could support such large-scale works. Then great numbers of skilled artisans and other workers who would be employed for years to create this spacious sculpture. They had to hew out courtyards, a vertical façade with decorative doors and windows, and perhaps figures of the donors, or – in the case of later caves – Buddha images. Inside the growing cave, pillars with elaborate capitals would have appeared at regular intervals out of the living rock and then, when they had penetrated far enough according to the plans, a stupa, sometimes with a figure of the Buddha, would have been carved. Nothing in all this work was built in the ordinary way of taking small materials and out of them constructing something larger. All of it was created by painstaking sculpture, a method that allowed no mistakes. Incredible skill! How long did it take to carve a temple cave? How many artisans worked on it? We shall never know, for the times in which we live, though having many wonders, have lost this art completely.

The Buddhist caves of Kanheri varied a great deal in size and function. Small caves were one-monk abodes, large ones were community halls. Large and generally high barrel-vaulted caves were temples with stupas as the focus for devotion, where the community of monks or nuns would gather daily to chant their praises of the Three Jewels and perhaps for meditation. No doubt lay Buddhist visitors also used these cool and impressive caves for their devotions. One cave among them had many long raised 'benches' in rock, leading one to suppose that it served as the refectory for those ancient monks. The caves were well preserved and their sculpture impressive. No doubt the original communities of monks and nuns had gradually dwindled until there were no longer any renunciate Buddhists to live and practise in them. Then occasional Hindu wanderers may have stayed there, and for hundreds of years these great monuments no longer rang to the stirring tones of Buddhist chanting. Perhaps we were among the first Buddhists to enter them again after so long a time. If there were any Dharma protectors still in residence they would surely have been delighted.[23]

Chapter Five

BRANCHING OUT

Among folk they are few
Who go to the Further Shore,
Most among humanity
Scurry on this hither shore.

But who the well-taught Dharma do,
Their Dharma according with Dharma,
From Death's dominions hard to leave
They'll cross to the Further Shore.

Dhammapada 85–6

Any advancement for the former Mahar community in the days of the British Raj depended on a connection with the Indian Army. Young men who joined had to learn how to read and write and their wives and children had also to attend school. In this way the army was a door to freedom from the bondage of outcaste status. Dr Ambedkar's family had used this door of escape, as had a scattering of other Mahars. This meant that, due to army service, by the time Dr Ambedkar died there were a number of literate older people who appreciated what education could achieve, as well as many keen members of the younger generation who already attended college and university. They were found particularly in those cities where the army had a large presence – a cantonment ruled by the army – one of which was in Poona.

It was this city that Sangharakshita made his winter headquarters that year, from which he and I went out to engagements in the surrounding areas. Sometimes due to pressure of invitations our ways parted and he would be taken by one group of people while my invitation took me in the opposite direction. For me this meant that, having listened to Sangharakshita's methods of teaching as well as the content, I was able to address gatherings myself, though – I must confess – with a certain degree of trepidation. Sometimes these meet-ings were small affairs; one in particular that I recall had an element of the humorous to me – though I took good care to show nothing of my amusement. It involved a large patch of dusty ground, a scattering of people, and a veiled notice board. My function was to bless this board and 'open' it. The board proclaimed grandiloquently that it was the site of an All-India Buddhist Meditation Centre. As I could not, no doubt due to the state of the finances, be invited to lay the first brick, or to cut the ribbon proclaiming the institution open, I 'opened' the notice board. With due ceremony and some chanting of Pāli protective verses the veil was removed and the well-painted board appeared. I have sometimes wondered if there were subsequent ceremonies cul-minating in the concrete manifestation of a building, or whether the ageing board still stands on that featureless section of land. I hope that the former is true.

At other times I had weightier duties to perform, such as the conver-sion ceremony I was asked to conduct.[24] I am using the word 'conver-sion' to apply to the change of religious direction by the former Mahars, though generally the word is inappropriate to use in connec-tion with all varieties of mainstream Buddhism.[25] In theistic religions, conversion means conversion from one belief or sect to another. More or less persuasion, and sometimes a resort to violence, may accompany such conversion. This does not sound at all Buddhist! While in Western countries individuals turn themselves into Buddhists through encoun-ters with Buddhist teachers as well as their own study and practice, in India only rarely did individuals take this step. It was more common for a whole social group, a whole village, or even, as in the case of the Mahars, a whole caste, to decide that henceforth they wished to be known as Buddhists. To authenticate this change, at least in their own eyes, as well as to raise their esteem in other social groups (though this might take generations), they tried to invite a famous Buddhist teacher to preside over the ceremony, in the course of which they would all declare themselves Buddhists. It is noteworthy, though, that they *invited* the teacher and from him *requested* the Refuges and Precepts. The decision is made by this group without any exterior pressure, as may often be found in conversions effected by missionaries of theistic faiths. Buddhist monks never engage in such missionary activity, as it would be a form of harmful conduct – the imposition of an alien religion upon people who no doubt already have their own ideas and practices. Such actions would run counter to the spirit of non-harm exemplified by the Buddha. Hence they must be *invited*, which presupposes that people wish to hear what they have to say and that formal teachings will be *requested* from them.[26]

So when this word 'convert' is used, for lack of anything better in English, these facts must be borne in mind. There appears to be no word in the Pāli language (and probably there is none in Buddhist Sanskrit) to express religious conversion in its common English meaning. The English-Pāli Dictionary suggests *parivatteti*, which literally means 'to turn around completely', but using it to translate 'convert' in its English sense would be to give this Pāli verb a quite new extension of meaning.

People might ask, 'Why did Sangharakshita involve himself to such an extent in the conversion of these people?' He could have pursued his quiet practice of meditation and literary works continuously in Kalimpong, but he chose not to. Many other monks in India, those from Ceylon and Thailand for example, made no such efforts. There are many ways to answer this question, though the most important aspect was no doubt his compassion. Sangharakshita saw people oppressed with miserable lives and his heart went out to them. They wanted to know what the Buddha had taught and he was capable of teaching them, so changing their direction: with the Dharma they would have the chance to see for themselves its benefits in this and future lives. Some of them would find their way out of the wheel of birth and death.

Next, perhaps, was Sangharakshita's feeling that he had inherited a great undertaking from Dr Ambedkar, whom he met several times. The great man knew that he would not live long, and that his followers would be shattered when the news of his death reached them. Who would continue the movement he had begun? No one except Sangharakshita appeared willing to inherit this work, but for him it was a sacred trust.

Other motives prompting Sangharakshita were less important, though they still require a mention here. He saw a chance that had not occurred for many hundreds of years for Buddhism's revival in the land of its birth, for the living Dharma to lighten the burden of sufferings and to lead many to the way beyond limitations.

Certainly he did not want any of them snared by devious missionaries and turned into parodies of western Europeans, like the Anglo-Indians, and to know nothing of their Indian heritage, or only to know of the negative aspects. Christians in India, as Sangharakshita knew from first-hand contact, had a reputation for blinkered narrowness when it came to other religions. The former Mahars and other groups of people inspired by Dr Ambedkar's example must not be lured away from the Dharma!

Last, there was Sangharakshita's devotion to the Bodhisattva ideal: 'Though the many beings are numberless, I vow to save them.' He could not be comfortable in his Kalimpong retreat knowing that many people, in those days mostly in western India, were starving for the knowledge of Dharma. Bodhisattvas do not consider their own comfort but work for the well-being of all creatures. This sums up very well the reasons why Sangharakshita devoted so much time and energy to Dr Ambedkar's followers.

I followed Sangharakshita in this because I considered his work of 'conversion' was wonderful and inspiring. I agreed wholeheartedly with what I perceived to be his motives and did whatever I could to help him.

Some time before the conversion ceremony which I went on to conduct, Sangharakshita, who had first been approached to conduct it, found, referring to his diary, that he had promised to attend another engagement. Therefore he asked me to perform this ceremony accompanied by some of the educated younger new Buddhists who were his trusted disciples and acted as his interpreters when he addressed gatherings. Until this event I had never been the principal speaker, so although I accepted the invitation with pleasure it was accompanied by some apprehension.

On the appointed day we set off on a fairly long journey. In the party was Mr Maheshkar, a young man who often translated for Sangharakshita, as well as Ms Kedari, a well-educated Buddhist woman, at that time a rarity in the community. As a novice I was wearing a set of freshly-laundered dark orange robes from Burma and had a newly-shaven head. Our party's gear included loudspeakers and several truck batteries, for we were going to an area with no electricity. A well-packed bus from Poona trundled through the dry landscape dotted with villages and small towns and after three hours deposited us at a large dam. When we had extricated all our gear from inside the bus and from the roof, we set off down a flight of steps leading to the water behind the dam. Waiting for us was an ancient motor-boat, perhaps of 1920s vintage, and in this we chugged slowly through the long flooded valley with its branches and islands until we reached a steep track leading down to the water's edge where two or three villagers were waiting. After exchanging traditional greetings with our hands together,[27] we slowly climbed the 200 feet or so and were invited to sit in the shade of a tree to wait for transport. The village that was our destination was only two miles or so away but as honoured guests we were not permitted to walk. Meanwhile, tea was served to all of us – and we waited.

By now it was late afternoon, but eventually we saw a procession approaching us, led by decorated ox-carts with a crowd of village men following. I was placed in the first of these carts, the decoration of which consisted of several stems of fresh-cut sugar-cane and banana-shoots with broad leaves. When everyone had been properly installed in this verdant splendour a band formed in front of my vehicle, which was to lead the procession. The instruments, both brass and wood-wind, had never been seen in any British military band. They were genuinely antique Indian pieces, one of which reminded me of the serpent, the bass wind instrument of medieval Europe. The music that emerged from their coils consisted of energetic renderings of tradi-tional Indian dance pieces – with no Bollywood influence at all. Going before this band were two lines of male dancers who danced us into their village with great vigour. From their gestures they were obviously clearing our path of obstructions, particularly demonic ones. It was an altogether most impressive welcome.

When we reached the village and were invited to sit and take tea again, I ascertained through careful questions that the oxen, the carts, the band, and the dancers all came from the high-caste warrior Maratha community. In this village there were only Marathas, re-nowned for their fierceness as fighters before the British gained control of the area, and the outcaste Mahars who did all the dirty work around the village. For some reason, though, relations between the two groups in this village were quite friendly, so that the Marathas had readily agreed to lend their support to this big event though of course they were not becoming Buddhists. When I learned of this unusual situ-ation, I cautioned my fellow Buddhists to be very careful in their speeches not to stir up any communal tension. It was common at that time for new Buddhists to rail at the oppressions they had suffered under the heels of high-caste Hindus. I have already mentioned some of the rules to which they were subjected and the humiliations they were forced to endure, and shall not repeat them here. None of these things, I warned them, were to be mentioned. We had not come here to be negative about the past, rather we would all be very positive regarding the present and the future. There is a procedure, I told them, in the monastic sangha to prevent different parties forming, arguments increasing and ill will leading to schism, called 'covering over with grass'. We will cover over the terrible past in the interests of communal harmony in the present and future. They all agreed that no words antagonistic to the Maratha caste would be spoken.

The 'function', due to start at eight in the evening, finally began about ten. A cloth-covered platform had been constructed and cushions placed upon it. Microphones were connected to ancient sound equipment, which obviously imprisoned a variety of enraged demons, from which wires led off into the darkness to distant loudspeakers. Light around the platform was provided by pump-up kerosene lanterns which roared away. They illuminated not only the speakers from far-away Poona but also the garlanded portraits of the Buddha Śākyamuni and Dr Babasaheb Ambedkar. Incense burned in front of the two pictures.

Below me, fading into the darkness, was a sea of faces, not only local people but also many from the surrounding villages who had journeyed on foot to be there. All the faces were topped by turbans, and one could not distinguish Mahar from Maratha – but all I could see were men. The programme opened therefore in a way that showed how different the Buddha-Dharma was from the customs of the Hindus. I asked the leaders of the community, both Maratha and Mahar, 'Where are the women?' They replied that the womenfolk and children were behind a nearby house. It was obvious they would see nothing and hear little of the proceedings, so I requested that the men move over to one side and let the women and children come forward. This was already a great revolution! The women were most pleased with this arrangement, while a lot of the men must have been amazed.

After this, I was introduced and delivered some brief instructions about the Three Refuges – Buddha, Dharma, and Sangha – and what it meant to go for Refuge to them. After this had been translated, those who were Going for Refuge were asked to remove their turbans. In this way Mahar men could be distinguished from the Marathas. Perhaps all the women present were Mahar.

The Going for Refuge ceremony followed, with people repeating the Pāli words I chanted, followed by a Marathi translation which they also repeated. After their undertaking of the Five Precepts as well, I was invited to give a Dharma talk. I confined my explanations of Dharma to subjects that would be easily understood by the audience as well as practical matters for everyday life. I did not explain any Dharma that might be controversial, though I certainly emphasized that the Buddha-Dharma transcended all the boundaries of human society – caste, for example. Of course, I spoke at length about the Three Jewels and Going for Refuge, including in the Dharma jewel a full explanation of Buddhist ethics. I hoped that by drumming in the value of the Five Precepts, real changes would come about in the lives of these people, both Mahar and Maratha. Following on from the harmony established by the practice of moral conduct, my talk continued with a long explanation of loving-kindness and compassion, enlivened by some illustrative stories. The Dharma talk concluded with the truth of impermanence explained on many different levels. All these subjects would make sense to people from both the communities present and perhaps lead to better relations between them. I said nothing about the worship of Hindu gods on this occasion, though later the twenty-two vows made by Dr Ambedkar, when he and his wife became Buddhists, were repeated. These included an abjuration to refrain from worship of these gods and from employing Hindu priests for ceremonies, as well as, among their wandering religious, to cease following Hindu forms of asceticism. After this explanation of Dharma was finished, it was the turn of my friends from Poona. It was as though my talk constituted the root text while my Mahar fellow Buddhists provided commentaries from various angles. For instance, Ms Kedari addressed herself mostly to the women and clarified for them how Dharma affects everyday life in the family.

By about 1.30 the next morning, all the guest speakers had finished their explanations, with one of them, I remember, raising a lot of laughter from the audience; and so the religious programme was concluded. As I was very tired, our kind hosts showed me a room in a house, I suppose a Mahar house, though I cannot now be certain of this, with a straw mat upon a mud floor, and there I slept soundly. The rest of the programme, of music, singing, and dancing continued until dawn.

Some time after this, when everyone had recovered from the all-night programme, country rice and chillies appeared with tea – this was breakfast. The people who brought the food explained as we ate that before the construction of the dam the village was sited in the valley where the land was more fertile. Their relocation to the barren uplands had adversely affected their wealth, though one could wonder whether the former Mahars of the area had been as greatly affected as the Marathas. Everyone agreed that the programme had been wonderful, awakening many of the Mahars to the pure practice of Lord Buddha's Dharma.

In that isolated village with difficult connections to the outside world some will still remember the night they became Buddhists, and some may be have gone on to deepen their knowledge of the Dharma. It is quite possible, though, that from that time in 1960 until now, thirty-eight years later, no Buddhist teacher has been there. Even in cities and smaller towns in India, Buddhists who could teach the Dharma were then as rare as hare's horns. Though at the time of writing this much has changed for the better for Buddhists in that part of India, still in remote villages such as the one I visited little may differ. For my part, I hope this Buddhist expedition led to great changes of heart for the former Mahars, as well as to improvements in their economic condition, but I trust that their friendly relations with their Maratha neighbours continue and have deepened.[28]

While Sangharakshita had guided many Mahars at numerous large gatherings to recite the Three Refuges and thereby become Buddhists, the village ceremony that I have described here was my only experience of this. Most of it remains clear in my mind, a joyful and treasured event which helped just a little to dispel ignorance and spread the light of the Dharma.

Another expedition which may have occurred at this time also remains sharply focused in my mind. I am not sure now, though, whether Sangharakshita led this party or whether I was the only monastic Buddhist. In any case it was an event worth relating.

Between Bombay and Poona lies the small railway station of Malavli where if one alights from the train no fewer than two famous Buddhist cave temples can be visited on opposite sides of the tracks, Karle and Bhaja. Our expedition set out from Poona on a local train, generally the sort that stopped at all stations – and often all places in between. I remember that about thirty or forty people accompanied us and that we got off the train and walked first towards the hills containing the Buddhist cave temple known as Karle, from its vicinity to a village of that name. What its original Buddhist name was no one now remembers. Even the outside, now ravaged by erosion, was impressive. A small fee paid to the local employee of the Indian Archaeological Service admitted us to the forecourt of the temple. And then what did we see? Tucked away into the outer pillars of this ancient excavation was a small and brightly-painted Hindu temple. That it should be built right up against the Buddhist monument was not altogether surprising, for Karle was obviously still a place of great power, but much worse was the fact that this was a temple where a bloodthirsty goddess was worshipped. At certain times of the year animals were sacrificed here. To say I was appalled would not express my feelings. Here – a place excavated for Buddhists to pay their homage to the All-Awakened One, who tirelessly taught:

> *All tremble at force!*
> *All are afraid of death!*
> *Likening others to oneself*
> *Kill not nor cause to kill.*
>
> *All tremble at force!*
> *Life is dear to all!*
> *Likening others to oneself*
> *Kill not nor cause to kill.*[29]

– was a temple for animal sacrifice. The very stones of the forecourt outside Karle's monumental Buddhist shrine were sullied with the blood of animals.

In classical commentaries on the Five Precepts, it is explained that breaking the first of them – 'not killing living creatures' – can be motivated by either greed, hatred, or delusion,[30] or – of course – a mixture of these roots of evil. Killing motivated by hatred is, alas, a common occurrence in this world, whether it concerns the destruction of one human being through murder, or masses of them, labelled as 'the enemy' in times of war. Killing rooted in the unwholesome power of greed can be seen in hunting animals for food, or of course in the murder of a person in order to get hold of their wealth. These motivations are common enough in Western society, but examples of killing on the basis of delusion, as it is classically explained, cannot so easily be identified. Of course, greed and hatred will only be given full rein when they are linked to delusion, but delusion itself may also be the dominant force causing the breaking of this precept. This happens, for instance, where people hold a religious view that a causal action that produces suffering will instead result in happiness for them. The sacrifice of animals is done with the desire to capture the god's attention so that some sort of happiness will manifest for oneself. Such beliefs are entirely contrary to karmic cause and effect, and are therefore muddled thinking, a type of delusion. Buddhists always teach that the karma of killing living beings brings the result of suffering for the doer.

The cave temples at Karle, the beauty of which will be described below, also illustrate our experience of saṁsāra, the wheel of birth and death. In this life the light and the dark sides are found inextricably entwined: the enjoyable and the painful, the beautiful and the ugly – leading of course to our grasping the one and rejecting the other. Grasping is greed. Rejection is hatred. These two are backed by delusion. Here again are the roots of evil. Of course, it is not necessarily the case that the beautiful is grasped and the ugly rejected, but without Dharma practice this is usually what occurs.

So – cultivating some equanimity for the Hindu intrusion – we entered the great cave shrine, all of it carved from solid rock. These days we cannot even imagine the process of carving into a cliff-face and creating as one goes pillars, arches, stupas, and images. Within its doorway, topped by a window letting light into the interior, was a pillared hall leading to an apse in which a solid stupa of rock was the focus of people's faith. It had no Buddha image, nor was there in sculpture by the entrance any trace of a representation of the Blessed One. This indicates Karle's very ancient origin, as well as the adherence of those monks who commissioned this work, or perhaps who worked on it themselves, to the oldest layer of Buddhist tradition that emphasizes that Awakened Ones cannot be depicted in images, only through symbols. For example, the lotus flower or bud indicated the future Buddha's birth, his Awakening was represented by an empty seat beneath a bodhi tree, his first teaching by the Wheel of Dharma, and his passing away or Final Nirvāṇa by a stupa.

The ceiling high above our heads was carved to represent curved wooden beams holding up a barrel-vault roof, in imitation of free-standing temple architecture which has long since disappeared. The magnificent pillars on both sides were topped by kneeling elephants with riders on their backs, while behind these pillars, running the whole length of the excavation and behind the stupa, was a processional passage for the practice of *pradakṣiṇa*, the respectful keeping of one's right side towards Buddhas and teachers while they are alive and towards their remains, symbolized by a stupa.

The stupa itself, austere in outline, with a round base elevating the original dome shape, was surmounted by a square *harmika* supporting a large parasol. Evidently of very great age, this symbol of the dignity of the Dharmarāja was slightly warped and, marvel of marvels, made of a wood that had endured the passing of at least a thousand years.

While we stood at the entrance of this temple, overawed by its perfection and sense of presence, with candles, incense, and flowers in our hands, we were told in no uncertain terms by the caretaker that 'worship' was forbidden in this place. As we were forty in number and he only one, his protestations could not succeed. We told him that this was a Buddhist place made by ancient Buddhists and that as we were living Buddhists we intended to pay our respects in the traditional manner. We also assured him that we would not leave so much as an incense stick when we left. Grudgingly, he conceded that we could go ahead. So for half an hour or so, after lighting candles and incense and placing them with flowers around the stupa, we chanted praises of the Three Jewels. Oh, the marvellous acoustics! Our chanting sounded like a troupe of devas from one of the heavenly realms. Then, to conclude it all, thrice we walked slowly in procession through the passage all around the temple, keeping the stupa on our right while recollecting the virtues of the Three Jewels. The whole practice was most moving, while our chanting seemed to awaken some slumbering energy that had endured there for many, many lifetimes. Afterwards, I wondered whether we were the first Buddhists to perform a puja there since the last Buddhists lived there – how many hundreds of years earlier?

Sangharakshita and I, at the end of this visit to Poona, returned to Bombay and after some time there boarded a train running north, then west, to Ahmedabad in Gujerat state. He had received an invitation from small groups of Dalits, not Mahars (who mostly lived within the boundaries of Maharashtra) but others who were also inspired by the clarion call of Dr Ambedkar. We were joined on this expedition by Vivekānanda. Vivekānanda was very unusual among his compatriots studying in India in that he had some understanding of cultures very different from his own. He was the only monk from Wat Thai who thought that the immense efforts made by Sangharakshita for the awakening of the former Untouchables were worthwhile – and who actually joined in and tried to help. He enjoyed travel and did not mind discomfort – travel and discomfort being almost synonymous in India. Muscular, jolly, and talkative, he was a good travelling companion. Unlike many Thais in monastic life who had been novices since their early teens, he had experienced the joys and sorrows of adult life before becoming a monk. In fact he had been a Thai kick-boxer and was physically very fit – he could snap into the full lotus posture without using his hands, but he confessed that when he sat in meditation he always placed a cushion in front of him. When asked why he told me that due to boxing blows he would sometimes pass out and lie there in the lotus position for hours. I believe that eventually he recovered from this obstacle. His colourful life before he left home and got ordained had included a grandmother who was a sort of witch, and a love of large and powerful motorbikes. He had a rich fund of stories to tell and recounted them so well, and with such good humour, that listening to him was most enjoyable. Dr Gottmann, of whom more below, wrote to me, 'Our cook was always afraid when Vivekānanda came, eating as he did a potful of rice good for a normal Indian family of six people.'

This rail journey was not at all pleasant for me as I had a rising temperature and felt very unwell. Sangharakshita was very concerned, but apart from getting off the train and interrupting our tour – which I did not wish to do – there was little he could do. When we arrived at Ahmedabad we were met on the platform by Yashodhara, a brahmin lady who sympathized with Buddhist teachings. We were to stay in her house during our time in the city. Sangharakshita, as soon as we had alighted from the train, asked her about a doctor, as by this time I had a raging fever, and she at once mentioned a married couple, both doctors, from Germany, who had established the Vasant Nature Cure Hospital – and were practising Buddhists! We went immediately to their hospital, where they examined me and concluded that I needed treatment for malnutrition – 'dystrophic' I remember was the technical term – and that I was suffering from a bout of amoebiasis. I was admitted to the hospital then and there, given my own room, and told to rest. The two doctors Gottmann, for that was their name, were most hospitable and treated me free of charge for a whole month. At the time I was admitted my temperature was around 41°c and, as can be seen from the photograph of the three monks, I was also thin and none too happy.

I suppose I shall never know what particularly good karma I had done in the past to experience such a fortunate connection with people so kind and caring. Without their help there is little doubt that my life would have ended in Ahmedabad.

With the expertise of the Drs Gottmann my return to health was assured. They treated me naturopathically – all kinds of pressurized water baths and earths were involved – but confessed that as they lacked some essential equipment in Gujerat they would have to expel the invaders in my intestines with one of the products of Bayer, the German pharmaceutical company. Exercises of various sorts were also part of the cure and I recall that towards the end of my stay with them I began to feel much better healthwise than I had in Bombay and Poona.

As I was then practising the Ten Precepts of a novice monk, the sixth of them forbidding meals 'at the wrong time' – that is, from noon till dawn the next day – I was used to taking no nourishment then. Both doctors told me firmly that while staying with them I must eat in the afternoon and evening as well if my strength was to be restored. I did as the good doctors ordered and so put a little more flesh on my bones.

Sangharakshita visited me regularly, bringing me news of his activities around the city. He was accompanied by a few of the new Buddhists who lived there. After he had left Ahmedabad to continue turning the Wheel of the Dharma in other places,[31] some of the younger men who spoke English continued to visit me. Later, when I was well, I delivered a lecture in one of the new Buddhist localities to an audience that was small by Indian standards. They found my 'Queen's English' rather difficult to translate into Gujerati and had to ask Dr Karl-Heinz Gottmann to cast my ideas into a language more nearly approaching Indian English.

Another visitor during my recovery was a young man from a wealthy Muslim family who had some attraction to the Buddha's teachings and had gone to hear Sangharakshita speak. His education had included not only the finest Indian private schools but also Oxford University, where I think he studied law. One day, talking about families, I learned that he had several brothers also with outstanding academic records. 'Oh,' I said, 'And do you have any sisters?' 'Yes,' he replied, mentioning how many there were. 'And where were they educated?' was my next question. 'It is not necessary to educate women,' was his astonishing answer. Though he had reached Oxford and obtained degrees there, this exposure to liberal Western culture had not made the slightest impression on his espousal of a male-dominated world. One side of him, at least, still lived in a traditional Islamic culture that asserted and protected male dominance. I considered this incident food for thought not only for Muslims but for Buddhists too.

Besides visitors, I had many other things to engage my attention in hospital. Dr Gottmann reminds me that at the time of my admission I was studying Guenther's translation of Gampopa's *Jewel Ornament of Liberation*, then recently published in London. In the evenings we discussed parts of it. The good doctor also requested me to prepare a summary of the Buddha's teachings contained in the Pāli tradition. Such a 'condensed survey' must have kept me scribbling away for weeks. I cannot now imagine how I managed to complete such a work without any books to consult, nor how those diverse and very rich materials could be compressed into one book. What happened to it, I wonder? In any case, its writing seems to have been part of my cure.

Besides discussing Gampopa's work with Dr Karl-Heinz Gottmann I enjoyed our more general exchanges of views on a variety of Buddhist topics. The doctor inclined towards Vajrayāna, being even then a disciple of Lama Govinda, the German Buddhist teacher who lived in the Himalayan foothills of Almora with his wife, Li Gotami. This lama later founded the Arya Maitreya Mandala, of which at the time of writing Dr Gottmann is the Vajra-master with the Sanskrit name Advayavajra. Lama Govinda, whom unfortunately I never met, was a good friend of Sangharakshita and they corresponded frequently. The lama also contributed to the *Maha Bodhi Journal*, produced in Calcutta, and to Sangharakshita's smaller publication, *Stepping-Stones*, which appeared for twenty-one issues from Kalimpong.

Looking back, it appears that my month at the Vasant Nature Cure Hospital was packed full of events! When I was pronounced cured and released from their kind ministrations, I arranged a little ceremony for the good doctors and chanted to bless their noble undertaking. The local Buddhists, though few in number, had asked me to stay with them in the city centre and this I did, walking over – every now and then – to visit the Drs Gottmann. I remember that my Buddhist friends there accommodated me in a two- or three-storey building, my room having access to a flat roof on which I usually slept. During this time, perhaps two or three weeks, I had small engagements round the city, such as name-giving ceremonies and teaching small groups of the scattered Buddhists.

Central Ahmedabad was a bustling place, rather different from the calm of the Gottmanns' clinic, but one day the noise level rose to quite remarkable heights with a barrage of screaming and wailing that continued for some hours. Enquiring about this racket, I was told that someone had died in a nearby house and that in the eyes of local

Hindus true grief could only be expressed in this extreme fashion. This led me to some reflections about the Buddha's Middle Way for transcending all extremes, contrasted with the common expressions in all parts of the world of unwholesome emotions. In this case I gathered that the 'grief' went on until the participants were utterly exhausted and could no longer demonstrate the depths of their love for the departed.

The city contained a strange mix of Hindus, Muslims, and Jains. The Muslims had borrowed many pillars from former Hindu temples for their mosques and continued to build in a way obviously influenced by Hindu architecture, though of course without any depictions of humans and gods. The Jains were much in evidence in the city too, having many temples and ashrams there. I was told about, though I did not visit, Jain 'animal hospitals' where sick or unwanted animals were kept by wealthy Jain merchants as a way of making merit. Even bedbugs, of which Ahmedabad had a more than usually voracious variety, were carefully collected and taken to these 'hospitals' where poor men were employed to feed them by lying down on bug-ridden beds. I reflected that this was a rather extreme form of *ahiṁsā* (non-harming).

Maybe it was at this time that I met a Jain teacher and his disciple at a Jain temple. I was curious to know his thoughts on the survival of the Jains in India in the face of Muslim onslaughts, contrasted with the disappearance of Buddhists once their great centres of study and practice had been destroyed. During the meeting we sat on mats on the marble floor – I was accompanied by a Buddhist who acted as interpreter while the Jain teacher had a young disciple with him. They were dressed in white cloth – at least, the outer layer was white.[32] Other layers which could be glimpsed were various shades of grey darkening to black. These monks never washed, an ascetic practice which made it advisable to sit a good distance away from them. Their heads were also adorned with a few long hairs which they plucked, not shaved, once a year – another of their ascetic practices. The older teacher had few of these hairs while his disciple still had a number of hair-roots still growing. At their ordination ceremonies, attended by large numbers of devotees to see how they faced the ordeal, *all* their head hair was plucked out. This is a practice that should be classified among the extremes of self-torture based upon the unwholesome roots, principally hatred, that motivate it.

The Jain *ācārya* adopted a superior rather than friendly attitude to me during this meeting, though of course he was a teacher of many years' standing while I was still a callow novice monk. In answer to my questions he said that the Doctrine of the Conquerors (Jinadharma, an expression also used by Buddhists) had survived invasion by Muslims because its lay-people were organized into Ganas, while Buddhism, he pointed out, had no such formal groups for householder devotees. Large monasteries, such as Buddhists developed in India (and of course very much later in Tibet), were the institutions most vulnerable to sudden attacks, and crumbled first. A worldly view of religions, any of them, is that when they are wealthy, well supported, and influential, they should survive for ages. In fact, though, as the Buddha warned but the monks perhaps had forgotten, 'gains, honour, and fame'[33] are a dire threat to the long continuance of the Dharma. Smaller and less obvious groups of practitioners – such as some of the yogis in India and Tibet – could weather the storm of oppression more easily. The golden roofs of Nālandā's thirteen-storey towers would have been astonishing to see and would no doubt have aroused great devotion among Buddhists, but they were also an invitation to any horde of barbarians that here was wealth to be had, and shrines to be pillaged. This was as true, I reflected, for the famous Buddhist monastic universities of ancient India as it was for the great monasteries with hundreds or even thousands of monks in the Tibet of the 1950s. The one faced Muslim fanatics more intent on plunder than conversion, the other Communist fanatics intent on destruction of an ancient culture by bringing low all those in high places within the hierarchy of religion and politics. Big monasteries fell first. What were supposed to be the bastions of Dharma actually crumbled most easily, a fact for Buddhists to contemplate.

The Jain teacher, with whom I engaged in no polemics, also crowed a little about Buddhism's 'weakness' and the strength of his own doctrine. The Jain religion, he said, could endure persecution in the land of its birth because of the practices (he meant the extreme asceticism) of its adherents, whereas Buddhism could not endure long in any place, though it travelled far in the world. In every country it was destined to be destroyed, as its principal practitioners – the monks – became lax and stopped attending to their ascetic lifestyle. I thought this attack upon the Buddha-Dharma ignored the truth of impermanence, which surely applied to all religions and their followers everywhere, whether they 'believed' in impermanence or not – and told him so. He did not have very much to say on this point, as no doubt he could think of examples of slack and corrupt behaviour in his own ranks.

Still, I thought later, after we had left those odoriferous monks in their spotless marble temple, it is true that the 'professionals' can attack and destroy a teaching from the inside more surely than peripheral lay followers. Later, in Thailand, I saw an old illustrated manuscript that depicted this – monks armed with swords and spears attacking the enthroned Buddha.[34]

Returning from one of my visits to the Gottmans – I walked the whole distance crossing the sandy river by bridge and then walking along its banks with the city's impressive medieval walls on my left – I came upon a contrast which is worth recording, as it illustrates a sort of shocking extreme. First came a little shanty village of cardboard and fragments of corrugated iron, all about four feet high, leaning crazily against the solid walls of the city. I asked my Buddhist friend who lived there. He replied that the men of this outcaste community were thieves and the women were prostitutes. There was no question of whether they wished to do these things: according to the Hindu caste system, this was their divinely ordained position in life. Caste, and the duties or 'dharmas' that it laid down, extended even to crime! We had only just passed this miserable encampment and rounded a bend in the city walls when we came upon a monstrous erection of glass, steel, and concrete – many million rupees' worth – a hotel that housed wealthy tourists. Upon enquiry I found that this unlovely structure was actually the work of Le Corbusier. The contrast could not have been more stark.

During my stay in Ahmedabad I remember going to the countryside only once, to a village to which Sangharakshita and I had been invited. One of the young Buddhists wished to take us to his birthplace there and so organized a small meeting of the outcaste community. When we arrived there after a long bus journey we saw that of course the high-caste Hindu houses were well built while the outcastes lived in poorer dwellings, though much better than the shanties I had seen around Ahmedabad's walls. All that I can now recall about the visit was the local government school, of which the villagers were rightly proud. All the children in the village attended this school, whether they were Caste Hindu or Dalit. This in itself marked a great change compared to the days of the young Ambedkar. At that time, if outcaste children had any chance to go to school they had to sit outside the classroom or huddle in a corner seated on sacking. Caste Hindu teachers at that time would not correct their books for fear of pollution. Well, times had changed attitudes just a little, for in this village school pupils sat together in class and played together as well. But caste prejudice still prevailed, for each community had its own water pot, the water for caste children being drawn from the Caste Hindu well, the Dalits' water coming from their community's well. As the Indian government had now officially abolished caste prejudice in its institutions and declared discrimination against outcastes to be punishable by law, there was only one water pot for the children on days when the schools' inspector made his round. But woe betide any outcaste child who was thirsty that day and drank from the Caste Hindu water! I was told that the government would not support any school in which caste discrimination was practised, hence this petty exercise in deception.

I rejoined Sangharakshita in Poona after my cure in Ahmedabad. We stayed in a large old-fashioned bungalow with wide verandas and plenty of space – it had formerly been a clinic also devoted to nature-cure methods – which was very suitable for the programme that we ran throughout March. Every each evening, apart from Sundays, Sangharakshita and I taught Dharma for about three hours to devoted Buddhists who were able to attend the whole programme. Indeed, it was designed as a training course for the new Buddhists who might in time become teachers themselves. At 7.30 each evening all those attending, between thirty and forty, went for Refuge and undertook the Five Precepts, followed by a short Buddha puja. Then began the lectures during which participants, if they were literate, were encouraged to take notes of all the topics covered. These included not only the principal doctrines of the Buddha-Dharma but also a commentary on all the 423 verses of the *Dhammapada*, of which a Maharashtrī translation was available. Buddhist history, canonical literature, some manners and customs, and an outline of monastic law were also covered. This seems a formidable amount of information to pack into about twenty-six evenings! It was however, greatly enjoyed by our audience, who appreciated all the information we gave them.

A tea break halfway through each evening was followed by a second teaching session. After each teaching, there was time allowed for discussion and quite a number of questions were asked, in contrast to the larger gatherings where this was very unusual. Mr Maheshkar acted as an excellent interpreter throughout the whole of this month, while I gave some of the talks. My time with Sangharakshita, during which he had delivered so many discourses upon such a wide variety of topics, had helped me to relax the shyness and nervousness that afflicted me when I was younger, so that my self-confidence increased.

The *Maha Bodhi Journal*, reporting this course, summed it up thus:

> For the trainees, most of them workers who came to classes straight from their duties in office and factory, the course was a means of great spiritual enrichment, while for the monks conducting it, it was a valuable experience which deepened their own knowledge of the Dharma and brought them into fruitful contact with their Buddhist friends in Poona.

Chapter Six

BANGALORE

Right worthy of gifts is the Sangha purified,
With pacified senses, all mental stains dispelled,
One quality alone with which all powers won:
Gone beyond desire that Sangha I revere.

A verse in praise of the Sangha Jewel

Sangharakshita had mentioned his former fellow 'wanderer' to me several times. Their practice of the homeless life together for two and a half years in South India is well described in Sangharakshita's memoirs.[35] While Sangharakshita had been ordained at Kusinārā as a novice and at Sarnath as a monk, Buddharakkhita, as his fellow wanderer was eventually named, travelled first to Sri Lanka and afterwards to Burma gaining his higher ordination as a monk there. On his return to India it was in Bangalore, in the southern state of Mysore, that he settled down to develop a branch of the Maha Bodhi Society. Sangharakshita told me his friend was a teacher of Pāli and the Theravāda Buddhist teachings contained in it. There had been a time, in the Hampstead Vihara, when I stoutly rejected the learning of another language to gain access to the Buddhist tradition, preferring in my ignorance to be content with the imprecise and often ancient translations already available. Sangharakshita made it very clear to me that without some knowledge of Pāli and Sanskrit my learning would be very limited. It seemed to me that he had neither the inclination nor the time to teach me a Buddhist language, so that if I was to learn one it would have to be with another teacher. There was then little choice in India, almost Hobson's choice, so I wrote to Buddharakkhita on Sangharakshita's advice, and asked the former to accept me as a pupil.

On my departure from Poona in April, therefore, I boarded the train which took me across the Deccan to Bangalore. It may have been this long journey which was lightened by a lengthy discussion with a fellow passenger, probably a brahmin who spoke English well and was learned in Hindu teachings. Our discussion, which I remember stretched over five hours, centred on whether the Buddhist view of Nirvāṇa could be equated with the Hindu conception of Paramatman, the Highest Self. I do not think we really resolved this issue! But he was able to quote many Sanskrit texts to me while I replied with quotations from the Pāli suttas, so the discussion was mutually educational. Though we disagreed on many points – which no doubt could still be further argued – we parted with good feelings when he alighted from the train. His name and where we parted now escape me, but I shall not easily forget the discussion. Where else except in India could one have such an extended debate on spiritual matters so that the time passed so profitably?

The train that took me to Bangalore was uncommonly crowded, even for the third-class carriages in which I was accustomed to travel. Perhaps this had something to do with the fact that this line was only metre-gauge with consequently narrower carriages. The further south we went, alongside changes in the landscape, there were differences in the food that could be bought at the stations where the train stopped for meals – a most civilized arrangement, as I have remarked before.

Ven. Buddharakkhita – he preferred the Pāli form of his name – was on the platform to collect me.[36] I accompanied him to the only Buddhist centre for many miles around, in a central area of the city called Gandhinagar. Perhaps it was appropriate, though this is a rather dualistic view, that the Maha Bodhi Society's acre of land was opposite the walls of the local prison – Great Awakening outside the bondage of saṁsāra! The Society's land was mostly planted with flowers, fruit, and vegetables, while the main building, then single-storey, occupied the rest. Like many Indian buildings which are intended to grow higher when finances make it possible, this temple-monastery building had reinforcing rods projecting upwards for the second floor. Also planned was a stupa, while a sapling of the bodhi tree was well established and growing tall. The building, for which Buddharakkhita had raised funds, was solidly constructed of local stone, and plainly intended to last a long time. In its centre was the temple, where we chanted puja morning and evening, while the wings contained accommodation, kitchen, and bathroom.

Altogether four monks stayed there, though at the time of my arrival I was still a novice. Besides our teacher, Buddharakkhita, there were two young Indian monks in residence, whom I used to call Sīla and Saddhā from shortened forms of their Pāli names, Sīlaratana and Saddhārakkhita. They were ordained as monks in April 1961. We spoke mostly English in the vihara, as Buddharakkhita's native tongue was Bengali, while my fellow monks spoke (I think) Hindi – and of course local supporters often resorted to English among themselves as they came from the multilingual south where Tamil, Telugu, Malayalam, and other languages, make for problems in communication.

Buddharakkhita was tall, physically strong, and of imposing appearance. His face was determined and could darken quickly with anger, but as though to make up for this, his smile was relaxed and heartwarming. Of his scholarship there could be no doubt, and his time in Ceylon and Burma had been well spent learning Pāli and the treasures of the Buddha's teachings set down in that language. If confirmation was needed of his excellent knowledge of Pāli then his translation of 'Kamalāñjali', literally 'Lotusing the Hands', a modern poem praising the Buddha in sixty stanzas, together with his explanation of unusual words, should be read.[37] When it came to teaching his treasure of Dharma knowledge, though, he was quite severe. He demanded that the lessons – every afternoon for two hours or so – be well learned. Trouble would certainly erupt if the Pāli conjugation or declension one was supposed to have learned by heart could not be repeated in his presence. As my ability to learn languages was limited I had to apply myself diligently so that I could repeat to him without mistakes: *Buddho, buddhā, buddhaṁ, buddhe; buddena, buddebhi/ehi; buddhassa, buddhānaṁ....* Sīla and Saddhā also had learning problems with Pāli, so we helped each other during our evening homework periods. Had the venerable teacher not been so fierce with his students, particularly with me, I doubt very much whether any Pāli would have lodged in our thick skulls, certainly not in mine. As it was, this side of his character helped me greatly in mastering this ancient language, unique in that only one tradition of Buddhist scriptures is preserved in it – and nothing else at all. I have always been grateful for his efforts to teach me the basics of the Theravāda Buddhist tradition.

Another aspect of our education at Bangalore was the writing of essays. I still have the two termite-nibbled Indian exercise books in which I recorded Pāli grammar and these essays. Though the first of these, entitled *The Pāli Language – an Outline of its History*, has no corrections, the second one, *Pāli Literary History and the Saṅgāyanas*,[38] has a number of sentences deleted. This meant that rather than following Buddharakkhita's precise instructions I had branched out with my own ideas learned from other sources. Such independence of mind, especially in a novice ordained only for a year, was not welcome. In fact, Buddharakkhita berated me for these elaborations on his teachings. In those days, his view of Buddha-Dharma was a narrow one which could be summed up in this way: 'Theravāda tradition is correct while all other Buddhist traditions are corrupt.' Even with my then limited knowledge, I could not agree with such a proposition – and so got into trouble. The sentences crossed out are still readable and present non-Theravāda views of such disputed matters as the cause for the great division of the Buddhist tradition after the second Saṅgāyana. Buddharakkhita would not hear of such things: he was concerned only with the Pāli tradition, which he equated with 'pure Theravāda'.

Because of this rigidity relations with him were not always easy. I remember, for instance, his dogmatic assertion that the suttas of the Pāli tradition – all of them – were the very words of the Śākyamuni Buddha. Such fundamentalism I found very distasteful, though I still respected Buddharakkhita for his learning. It could not even be argued to him that portions of many suttas were narrative and could not therefore be the Buddha's words. At such a suggestion he would react angrily and deliver a lecture on how conceited I was (probably true) to differ from his traditional learning.

Referring again to my two old notebooks, I see that my third and fourth essays, 'The Analysis of Pāli and Vibhajjavāda'[39] and 'The Khandhas',[40] contain no deleted passages. Obviously, by that time I had concluded that Buddharakkhita's anger should not be aroused, so I would keep non-Theravāda knowledge to myself and not write – and certainly not speak to him – about such things.

Besides Pāli language and general Buddhist study from a Theravāda perspective, we also had lessons on the Abhidhamma. While I enjoyed the first two subjects, the study of Abhidhamma – the philosophical analysis and synthesis of all the momentary events, or *dharmas*, that continually arise and pass away – I found dry and uninteresting. Perhaps my negative reaction to it was fuelled by Buddharakkhita's insistence that this highly complex system was also the word of the Buddha, just as the Vinaya and Suttas were. I could not believe such an assertion, which ran counter to scholarly evidence, even though it was supported by Pāli commentators of such great stature as Buddha-ghosa. Another reason for my aversion to this study was its numerical nature. At school, mathematics was not one of my best subjects and though in this case the maths required were only addition and sub-traction, still I disliked what I termed privately 'Buddhist arithmetic'. No doubt it could be a skilful means for interesting mathematicians in the Buddha's teachings, but to me it seemed only a system that tried to account for all manner of things left unexplained by the Buddha's teachings in the suttas. In the suttas it is very clear that the Buddha taught the Dharma for the Awakening of his listeners and felt no need to weave all his diverse teachings together so that they would fit into one coherent system. Abhidhamma, by contrast, seemed to me like a straitjacket intended to stifle enquiry and more likely to lead to the writing of learned treatises than to the actual experience of Awakened Mind. Once, as I recall it now, I did challenge my teacher on a philo-sophical assumption made in the Abhidhamma, at which he exploded in anger.

These Abhidhamma studies, perhaps due to my sceptical approach, ceased shortly afterwards and we never finished fitting the intricacies of this Buddhist arithmetic together. I was very glad when they were discontinued, for I could see no point in filling my head with such arid material, which on the one side would be quite useless for teaching purposes (the audience would go to sleep), and on the other seemed to me to have little or no application to personal Awakening. Surely a spiritual experience which was classified and named by Abhidhamma analysis would lose its wonderment, its power of spontaneity.

Fortunately, our emotional life at the vihara was refreshed by the regular pujas, morning and evening, that we chanted at the shrine in the middle of the building. In another battered exercise book, this one from Britain, I have a record of the puja that we chanted. All the material was from the Pāli tradition, chanted in Pāli, and apart from passages drawn from the suttas, consisted of verses composed in Sri Lanka. The style of chanting was also Sinhalese, as was the layout of the shrine. In front of a modern reproduction of an ancient Indian Buddha image was a sort of concrete shelf for the flower offerings, oil lamps, and incense burner. Though aesthetic considerations should make shrines places of real beauty, this concrete structure was not very inspiring, like much modern Indian construction. The chanting, how-ever, made up for this deficiency, for Buddharakkhita had a good voice for it and I very much enjoyed joining with him and my fellow monks.

At other times I could be found in the centre library scribbling away with open books all around me. The library, quite an extensive one, was the place where I began to collect all sorts of quotations from many Buddhist traditions which would eventually be placed in order and joined together with my comments to produce my first published book, *Tolerance, A Study from Buddhist Sources*. This work was born of conversations with Sangharakshita, and perhaps the rather *intolerant* atmosphere at Bangalore Maha Bodhi Society added piquancy to its composition.

It must have been in that library that I wrote a rather ferocious piece of criticism published in the *Maha Bodhi Journal* (June 1961) as 'Some Modern *Mithya Drishti*' (wrong views). This appeared in reply to an article appearing over three issues of *The Golden Light* (published, I believe, in Malaysia), authored by an educated Thai layman whose 'Buddhism' seemed to be based mostly upon Western sources rather than his own native tradition. I noted that in his meanderings through what he called the Dharma, he drew mostly upon the *Bhagavad Gītā* (a Hindu work with many un-Buddhist ideas), strains of Theosophy, and pseudo-Zen (the third or Western school, the two major Japanese schools being Rinzai and Sōtō). The last refers to Christmas Humphreys' attempts to 'explain' the Zen tradition. That article, 'The Buddhist Way of Life for Modern Man', was really a complete mishmash of ideas and seriously distorted the Dharma. While such confused 'explanations' of the Dharma certainly do not lead to clarity, I doubt these days if I would spend time writing such a long reply, occupying more than ten pages of the *Maha Bodhi*. I wonder if I showed it to Buddharakkhita? Probably not, as Mahāyāna is also mentioned in connection with Right View.

From my arrival in Bangalore in April until the middle of July I remained a novice, though Buddharakkhita wanted me to ordain as a monk. I, however, was not sure that I was ready to undertake the monk's 227 precepts rather than the ten of a novice. Though many of the monk's precepts are matters of good manners – no problem with them – or of restraining desires for food, sex, and indulgence – much more difficult to manage – there were also a great number that had little or no bearing on modern life, especially on life in a Western country.[41] I doubted whether the burden of these extra precepts would make my monk's life more enjoyable or harmonious.

In any case, no ordination could take place in the absence of the number of monks required in the Vinaya. For the Middle Country, the

Buddhist heartland of the Gangetic Valley, ten monks were needed, three of whom had to be senior and well qualified. As Bangalore did not count as Middle Country, only five were needed, but there were only three at the vihara: Buddharakkhita, Saddhārakkhita, and Sīla-ratana. One or two more might have been invited from Madras where a few Sri Lankan monks resided, but it so happened that the abbot of Wat Thai at Bodh Gaya, accompanied by one other Thai monk, Sukitti, was touring India. Buddharakkhita therefore invited them to come and stay at the Bangalore Vihāra (we moved out of our rooms to make space for them), and in particular invited the abbot to preside over the ordination procedure. This ceremony took place on 12 July 1961,[42] so my ordination booklet from the Maha Bodhi Society informs me. It even notes the time when I became a monk as 4 pm on that day – though I see that, perhaps anxious to be more precise, I have added the words, 'actually 16.38 hrs'. The signature in Thai of the presiding monk follows – 'Phra Dharmadhirarājamahāmuni' – and then that of my teacher who signed himself simply as 'Buddharakkhita'.

The ordination ceremony took place in the garden surrounding the main building. In this garden was a curious structure with a concrete floor, and four concrete pillars holding up a concrete roof. I was told that this was the *sīma*, literally 'an area defined by a boundary'. It may have been previously established as a venue for legal Vinaya acts of the Sangha by the required number of monks – but I rather think that in fact its consecration happened just before my ordination. The monk sangha sat under the roof, which was just large enough to shelter us all from the sun. The whole ceremony took about an hour, and as the presiding elder came from Thailand it was performed Thai-style.

By the end, I found myself a monk with the new name, Khantipālo, 'one who keeps patient'. This name was arrived at by consultation with Buddharakkhita. I had the notion of a name incorporating the word *kataññutā* or 'gratitude', a virtue that particularly appealed to me, but in Pāli it is a feminine noun, and Buddharakkhita opposed the use of feminine nouns in monks' names. He pointed this out and proposed instead a name containing *khanti* or patience. No doubt he considered that my impetuous youthful nature could benefit from some patience. So Khantipālo I remained during my stay in India, through eleven years in Thailand, and nearly twenty in Australia. Though no longer formally a monk I still use Khantipālo as my name, and perhaps after all these years there is a little more patience as a result.

But how did I feel then, when the ceremony was complete and I was a fully ordained monk? I had had no expectations of any sudden spiritual blessing descending upon me or welling up from within, and indeed the ceremony, though well chanted and conducted without any faults according to the legal standards established in the Vinaya, was just a complex legality – and that was all. I cannot remember feeling either pleased that it had been accomplished without any forgetfulness on my part, or otherwise. Even then, in the back of my mind, something seemed to be missing – perhaps it was that very inspiration, the Dharma-eye itself.

In this the ceremony was in great contrast to my novice ordination, or more literally 'leaving home', under the very different circumstances of London. The same ordination booklet tells me that this took place on 7 March 1959 at 'The Sangha, 50 Alexandra Road, London, NW8, England' only a year earlier. What had been the dining room on the ground floor of this Victorian house had been turned into the Dharma teaching room. There was no meditation room because there was no community meditation; chanting or puja was not part of daily life in the house, and there was no shrine. A Buddha image may have graced the marble mantelpiece, but otherwise there was no trace of the oriental, apart from the shaven heads of the monks and their orange-brown robes. Three monks resided there: Paññāvaddho, the most senior of them and my teacher; then Vimalo and Dhammiko, German twins ordained in London by a visiting Thai abbot who divided his own name, Vimaladhamma, for them.[43] Also resident in the house was an elderly nun, Jhānānandā, who had originally been ordained in China with the name Tao Lo, the the notorious Chao Kung[44] being her teacher. She wore the brown robes of a ten-precept nun though she was actually a fully ordained bhikṣuṇī.

As there were only three monks, and Paññāvaddho was himself still junior in terms of the number of Rains spent in the Sangha, he decided to invite Ven. Dr Saddhātissa of Sri Lanka to be my formal teacher for this ordination. I had already memorized the request for novice ordination and the three Refuges with the Ten Precepts – all in Pāli, of course. The request was in Thai style, as Paññāvaddho had been there briefly and brought back their tradition. The event was publicized, and even a reporter turned up. His editor allowed this event an inch of a column in a national daily – where I was described as a 'scientist' because, I suppose, of my connections with the Royal Botanic Gardens, Kew, in which I had been a humble student-gardener for two years.

7 March had mostly worn away by the time of my ordination. At seven in the evening it was cold; the thin white cloth in which I requested the Refuges and Precepts did nothing to keep the warmth in, and I was nervous. About thirty-five people attended the ceremony, the most important of whom, for me, was my mother, seated in the front row of chairs. From her I received the bundle of robes, Burmese dark orange ones, as well as a bowl, also from that country, donated by my kind friends, Mr and Mrs Tennakoon from Sri Lanka.

Ven. Dr H. Saddhātissa Mahāthera sat flanked by the other three monks while I knelt at his feet and bowed my head to the floor. So far, so good. Then in a wavering voice due to the cold – probably to a particular cold that I had then, and the strangeness of the whole event – I began to chant the request. The Venerable then smilingly corrected me – for I had learned a Thai order of words, while he was accustomed to a Sri Lankan form. I really wished that the floorboards might open and swallow me. I tried again and he demurred, but slightly this time, and then told me to continue in the way that I had learned the request. All went well after this.

Bowing at the feet of my mother as I received the robes from her was a moving experience. She too had tears in her eyes, but they were tears of joy, not of sadness. Mine were the same, for although my training in horticulture had been interesting, I was now turning my life in the direction of liberation, an incomparably better goal. When I returned to the crowded room wearing those robes and carrying the bowl, though the emotion in me was still deep and strong, there was also a calm strength, and my repetition of the Refuges and Precepts was clear and steady. A strong contrast to my full bhikkhu ordination indeed.

But having attained the status of a monk, just over a year after the London ceremony of leaving home, I continued to harbour doubts about whether this eminence was of much use. At Bangalore I do not recall that it made much difference to my life. At every turn of the moon's phases, full moon and new moon, it was the monastic practice at Wat Thai, Bodh Gaya, for the monks to gather and listen to one of their number reciting – at high speed and without a book – the *Pāṭimokkha*, the 227 precepts of a Theravāda monk. In Bangalore, as no one knew them by heart, the 227 precepts were read out in Pāli by Buddharakkhita. Before this fortnightly ritual we did confess to each other, but in a such a general way as to make it meaningless, while the actual list of precepts, all chanted in Pāli, could only be understood if one had mastered this ancient language. Though I listened, in the course of my monk's career, to the Pāṭimokkha some hundreds of times, even when I did know Pāli I cannot honestly say it made me a better or more purified monk. Like the monk's ordination ceremony it was just one more ritual to be performed. The principle in such matters seemed to be: make no mistakes and get it word perfect. These matters seemed to have nothing whatsoever to do with a change of heart. I reflected that undertaking such a burden of rules, some of which could not be kept since they could no longer be broken,[45] seemed merely the repetition of an archaic ritual and, for most monks, one they did not understand. Still, I listened to it, as custom demanded, all through my time in Thailand and from 1973 onwards while I lived with Thai monks in Australia. But when, after 1978, I established Wat Buddha Dhamma in the bush outside Sydney, it was the first dead wood to be abandoned.

During my remaining time with Buddharakkhita I became more aware of the power of caste and how it could easily insinuate its tentacles into the Indian Buddhist community. My teacher came from a Bengali brahmin caste, a fact which no doubt had contributed to his attainment of a good education and made him eventually an impressive Dharma teacher. Around him in Bangalore there were many outcaste communities with whom he had little or no contact, either because he retained some lingering brahmin prejudices against them, or, more likely, because as a former brahmin they distrusted him. In this way he was more isolated from potential Buddhists than Sangharakshita, who had no such caste background. The people who came to listen to Buddharakkhita's 'sermons' were all Caste Hindus and intended to remain so. They enjoyed his perorations and generally agreed with the Dharma he explained. They thought his conduct admirable in that he was both vegetarian and celibate, but if they classified him at all it was as another kind of Hindu, one to be listened to respectfully but certainly not one to follow to the extent of declaring oneself to be Buddhist. Some of them were wealthy and supported the Maha Bodhi Society in Bangalore generously – I remember going with Buddharakkhita to one or two of their houses for lunch – but we never went for alms among the outcaste communities. In this, Buddharakkhita followed the lead of other monks at Maha Bodhi Society centres, most of them from Sri Lanka, who pursued wealthy patrons among the Hindus (who would never be Buddhists) but neglected the Dalits who might in some cases be prepared to go for Refuge to the Buddha.

Buddharakkhita would have liked me to stay on at his centre indefi-
nitely. I decorated the shrine artistically and looked after the library –
one of several collections of Buddhist books that I have ordered and
applied myself to learning and practising from. With the others, I had
a retreat of seven days dedicated to insight meditation in the Burmese
style before Wesak, the celebration of the Buddha's Awakening. Apart
from this I sat in meditation with the other monks every morning and
after the puja in the evenings.

In various ways, though, I was not happy in Bangalore. I did not
enjoy the constriction of Buddharakkhita's sectarianism and dreaded
his outbursts of ill humour. Though I was not looking for a 'perfect'
teacher – indeed I do not think I believed that such a person existed,
in spite of reports from Burma and Thailand about Arhant monks –
still it was important for me that whatever blemishes a teacher had,
they should not lead to inflicting on me or others pain and suffering.
I was dismayed on one occasion to see my teacher thrash with a cane
a lazy Indian would-be novice – a quite useless fellow who merely
wished to use the monk's robes to get a livelihood.[46] At first
Buddharakkhita's strokes were motivated by anger at this fellow's
negligence, but after the first few I saw some sadistic enjoyment in my
teacher's face. That a Buddhist teacher could enjoy the infliction of
suffering I found too painful to watch. This event unsettled me and
undermined whatever confidence I had in him up to that time. Though
he never laid violent hands on me personally, merely uttered very
angry words, I learned subsequently that many of his disciples either
fled from the Bangalore Vihāra or were thrown out by him. That I
lasted there for nine months seems something of a record.

Perhaps this is the place for some reflections on Dharma teachers. I
mentioned above that I doubted the existence of perfect teachers – and
even if they were perfected in every virtue, power, and Awakening,
how would the mind obscured by greed, hate, and delusion, which
judges everything conditioned by past experience and present expectations, know them? As the Buddha said, 'It is by living with a person
that their virtue can be known, it is by business dealings with a person
that their honesty can be known, it is in adversity that a person's
fortitude can be known, it is by discussion with a person that their
wisdom can be known; and then only after a long time, not a short
time, only after careful consideration, not when it is lacking, and only
by one who is wise, not by a dullard.'[47]

In this memoir I speak about two of my teachers and I have praised their virtues as I perceived them. Unfortunately I have had to mention the dark side of Buddharakkhita, as this accounts for my leaving his vihara. Generally, though, I believe teachers' good qualities should be reflected upon and spoken about, while their negative aspects should not generally be discussed, on the principle that 'those who live in glass houses should not throw stones'. Who indeed will be immune from all blame once the stones begin flying? Also, there are many places in the sūtras where the painful karmic results of insults and threats against those who are blameless are made abundantly clear. Even when teachers are somewhat to blame, still those are their own karmas for which they will receive a result – blaming them will not mend the situation.

Dharma teachers who harm neither others nor themselves (how else would they be called Dharma masters?) should be held in reverence and respect. Those who have been my teachers in this life, whether or not they could be considered 'perfect', I place above my head out of gratitude for all their efforts on my behalf. Without them, where would I be?

If, however, one prefers to see the dark sides of teachers, or what one takes to be their dark sides – and certainly I have met Western disciples of Dharma masters who have made a speciality of this – not only is such action very negative in the present but traditionally it will also guarantee that one will have little or no contact with teachers in future lives.

After the Rains at Bangalore, and not without a good deal of regret – which translated into staying another two weeks or so – I informed Buddharakkhita that I wished to leave. Of course, he asked me where I would go, for a young monk of under five Rains is supposed to live with a teacher, a monk of at least ten Rains who is well versed in Dharma and well practised. I told him that Sangharakshita had invited me to stay at his vihara in Kalimpong, at which he exclaimed, 'Ah, you will study Mahāyāna and eat in the evening' – apparently the two most serious lapses of morality that he could envisage.

On the appointed day, 8 November 1961, I therefore paid my respects to his feet, took leave of my fellow monks with whom I had developed a close friendship, and, with a ticket bought from the vihara's funds, boarded a train that took me to Madras, from where I could travel to Kalimpong.

Chapter Seven

KALIMPONG I

For laying hold rightly to this mind-jewel,
Puja I make to Tathāgatas all,
To that Dharma of Truth – jewel without flaw,
To those oceans of virtue of the Buddha born.

Bodhicāryāvatāra ii.1

I arrived in Madras the next day, and went straight to the Maha Bodhi Society vihara, where I was welcomed by a hospitable and kindly senior monk from Sri Lanka. On my second day, which happened to be my birthday – though I doubt whether anyone else knew that – he took me to see the Theosophical Society's headquarters, which is in a beautiful park-like setting. There were huge flowering trees and well kept gardens in which the various buildings, including, I think, a Buddhist shrine, were scattered. This kind monk helped me with the purchase of a ticket to Calcutta and got me aboard the immensely long train which would take the best part of three days to get there. Though called an express, it was leisurely by the standards of travel in our more hurried times.

I thought I had immediately set out to return to Kalimpong from Calcutta, but extracts from the *Maha Bodhi Journal* that Sangharakshita sent me prove these memories wrong. Apparently within ten days of leaving Bangalore I was again in Ahmedabad where the *Maha Bodhi* records that I went 'for a short visit'. Now if I had known in Bangalore that I was to go to Ahmedabad, I certainly wouldn't have gone to Madras and Calcutta, a very long way round! But it seems clear that that is what I did. Just why remains a bit of a mystery. In any case it involved me in a long loop of a journey through India's west and north-west before returning to Kalimpong.

After Ahmedabad I went by train through Rajasthan, my only visit to this area, and was met at Ajmer station by a Buddhist, Rahula Sumana Chhawara. He had been instrumental in turning his small community of Kolyas in the direction of Buddhism. When Buddhists hear the name in its Pāli form, Koliya, they think immediately of the Buddha's maternal family, who were from that clan. It was claimed by this small group – far away from territory that would have belonged to those ancient relatives of the Buddha – that in fact they were the living representatives of that line. Though this would no doubt be hard to prove, still the similarity of names seemed a good reason to become Buddhist! Sri Chhawara was very active in inviting teachers to visit – Sangharakshita had already been there – and the group had a good Buddhist library.

Delhi was my next stop, where 'in a western part of the city' of which I have now no recollection, I delivered a lecture on the anniversary of the death of Dr Ambedkar. Perhaps that 'western part' was around the Kutb Minar, an impressive Muslim tower, for I do remember visiting a senior monk of Cambodian origin, Dhammaweera, who had settled nearby. The impressively walled area, said to have been a pleasure garden in Moghul times, is where he lived and meditated, in a pavilion inside its walls. From his meditation upon lights he had developed certain abilities, one of which was to cure serious diseases through light. Even then he was much in demand. Later he went to somewhere in California, I believe, and many years later I met him at the City of Ten Thousand Buddhas, which is just outside Ukiah. By that time he was 104 years old and still able to walk and teach.

During this visit to Delhi I stayed with Mrs Freda Bedi, an English woman who had founded a school for young Tibetan refugee lamas. About twenty of them were accommodated and fed in a large old-fashioned bungalow in a Delhi suburb. Here they not only continued their traditional studies but also learned English and Hindi. Among them I remember only Trungpa Rimpoche and Akong Rimpoche, both incarnate lamas from Tibet and abbots of important monasteries there. Trungpa, then in his late teens, had a magnetic personality. In his maroon robes and short black hair he appeared very alert, very present. His broad face had a pair of penetrating eyes and a wide mouth that softened into frequent smiles and laughter. I sensed that his intelligence could easily distinguish falsity and deceit in others.

Indeed, I remember thinking that when he grew a little older and had learned more English, he would certainly attract Western disciples who would no doubt find him a formidable but compassionate teacher. I felt a strong attraction to Trungpa in particular and talked to him several times, as much as his broken English and my complete absence of Tibetan would allow. Somewhere in India, at one of the numerous stalls selling Tibetan artefacts which the refugees sold to obtain food or medicines, I had bought a jade mālā of 108 beads with the traditional counters made of the same material. It was of a particularly beautiful shade of green and I had acquired it as I was interested in doing some Green Tārā practice – mālās and the colour of the deities visualized are sometimes correlated. However, at the end of these meetings with Trungpa I gave him this mālā, which he seemed very happy with and no doubt used for his own practices.

In Calcutta, the Maha Bodhi Society put me up for a night or two before I set off northwards, again by train, to Siliguri. In those days, due to the emergence of East Pakistan, the direct line to Siliguri was broken and the Ganges had to be crossed, first by walking over the nearby sand-dunes, then by an ancient ferry, then more wastes of sand. I came to appreciate their inexpressible extent reflected in such phrases from the Mahāyāna sūtras as 'the merit from the practice of [whatever virtue was being commended] will amount to equal the number of sand grains in the Ganges'. A formidable amount of merit! These dunes over which everyone struggled with their baggage (or hired a porter to transport it) led to the gangplanks of a huge dinosaur of a paddle-steamer. When everyone was on board it took us across with much wheezing and churning. Perhaps it illustrated another Mahāyāna teaching – that one should not just gather wood for one's own little raft to cross to the Further Shore but rather construct a mighty ship to transport all living beings without exception across the ocean wastes of saṁsāra. Eventually, to the exhausted passengers, this other shore appeared, alas, to be as little welcoming as the one from which we had set out. Having finally found the other train, we continued our journey. As the crossing was by night with few lights around, the successful completion of the whole ordeal, ending with the spreading of bedding on a wooden rack and the horizontality of the body, was most satisfactory – even if it cannot quite be equated with Nirvāṇa.

It must have been towards the end of November that I finally arrived at Triyāna Vardhana Vihāra. As this was my second visit to the vihara, I got to know Sangharakshita better, and his character came more into focus. I particularly appreciated the example he set of diligence and effort, which was evident both in the Kalimpong vihara, where it manifested as literary activity, and in his teaching of the Dharma, particularly to the former outcastes. He could be very single-minded, so much so that sometimes a meal would be accompanied by very few words indeed, occasionally by none at all. Being silent with him did not feel uncomfortable, however, for I was aware that his mind was fully engaged in the contents of whatever he was then writing. If this abstraction continued over longer periods, though, I could experience him as rather distant, and hard to contact. This may well have been compounded by my own introspective nature at that time.

I also noted his mindfulness. He was someone very much aware of his actions and words; 'well-considered' would be a good description were it not that they were also spontaneous. This spontaneity was specially in evidence in his dealings with the many and various people he met on his teaching tours, when he could switch from one approach to another, depending on the person he was addressing.

His kindness was another aspect of his character that was immediately apparent. He cared how people were, and his enquiries after their well-being were warm and genuine. This kindness, however, was tempered by a strongly ascetic inclination so that it never became cloying. His mode of life as a monk reflected on one side the Buddha's famous 'Discourse on Loving-Kindness',[48] but on the other his frequent exhortations to his wandering followers to have few wishes. As a result of this, there was no luxury to be found in the Abode Where the Three Vehicles Flourish. This relaxed asceticism had no grimness attached to it and I never felt that Sangharakshita was compelling himself to be simple and contented. His was a natural practice of the Buddha's exhortation to the monks: 'Be my heirs in Dharma, not my heirs in material things.'[49]

Allied to his kindness was a gentle and non-hurtful sense of humour, especially evident in difficult travelling situations. It would be hard to find examples of him being upset by unexpected or potentially troublesome events. A good deal of equanimity manifested then, spiced by a flash of humour and a ready smile. Once, on such an occasion, a verse of Sangharakshita's translation of the *Ratana Sutta* came to my mind and I thought it described him well:

> *Just as the firm post at the city gate*
> *Doth stir not though the four winds on it blow,*

So do I call him a good man and true
Who sees experientially the Noble Truths.
Yea, in the Order shines this glorious gem;
By virtue of this truth, may bliss abound![50]

I was also impressed by the range of Sangharakshita's mind, both in his private conversations with me and in his public discourses. Here, I thought, is a teacher who has realized at least some part of the Dharma's truth, for his teachings were both wide-ranging and deeply penetrating. I enjoyed the experience of listening to his words, which flowed from a mind that evidently had few boundaries, few limitations. Just one example of this were his explanations of the 'three vehicles' (*yāna*) which I heard from time to time.[51] Although he adopted this triad for the classification of the Buddha's teachings he did not do so in a dogmatic way, nor, copying the Tibetans, did he arrange the *yānas* in a hierarchical order of ascending importance. Rather Sangharakshita took from each *yāna* what was important for practice and what was digestible by his listeners. In this way, the Hīnayāna – of which Theravāda is the only living example – was in his eyes of the greatest importance in that its texts, the Pāli suttas, teach the basic doctrines of the Dharma. The Mahāyāna sūtras and treatises map out the Bodhisattva path in detail – and to that end one may or may not be part of a monk or nun sangha. While this ideal is present in the Pāli suttas, more emphasis is given there to the liberation of oneself as an *arhant* in the context of a monastic sangha. Timewise, the Pāli suttas emphasize liberation through renunciation in this life, while the Mahāyāna Bodhisattva path makes the practice of the perfections stretch over many, many lives. Finally, the Vajrayāna re-emphasizes Awakening in this life with the special methods that it employs. All beings will still be saved but more speedily, while one's own attainment as a *siddha*, one who is truly capable, may quite possibly take place after living an unusual, even eccentric, lifestyle but one in which there is great devotion to one's teacher and, beneath the façade of nonconformity, the constant dwelling in emptiness.

These vehicles were not just concepts for Sangharakshita. He embodied the Theravāda ideal of a renunciant while energetically manifesting the Bodhisattva's heart of compassion. To complete his three-*yāna* practice he had many initiations from Tibetan masters into the Vajrayāna and used this wisdom during his meditation.

These various aspects of Sangharakshita's character naturally stimulated my friendship with him. My Dharma practice was certainly helped by living with him for, as I noted above, he was an example of a monk who lived for Dharma, not for worldly things. Although I later met other senior monks of whom this could also be said, they were Thai speakers, while Sangharakshita communicated in my mother tongue. It is hard to imagine what my own development in Dharma would have been like without his example or his clear communication of the principles of the Dharma in a language that we shared. I respected his profound knowledge and was deeply impressed by his practice.

Our relationship in the Kalimpong vihara was a mixture of both master–pupil and fellow practitioners. While Sangharakshita was obviously a teacher he was not a typical Indian-style guru. He did not encourage in me, or in others, guru devotion, unlike the teachers of more traditional forms of Buddhism. In those, pupils would be expected to wait upon their master, clean his room, wash his robes, and so on, but I never did any of these things for Sangharakshita. His room was a kind of sanctum into which few people ever entered, myself included. While Buddharakkhita tended to be more of a guru-type, exercising authority over his pupils, Sangharakshita shared his knowledge and lived his life in such a way that living with him felt for me as though we were fellow practitioners upon the path.

I could then ask myself what I contributed to Sangharakshita's time in India, or, since I did little for him personally, was my presence perhaps a burden? I think it was not, for we could, when it was convenient, have intelligent conversations on the Dharma, some of which took place during or after meals, while others occurred while walking into Kalimpong and returning to the vihara. We did this regularly in connection with Mr Chen's book (which I shall talk about later) and developed a close co-operation. On other occasions during his teaching tour, I helped with his Dharma engagements, while in Kalimpong I supported his determination to stop the Christian missionaries from converting poverty-stricken Tibetans and other Buddhists.

I do not know now whether it ever occurred to me to ask myself what Sangharakshita thought about me then. As he was very perceptive regarding people, I guess he thought of me as a sincere student of Dharma, one who was even then deeply committed to the truth represented by the Three Jewels. I suppose he found me fairly intelligent but rather shy and uncertain of myself, though he may have thought me very willing to learn and open to ideas quite new to me. Though I had quite a conventional upbringing, its suburban stodginess was fortunately relieved by a dry sense of humour, as Sangharakshita has recently reminded me. Whatever other changes have taken place in me since then, the humour, I am glad to say, has remained.

For a brief time I was the only monk in the Kalimpong vihara, but Sangharakshita returned during December. I am sure that he returned then, as on 2 January 1962 my old puja book records that I received 'The combined method of Brahmavihāra and Buddhanussati according to the method of Dudjom Rimpoche', of which I recorded only the second of the three methods in this practice.[52] As these three are said to be 'for those of low, middling, and superior intelligence', it may be assumed that I was of middling capacity. I do not think that Sangharakshita and I actually went together to Dudjom Rimpoche to receive this instruction – though the Rimpoche certainly lived in Kalimpong at that time. It is more likely that Sangharakshita shared this teaching with me and that I copied it from his notebook. Though occupying only a page and a half in my book, the practice could be expanded to fill an entire day. Although I do not remember using it in this expanded fashion, I did try practising it in more condensed form during our two periods of meditation each day.

The word 'practice' appears in a group of three in the Pāli commentaries: Thorough learning, practice, and penetration wisdom.[53] Sangharakshita and I practised together – not just in the sense of sitting meditation (valuable though that exercise is, there are but few in this world who can afford the time to sit for many hours every day), but in the sense of practising the various aspects of the Dharma with mindfulness all the time. This is the translation of the Pāli word *patipatti*, not just sitting meditation.

The shrine-room of the vihara where the two of us sat in meditation was quite small. Perhaps five or six others could sit in it comfortably, and occasionally – especially on full moons – we had this many, who sat with us in meditation after puja. However, the early mornings usually saw only two monks sitting there. Still, our shrine-room practice could be called the most concentrated of the day. When we closed the door to the veranda few sounds could be heard, maybe muted birdsong if it was light enough, or sounds of foot-travellers to the nearest village, but within the room there was an indescribable natural silence. And though it was an ordinary enough small room, within it was a presence, a sort of 'shiningness' hard to put into words.

The focus of the shrine was a particularly endearing standing Buddha image about two feet high, gilded and painted. Its right hand was raised in what is often called the gesture of blessing, but should properly be called the *mudrā* of non-fear, an expression of loving-kindness. The left hand loosely held a corner of the reddish-brown robe, while upon the lips of the gilded face played a rather mischievous smile. It is as though this Buddha was saying 'Look! Do wake up, will you? It is all here and now. Where else do you think you can do it? But of course there's no you to accomplish it and no present time to do it in! What will you do? What will you do?' Sangharakshita told me the Buddha was made of clay and therefore quite fragile, also that it was a gift from Lama Govinda. How it survived the long journey from his ashram in Almora to Kalimpong unscathed I cannot imagine.[54] One could say, from its poised presence, that it radiated that peace and awareness which pervaded the room, or alternatively that the Buddha helped to generate in the hearts of those who practised there that quality of illuminated presence. The shrine was beautiful and well maintained, though there were no signs of conspicuous display, as one sometimes saw in the houses of wealthy Tibetans. One or two *thangkas* adorned the walls, while the standing Buddha ever waited for us, patiently, to see what he had seen, to know what he had known.

Our puja was similar to the one I had been used to in Bangalore in that we chanted passages and verses from the Sri Lanka Pāli tradition. Three or four pages in my old puja book are devoted to the carefully copied *Ratana Sutta* with Sangharakshita's English translation inter-linear with the Pāli text. We chanted this frequently in Pāli. Chanting in English, something I now find quite natural, did not play any part in our puja then. As this was the Abode Where the Three Vehicles Flourish, other chants were added and my puja book records the beautiful Sanskrit verses of offering – twelve of them altogether – from the second chapter of Śāntideva's *Bodhicāryāvatāra*, as well as Sangha-rakshita's translation. I still chant these Sanskrit verses for full moon pujas nearly forty years after I first heard them. Also part of our puja then was the 'Heart of Perfect Wisdom' – the *Prajñāpāramitāhṛdaya Sūtra* – which we chanted in Sanskrit. Though I no longer use the Sanskrit, an English translation is part of my present puja – chanted with a wooden fish in the way that Zen students perform it.[55] From that time there is also a selection by Sangharakshita of Pāli *Dhamma-pada* verses which I recall chanting regularly with him.[56]

While the first two vehicles were well represented in our pujas, the third one, the Vajrayāna, seems to have been absent, unless one counts chanting of the mantra of Prajñāpāramitā – of which more below – as representing this. Particularly with regard to Vajrayāna, I find on closer inspection of the old puja book that it contains a piece of ancient-looking paper with Sangharakshita's clear writing of the hundred syllable mantra of Vajrasattva. The mantra is in red ink and capitals while a 'translation' is given in ordinary script and blue ink. Perhaps we recited this on special occasions. (Some of the practices that I do all these years later employ this long mantra to great effect.) There is also Chandragomin's *Tārādevīstotra-puṣpamālā*, the 'Flower-Garland Hymn to the Goddess Tārā', covering all of six pages in Sangharakshita's English translation. Though I have no recollection of chanting this, it is possible we did. At the beginning of this hymn there is a note that says 'from Chattrul Sangye Dorje (Nying-ma-pa)' with no date given. As I suspect I never met that teacher, perhaps Sangharakshita gave me this Garland of Flowers to copy as a support for my Tārā practice.

I received many texts like this from Sangharakshita as well as all manner of information upon diverse Dharma subjects. Before meeting him I had read a few Mahāyāna books, such as were available in those days. I recall reading Evans-Wentz's Oxford series in Britain, though much of their meaning and all the practices connected with them passed over my head. As well as these I had begun to study that rather laborious work, Gampopa's *Jewel Ornament of Liberation*, during my novice days at Alexandra Road. As I lacked the traditional commentaries and more importantly lacked learned teachers, these works were of limited value, apart from acting as reminders that there were other sorts of Buddhists who looked at the Dharma in ways differing from Theravāda. In Sangharakshita I found a teacher who had learned and well practised many of these Mahāyāna traditions and was very able in explaining them. My horizons were immeasurably widened by his expositions of the Dharma. It does not seem too fanciful to compare the physical horizons of the Dharma places at which I stayed in those early years – flat and suburban in the case of both Alexandra Road and Gandhinagar – with the magnificent vistas from Triyāna Vardhana Vihāra. It was as though the view from the windows or garden of this vihara somehow corresponded to the wide and impressive Dharma view of the teacher there.

Behind and above the vihara was a sharply descending dirt track connecting a village with one of the winding roads into Kalimpong, so that the back of the bungalow was almost dug into the hill. The front had a veranda that ran outside the three principal rooms. Sangharakshita's room came first, the shrine-room was in the middle, and the dining room last, from which there was a door to the kitchen. Conspicuous in Sangharakshita's room was a desk with its manual typewriter, some well-stocked bookshelves, and around the walls a series of eight fine *thangkas* of Padmasambhava. My own quarters were not in this *pukka* – that is, solid brick and stone – building, but in another structure akin to the local villagers' houses in bamboo, thatch, and mud-plaster. This building lay higher than the vihara itself but only a few yards away from it. Surrounding the buildings but mostly on the western side, which fell steeply, was a four-acre garden of terraces. The lower ones were planted with a particularly luscious variety of tangerine – about a hundred well-established trees grew there. In season these provided not only some fruit to the inhabitants of the vihara but also a small annual income. Bamboos from a large clump also brought in some income, while excess vegetables, especially pumpkins, grown on terraces nearer to the house, were sold as well. The nearest terraces had some flowers which would grow in Kalimpong's frost-free climate. Winters were cold but never icy, so that a wide variety of plants, bushes, and trees flourished there. Though the native flora was rich in ferns, orchids, and other Himalayan specialities I remember none of these being in the garden unless they grew upon the huge cypresses that framed it.

Apart from us two monks there was only the cook living there, who was a young Tibetan. He lived in a narrow room near the kitchen. Occasionally, educated young Nepalis who had been Sangharakshita's friends and pupils from the Young Men's Buddhist Association turned up and would share a meal and sometimes stay a night. I myself felt most fortunate to stay in this Dharma place, though the physical conditions were not always easy to endure.

Sangharakshita had to stretch a slender budget to cover living costs at the vihara as well as his travel and other expenses. One consequence of this was that the food there was both simple and limited. Meals at Wat Thai were rich fare indeed, while those at Bangalore were banquets compared to the ascetic diet in Kalimpong! Because of this stringency, and the winter climate, we did indeed have some soupy rice in the evenings, ignoring the Vinaya's injunction to cease eating at midday. This rule, quite reasonable for a tropical climate such as Sri Lanka, as well as for contemplative life in which much energy is not expended, is out of place in colder climates and more vigorous occupations. Most monks who kept this rule and therefore fasted from midday to dawn would never have been able to undertake Sangharakshita's workload, as when he addressed one mass meeting after another in the wake of Dr Ambedkar's death. I had my own, very active, programme, especially when I had started work on Mr Chen's book, and I remember fortifying myself from time to time with the delicious round bread from Amdo and even buying strings of iron-hard Tibetan cheese, both to be found in the Kalimpong bazaar.

Tibetan lamas and other monastics usually had something to eat in the morning and another meal in the early evening. This adaptation seems not to have adversely affected their spiritual practice. In fact, those countries where this rule and many other 'minor regulations'[57] were stringently kept were not noted in historical records for the production of marvellous and saintly teachers, while other lands adhering to the spirit of the Vinaya rather than to its letter produced large numbers of extraordinary realized beings. Sangharakshita took a view which coincided with the Tibetans', and insisted that the 227 or 252 rules of a monk could be adapted to the changed circumstances of today's life, in contrast to those emphasizing rigid adherence to regulations made in very different times and places. This practice seemed to me a very proper attitude, and as the junior monk in the vihara I followed Sangharakshita's example in this matter.

It seemed to me then that a rule such as this (secretly broken by many Theravāda monks in India), which was impossible to keep outside monastic walls – on long railway journeys, for instance – should be approached flexibly. No moral principles will be sacrificed if one eats at one minute past midday, or for that matter at several hours past the deadline. In fact, I noticed that the strict keepers of the rules became quite disturbed if they could not adhere rigidly to them – not, one would think, the best attitude to cultivate in spiritual life. Though I was then quite a newcomer to the monastic sangha I did not consider that rules should be followed just because tradition ascribed them to the Buddha. Blindly following traditions seemed to me at that time, as it does to me now, to be the antithesis of Buddhist practice, a method guaranteed *not* to produce wonderful, Awakened people. While the sentiments of the Buddha's discourse to the Kālāmas,[58] ('Do not (believe) on the basis of tradition, etc., but test the results of practice to discover whether greed, hate, and delusion grow or diminish'), may have influenced my attitude in this case, I think it was from Sangharakshita's lips that I heard for the first time the famous and apposite Buddhist Sanskrit verse:

> As one who's wise with gold
> Smelts, cuts, on touchstone rubs,
> So, monks, accept my words
> By wisdom, not belief.[59]

In the last line 'not belief' is more literally 'not as one would accept the words of a guru',[60] that is, not blindly following those whose pronouncements are deemed by worldly standards to be weighty.

Though my previous teacher, Buddharakkhita, feared that I might depart from the strict path of a monk's practice and so eat after midday in Triyāna Vardhana Vihāra, the nature of the food – rice and dal, vegetables and potatoes, as I recall it now, as well as the mountain climate, made our evening repast necessary. These words upon this minor rule may seem more than are justified, but point to the principle in the case rather than mere reliance upon the rule. If one's principle is to live strictly by the rules – and if this can be done quite naturally so that emotion and energy are relaxed – that is fine. However, if adhering strictly to the rule means that one becomes full of the pride of so-called 'purity' so that one looks down upon others, one's prideful attitude results in growing tension and disharmony both in oneself and with other practitioners. This contrasts with what I see as the true principle of practice: Dharma practice means one neither harms oneself nor harms others, in fact great benefit comes to both. The core, the essence, is to be practised while unimportant matters connected with Buddhist history and culture in many different lands may be questioned in the light of present conditions. Human beings, though, while still unawakened, do need some indications of what is wholesome to do and what is not. Such formulations of basic Buddhist morality as the Five Precepts or the Ten Pathways to wholesome conduct are very useful and necessary. Effort made to practise them skilfully in everyday life can only result in the increase of happiness and the decrease of tension for oneself and others. Even then, having practised such moral precepts for many years, one should not become proud of them, or inflexibly attached to them. While they are generally beneficial there may sometimes be situations where a rigid adherence to them would not be for the best. This is where wisdom needs to be employed in Buddhist ethics.

Buddharakkhita had also feared that I should learn Mahāyāna by leaving his vihara and going to Kalimpong. Certainly the area around Sangharakshita's vihara promised more exposure to Mahāyāna than Theravāda. Indeed, those Himalayan foothills were home to a mixture of both these vehicles, and Vajrayāna as well. Around Kalimpong, Theravāda (the pure unadulterated form of Buddhism, as its proponents were wont to praise it) was particularly hard to find. All the Buddhist temples in the Kalimpong area clearly belonged to the mix of the three *yānas* which we are accustomed to call Tibetan Buddhism. This is not to say, of course, that because so many statues of Avalokiteśvara, the Lord of Compassion, were found in those temples, or because they contained quantities of block-print Buddhist books in Tibetan script, or again because many maroon-robed figures inhabited them, that the Dharma was flourishing and its followers all knew the meaning of their chanting, the contents of their holy books, and so on. In fact, the local varieties of three-*yāna* Buddhism were notable for their lack of understanding and for the mere performance of rites. In this respect, the Tibetan exodus from their own land was a blessing to the Buddhists of the Kalimpong area, as many great teachers from beyond the Himalayan snows consequently came to live there.

In my own case, too, their presence was also to be of great benefit, as I shall relate. From day to day at that time, however, my Dharma-life was enriched by living with Sangharakshita and slowly absorbing his teachings. It was not that he specified times each day when he would teach, as was my experience in Bangalore; rather that discussions on the Dharma arose out of circumstances in a natural and relaxed fashion.

Our talk, I remember, was mostly about some aspect of Dharma with occasional diversions into the doings of local personalities and international politics, where these impinged upon Dharma practice, as in the case of the Chinese invasion of Tibet. Sangharakshita also told me about the involved politics which surrounded the heirs of Dr Ambedkar. Certainly our conversation could not be described by the list of 'animal talk' – so called, the commentaries tell us, because it goes on all fours and is not upright. For instance, in one of the suttas there is a description of a non-Buddhist assembly of ascetics:

> *Poṭṭhapāda was sitting with his crowd of wanderers all shouting and making*
> *a great commotion, indulging in various sorts of 'animal talk', such as about*

> kings, robbers, ministers, armies, dangers, wars, food, drink, clothes, beds,
> garlands, perfumes, relatives, carriages, villages, towns and cities, countries,
> women, heroes, street and well-gossip, talk of the departed, desultory chat,
> speculations about land and sea, talk of being and non-being.[61]

As we lacked all access to the modern media (the above list covers rather well all the topics discussed in papers, on radio, and on television), we had little worldly stimulation and no interest in these matters.

Sangharakshita's routine began with an extended period of contemplation and writing in his room. Precisely how long this took I cannot say, and it probably varied with circumstances. He would light his kerosene lamp – the vihara had no electricity – in the small hours of the morning, and continue writing or rewriting whatever volume he was then engaged on. Those were very quiet hours at the vihara, suitable for every aspect of Dharma work, when no interruptions would impede the task in hand, whether it was meditation or the writing of a poem or a new book.

Some time around dawn the two of us would enter the shrine-room, make our prostrations and offerings to the shrine, and then sit on our seats on either side of the Buddha image. Perhaps an hour of sitting meditation followed, but for me it usually passed rapidly, such was the peace and sparkling vitality of that place. Our meditation complete, we chanted the morning puja and then had breakfast – often, I think, of a thin rice-porridge.

If the day was not to involve travelling or visits, the morning was taken up with correspondence or possibly more writing. During the morning and afternoon this was punctuated by walks in the garden or, when it was wet, stretching our legs on the veranda. It was during this time that I read the first of Sangharakshita's long books, a work derived from his lectures in 1954 at the Indian Institute of World Culture in Bangalore. I found *A Survey of Buddhism* an enjoyable and stimulating read that certainly helped me to expand my horizons and view the Dharma with all its manifold connections in a more profound way. Though the sources for some of the quotations were the older, less accurate, translations of the Pāli Canon, and though other sources beyond this canon were then very limited, Sangharakshita managed to illustrate his work with an impressive array of authorities. One thing that I noticed recurring throughout the book was a certain negativity towards Theravāda, the 'organized religion' of southern Buddhist countries. No doubt this was based upon what he had observed of

Buddhist monastics in Ceylon and India. This comes to a climax in a passage where the hypocrisy of many monks is highlighted, and was, I then thought, an unjust attack upon the whole monastic sangha (to which I was quite attached) for the sins of a few misbehaving monks. After my three years in India, I stayed for the next eleven in Thailand, where some of Sangharakshita's strictures certainly did apply. What really inspired me there were the forest teachers of meditation who led lives far from the bustle of Bangkok and who in fact condemned what passed for 'Buddhism' there. One of them, Acharn Mahā Boowa, was fond of remarking that formerly there was only *one* Devadatta (the Buddha's cousin who sought to destroy the Dharma), but now in town monasteries there were four: television, radio, newspapers, and loud-speakers.

At the vihara, lunch was taken at about midday and was a more substantial meal but, depending on the cook and the finances, still a fairly austere one. The advantage of this was that one's body was not so heavy with food, so we avoided the effects of sloth and torpor. Afternoons resembled mornings, though it was then that visitors were more likely to arrive. Sangharakshita usually talked to them on the veranda where there were seats, or, if the weather was inclement, in the dining room. As evening approached we partook of another soupy preparation and then performed the evening puja, followed by an hour or so of meditation. Sangharakshita went to his room on these ordinary days after the meditation and then read for a while before putting out his lamp. I retired to my room in the other building where sometimes I read, sometimes meditated further or, if I was very tired, slept so that I could get up early the next morning.

It may be noticed that in this account of a typical day at the vihara our devotion to the Dharma was expressed mostly through speech (puja, Dharma talk) and mind (meditation, contemplation), but little through the body. Of course, we bowed before the shrine three times but there our physical expressions of devotion to the Dharma ended. I do not remember that we did any *mudrās* (hand gestures) apart from the *añjali* or lotusing the hands at the heart, nor did we perform the long prostrations, 100,000 of which form part of the preparatory prac-tices to tantric meditation. Having been accustomed to quite strenuous work in horticulture, as well as having then the energy of youth, I would have welcomed some Buddhist practices like these.

Though changes to our routine occurred when visitors arrived, or with our expeditions to town, during the Rains – worth a capital letter in the case of Kalimpong – interruptions were very few and days could pass without seeing visitors and without Sangharakshita and I going anywhere. The rain drummed on the roof, or sometimes the fog swirled about the vihara and everything – robes, paper, and the table-top – was damp. It was not an enjoyable time in the way of the world but it was very profitable for Dharma practice. Meditation deepened, while written pages of books mounted up. Our life at that time brings to mind that verse of the *Dhammmapada* (99):

> *Delightful are the forests*
> *Where folk do not delight,*
> *There the passionless do delight –*
> *For they're not pleasure-seekers.*

As I have noted already, the vihara was 'separated' from worldly happenings in various ways: its distance from Kalimpong sheltered us from bazaar news, while events of a larger nature filtered through to us only slowly. Sangharakshita read no newspapers regularly, there was no telephone, and the vihara had no radio. Television, of course, had still to arrive in India. There were few causes for distraction and much Dharma work could be accomplished.

A great deal of my writing at that time comprised my first book to be published, *Tolerance, a Study from Buddhist Sources.* I shall have more to relate about *Tolerance* later, though a true story from its appendices took place at about this time. No doubt the inclusion of this incident in the book was intended to emphasize the Buddhist attitude to religious tolerance; it certainly says something about mine at that time.

The story concerns a young ex-Rāmakrishna celibate practitioner who had the noble aspiration to become a Buddhist monk, and with that purpose journeyed up from the plains to the hills of Kalimpong. Before taking the monk's ordination, however, one has, of course, to be wholeheartedly Buddhist. This man had a deep regard for the Buddha in a rather vague and devotional way, common among Hindus. He had read the *Dhammapada* and accepted it as something like the *Bhagavad Gītā* of the Hindus, not in fact a very good compari-son. Still, he was anxious to learn, so we explained the contents of our puja to him. He did not object to the traditional Pāli verses which in English translation read:

> *No other refuge shall be mine*
> *The Buddha is my refuge true....*

There are similar verses stating that one's refuge is also in the Dharma and the Sangha. In the course of explaining *sole* refuge in these Three Jewels, the *Dhammapada* verses 188–9 were quoted:

> Many a refuge do they seek –
> On hills, in woods, to sacred trees,
> To monasteries and shrines they go,
> Folk by fear tormented.
> Such refuges are insecure,
> They are not supreme.
> One's not free from dukkha[62]
> When to these 'refuges' gone.

During his reading, though, he chanced upon an unpublished manuscript of mine entitled *The Buddha's Middle Way*, in which he read that, contrary to the usual Hindu beliefs, the Buddha was not one who had said nothing about God; in other words, he was not an agnostic. On the subject of a Creator God, the Buddha made some very forthright pronouncements, and besides calling belief in such a being a false view, there are several discourses of his in which the poor Creator is shown, with mild ironical humour, to be the subject of his own delusions.[63] On this matter I quoted the Jātaka verses to him:

> If he indeed has Lordship in the world,
> God, Lord of beings all and humankind,
> Why in the world has he arranged travail?
> And why for all is there not just happiness?
> If He indeed has Lordship in the world,
> God, Lord of beings all and humankind,
> What purpose had He made a world of lies
> With fraud and faults, with what's unjust as well?
> If He indeed has Lordship in the world,
> God, Lord of beings all and humankind,
> Unrighteous is that Lord of beings then
> Who wrong arranged and not the Dharma true.[64]

But the would-be monk did not welcome this instruction, clinging as he did to the Hindu idea that all religions can be subsumed in Hinduism, while possibly holding the view that Buddhism is just another Hindu sect. It follows from these views that all religions should be equally respected. One day, as we returned to the vihara from Kalimpong town, this young man and I passed a Durga temple, and he asked what sort of temple it was. I told him that it was a temple of the goddess Durga, at which he proposed to go in and pay his respects to the image and the swami living there. I pointed out that a Buddhist monk could not enter such a place where animals were frequently sacrificed (except perhaps to liberate them), and that it would contravene my Refuge in the Three Jewels to do so. This candidate for ordination had some difficulty with this and dropped behind a little – maybe he put his hands together revering Durga while standing on the road. When he caught up he started an argument based on numbers. 'Four hundred million Hindus worship this goddess ...' – as though numbers could assure one of the ultimate truth. In reply to this I said something about delusion and how everyone in the wheel of birth and death was overcome by it. Mere numbers never prove the truth.

Nearer to the vihara another discussion started, during which he accused Buddhists of being 'fanatical'. I was surprised, for I had never thought of Buddhists in this way, so I asked him, 'In what way are Buddhists given to fanaticism? We have not killed others of our religion as "heretics", nor have we forcibly converted others. There are no Holy Wars [a complete contradiction in terms for Buddhists] in our history; indeed, the beliefs of others have been respected though not, of course, agreed with.' It turned out that the former Rāmakrishna devotee objected to the Buddhist conception of Right View, a position which needs to be understood clearly; moreover, if that View is attacked, then, depending on circumstances, the Buddhist position needs to be made clear. As he could not let go of his all-religions-are-the-same view and found that Buddhists disagreed with it, one day he quietly disappeared.

It was during this stay in the vihara, in February 1962, that an event which was proclaimed as world-shaking occurred – one that certainly brought India to a standstill and resulted in chaos on every form of transport. For many months Indian astrologers, most of them brahmins, had been predicting doom to the world generally and India in particular on the basis of the conjunction of eight planets in one zodiacal sign. This Ashtagriha[65] was certainly a rare event and all the pundits agreed that various sorts of disasters would come about – earthquakes, furious storms, tsunamis, and so on. Large-scale destruction would result and the loss of human life would be very high. Although Nehru, then the Indian prime minister, and other educated sceptics, broadcast repeatedly against these ideas, many more Indians believed in the coming disasters than disbelieved. The result was that huge numbers of people decided, as cities particularly were to be destroyed, to migrate to their ancestral villages, a mass movement which packed buses, trains, and planes for a week before the dreaded three days of doom.

Meanwhile, brahmins, who were the effective authors of this stampede, organized Vedic rites to propitiate the gods and stave off the impending destruction. These rites consisted of a *homa* or fire-sacrifice of grains and foodstuffs generally, fuelled by the pouring of ghee, the butter-oil in which the best Indian food was cooked. At the same time, they appealed to the public to fund these rites (and no doubt their own pockets) generously, so that it was common to see parties of brahmins going from door to door collecting anything valuable. People's fears had been aroused to such an extent that they gave not only money but also gold, jewellery, and gemstones to these supposed experts.

Brahmins could now benefit whatever the outcome: if disasters actually befell India they could claim, 'Well, we warned you to give but you were just too stingy so the gods were not pacified with your poor offerings'; while if nothing extraordinary happened they could crow, 'See how efficacious our rites have been in averting this Ashtagriha and saving you all.'

Buddhists in India saw that the whole operation was a swindle driven by greed and superstitious fear. Sangharakshita preached against this in the Kalimpong area using the text: *Kiṁ karissanti tārakā?* (What indeed will the stars do?)[66]

This line comes from a Jātaka verse, the sentiment being from the more sceptical end of the Buddhist spectrum. Every Buddhist country, of course, has its astrological system, even though consulting the stars is listed by the Buddha among the low arts unsuitable for cultivation by his disciples. Tibetans were no exception, and had a complex form of astrology based partly on Indian models but with much other material included. Tibetan astrologers concluded that the Hindus had got it all wrong, and that in fact the Ashtagriha was a most auspicious event, and therefore derided the brahmins' claims of doom. This should cause one to reflect that if all systems of astrology – Western, Chinese, Indian, Tibetan, to name a few – cannot agree on the interpretation of an astral event, either their practitioners are all deluded or only one system is correct (probably the one which is native to one's own culture!) and others definitely wrong. Scepticism seems justified. More about this Ashtagriha is found in the next chapter.

It was during this time, though I cannot remember why at this precise time, that I went to Sikkim for a few days. At that time Sikkim was still a semi-independent principality with its own Buddhist royal family. They had not agreed to the take-over of their state at the time of Indian independence, though India later 'absorbed' Sikkim whether or not people there wanted it. While in Sikkim, I stayed at the Institute of Tibetology, a large building in somewhat traditional style outside the capital, Gangtok. As this invitation came from the Sikkim government I was hospitably received and comfortably lodged. My Indian visa stated that I could only stay on Sikkimese soil for three days, as it was a politically sensitive area with a high frontier to Tibet, at that time recently taken over by China. In fact, this was the nearest I got to seeing Tibet: from the Institute it was possible on a fine day to see Nathu-la, the mountain pass into Tibet.

Though I find it rather inconceivable now, my main purpose in going to Gangtok was to deliver a lecture to the assembled officials and important people of Sikkim headed by the raja and his son. This event took place in the royal palace where on two occasions Sangharakshita had delivered lectures. My own address to the distinguished audience was upon the interdependency of the three yānas and I shudder a bit as I write this, wondering what nonsense it was that I spouted then. It was not that I had no learning on the subject, for my knowledge of Theravāda (representing the Lesser Vehicle) was quite good, though what I knew about Mahāyāna then was surely patchy. As for the Adamantine Vehicle, Vajrayāna, I doubt if then I could have said anything useful at all. These doubts notwithstanding, the lecture went off quite well; at least, the Buddhist audience was very polite and attentive.

Getting into Sikkim had been quite easy – by way of jeep which descended many thousand feet from Kalimpong to the River Tista, getting my visa checked at the Sikkim frontier, driving through dense rainforest hanging with all manner of orchids and ferns – and then rising up a long winding road to Gangtok. Getting out while the Ashtagriha fever raged and my visa was still valid was quite another matter....

All transport in India – train, bus, and plane – stopped for about three days while the gods were being placated with pourings of ghee. If at that time the Chinese army had decided to invade India, it would have been a walkover. Even Indian army units, prominent in border-area Sikkim, were fervently engaged in *homa* rituals, while jeep drivers, mostly from Hindu Nepali backgrounds, were doing the same. The road out of Sikkim was empty of all traffic, and it was only through the concerted effort of a number of officials that a driver could be found to take me. In the hillside army camps and in villages everywhere little fires were burning, consuming precious foodstuffs and quantities of ghee – and the brahmin ministrants themselves had no doubt done quite well out of this event. Ghee was in short supply in India for months afterwards.

While I returned safely to the vihara in Kalimpong on the last day of the Ashtagriha, the entire population of India was 'saved' by the performance of brahmin rituals. No earthquakes, cyclones, or other manifestations of the gods' displeasure, afflicted India. It could be concluded, therefore, if one was a Hindu, that the Vedic fire-pujas had been very efficacious. A colossal amount of wealth had changed hands, mountains of food had been destroyed, and superstition had been considerably strengthened – what a fine result!

Chapter Eight

NEPAL PILGRIMAGE

Who's overpassed this difficult path,
Delusion's bond, the wandering-on,
Who's crossed beyond, contemplative,
Craving not, no questions left,
No clinging's fuel so cool become:
One such I say's a paragon.

Dhammapada 414

Shortly after these events, I set out on another, much longer, expedition from the Kalimpong vihara. I had heard from Sangharakshita about the journey he had made on foot in Nepal,[67] inspired by his teacher U Chandramani, and he encouraged me to undertake a similar route. Perhaps he considered that a solo pilgrimage of this sort would mature my self-confidence. It was certainly good for cultivating a degree of detachment from familiar surroundings, getting out of a settled monastic life, and returning, as closely as this can be managed in these days, to the ways of the wandering sangha in the time of the Buddha.

While my journey was solitary, Sangharakshita's was with Buddha-rakkhita. Though their route was similar it ended for both of them in Phalpa Tansen, while mine continued to Pokhara. They encountered the rigidities of rule, especially of caste laws, under the Rana prime ministers, but by the time I went to Nepal those dictators had been overthrown and a more democratic system prevailed. Both Sangha-rakshita and I suffered from 'wind balls' in the intestines, as I shall relate of myself, which made our pilgrimage difficult. Finally, among these contrasts and similarities, as I followed the footsteps of my two predecessors, I met many of the same Buddhists. They remarked frequently to me on their memories of the two foreign monks, and once at least I was mistaken for Sangharakshita. During this journey, which began on 5 March and ended on 15 June, I kept a sort of diary eventually called 'Reflections of a Pilgrim', with entries made for most of these days. It occupies two hardbound Indian exercise books and contains, besides observations on persons and places, my views on all manner of events and the occasional book review. I have drawn extensively on its pages in recounting this pilgrimage.

The first entry contains this laconic note: 'Started auspiciously – great storm and then at exact time, sun came out.' A small, jolting bus took me to Siliguri, and some hours after boarding the train there I repeated the crossing of the Ganges in the reverse direction, from Manihari Ghat to Sahibganj on the ancient paddle-steamer. The very next day saw me in Calcutta, no doubt to obtain the necessary Nepali visa, where, while staying at the Maha Bodhi Society, I found time to write a stinging review of *The Christian Approach to the Buddhist – An Outline*, a booklet by the Rev. George Appleton. This review starts out with a quotation from the author: 'In the last resort it is only people from within a religion who can finally tell you about its heart and mind.' I noted that though the author was sympathetic towards Buddhism he had made many errors in trying to 'approach' it as a Christian. In fact, I found no fewer than ten places where the author's understanding of the Dharma was defective, even though he had lived in Burma for many years and come to respect Buddhism and admire so many of its followers. This review was finally published in the May 1962 issue of the *Maha Bodhi Journal*, though now I wonder whether such criticism had any good result. Certainly it reveals to me how critical I then was of Christianity and how little prepared I was to consider its strengths. It is, of course, quite one thing to criticize a religion abstractly in a book review, but quite another to discuss their faith with sincere believers. Perhaps it was due to the short time that had elapsed since my own change to the Buddha-Dharma's view, a mere eight or nine years, combined with what I saw of the missionaries' ravages in India, that led me to have not the highest opinion of Christianity.

Another recollection from this time in Calcutta seems worth recording for the light it sheds on some Hindu attitudes to Buddhism. One day I had walked from the Maha Bodhi Society to the Burmese temple about a mile away. As I was walking back on the crowded narrow pavement and passing a Bengali sweetshop, a large brahmin in voluminous white dhoti and long shirt sailed out and collided with me. Immediately he brought his hands together and bowed apologetically saying, 'Please forgive me, Swamiji.' He explained that he was in too much of a hurry and also that he often went to the Maha Bodhi Society. Then he asked me to wait, promising a lift in his car, and disappeared back into the shop. On emerging he presented me with a box of fine Bengali sweets (all of them special preparations of milk and sugar and very rich), and guided me to his Morris Minor. When both of us had folded ourselves into the vehicle he began the slow drive back to Maha Bodhi, avoiding straying cattle and overloaded buses and trams, as well as the many pedestrians who preferred to walk in the middle of the road. While performing this feat he chanted in flawless Pāli the Three Refuges and the Five Precepts, and then declared himself a great devotee of the Buddha. From the way he spoke it was obvious that he frequently went to hear discourses on the Dharma and appreciated their value for his daily life. He also informed me quite modestly that he was a High Court judge. Drawing up at the curb outside the Maha Bodhi, he excused himself from accompanying me inside and paying his formal respects, saying 'I must rush off! My son is about to take his final legal examinations and we have to go to the Kali Temple to offer sacrifice!' He left me hurriedly, leaving me to digest what was for me his strange mixture of admiration for the Buddha and his Dharma with adherence to the bloody rites of the Kali Temple. This was a clear case, I reflected, of attachment to rites and vows, one of three barriers to initial insight into the Dharma's Truth. 'Rites and Vows' does not point to a blanket condemnation of all ritual activities, as some Buddhists have supposed. Rites such as the killing of an animal to please the gods, and vows like undertaking self-punishing penances, do not agree with Dharma. These causes will never deliver the desired results and so, even if they are supported by ancient tradition, they need to be abandoned.

By the beginning of April I had reached Kusinārā, the site of Śākyamuni's Final Nirvāṇa, and stayed there with the 87-year-old U Chandramani Mahāthera from Burma, the same venerable monk who had officiated at the conversion ceremony of Dr Ambedkar and his followers in Nagpur. Among other reflections around Kusinārā I have written: 'How many unknown bhikshus lived and died here? How countless their numbers and unknown their names. The majority may have been ordinary but even the learned and the wise, we know them not. Their dust is under our feet.'

From there I went to Lumbini, the border crossing into Nepal was 'just one bamboo pole across the road. After a few minutes at the border some sort of officer was found who came into the bus and asked desultory questions. He seemed satisfied that we were not saboteurs and so on.' Rummindei, as it is now called, the historical Buddha's birthplace, was in ancient texts known as Lumbinivana, the forest of Lumbini. It is notable now for its absence of trees and generally barren appearance. This celebrated place had ruins of monasteries, an 'old' Hindu temple holding a much older stele of Queen Mahāmāyā giving birth to the Bodhisattva, the battered Aśokan pillar, and an unfinished and rather jerry-built Nepali temple inhabited by one monk. In the grassy wastes which represented Lumbini Forest there was also a poorly constructed pillar put up to commemorate King Mahendra of Nepal's recent visit to Lumbini, and an ancient steamroller made by Burrells of Thetford, Norfolk, in which town part of my schooling took place. It seemed that the steamroller, though rusty, was likely to outlast the pillar. I wrote: 'Soon guides will be able to point out to credulous pilgrims the very engine used by Emperor Aśoka to make a road here.'

More encouraging than the stagnation that then prevailed, and perhaps still does in spite of grand United Nations plans, was the sight of the hills towards which I hoped to go – what a joy, and only twenty miles away! In the morning – before dust obscured the horizon – there were Everest and Dhaulagiri rising white beyond blue hills. I am always happy among hills and mountains. I hoped soon to be there!

After a number of days exploring the whole area of Lumbini, mostly on foot, the kind Nepali monk, Ven. Anuruddha, showed me the way to Bhairawa one morning before dawn. All was cool before sunrise. This and sunset are the best times of the Indian summer day. Cool breezes blow and birds sing out of the stillness. Bullock carts out before us moved slowly along the road. There was of course dust everywhere, but this road proved more interesting than others I had recently trodden. 'The reeling road, the rolling road that windeth round the shire', with many clumps of trees, especially mangoes. Until we parted, our conversation was upon Buddhist 'vehicles' (*yāna*), with my friend expressing some common Theravāda misunderstandings: Mahāyāna has no (monastic) sangha; Mahāyāna (followers) keep no precepts; Theravāda is the earliest and purest tradition; A monk taking Theravāda ordination must profess Theravāda doctrine. I no doubt countered these ideas with some vigour, as such statements really display a good deal of ignorance. Yet we parted in a friendly fashion, even though we disagreed on some points such as these.

Eventually, around lunchtime, I arrived in the rather dingy provincial town of Bhairawa, still on the flat Nepali Terai with the foothills only a little nearer. After eating in a fly-blown café, I sought out the Nepali police who would determine whether I could proceed walking into Nepal or not. My visa stated very clearly, 'by air from Patna to Kathmandu only'. At the police station I was an object of great curiosity. Are the diagrams in this book some sinister plans? No, just Abhidhamma charts learned from Buddharakkhita. Well then, is that object carried in its sling a bomb? No, just a monk's bowl for food. I was finally shown into the office of the police commander, an officer who it appeared was trained in the military tradition of Sandhurst: immaculate jacket and shorts, gleaming brown leather belt with brilliant brass and shining shoes. He rose as I entered exclaiming, 'An English sadhu!' After questioning me closely he told me that it would be fine if I walked to Kathmandu – in spite of what my visa indicated. Would he, I asked, be prepared to write a letter authorizing this journey, one which could be shown on the way to other police commanderies? He was pleased to offer such a letter. My pilgrimage could proceed!

A police officer then kindly assisted me in getting transport out to Bhutawal (or Butwal), a town that nestled at the very foot of the Himalayan foothills. He found me a truck piled with merchandise and people and we proceeded out of Bhairawa at the modest speed of 10 m.p.h. on a road which was a peculiar mixture of loose dust and projecting boulders. It took all of two hours to cover fourteen miles. This was to be the last mechanical transport I took on this journey until I reached Pokhara. Nepali roads, in those days, just petered out when they reached the hills to be replaced by footpaths and bridleways. This particular road, if it was worthy of such a title, actually did not even go all the way to Bhutawal. I have a vivid memory of the light fading and the truck eventually lurching to a stop in the dark. Some way off, the kerosene lanterns of Bhutawal shone out, but between us and the town there was a river to cross. No bridge spanned it and no boat plied for hire. Everyone rolled up trousers or caught up skirts – the latter applied to me – and felt their way across. The stream was only knee-deep and its bottom sandy, so in spite of the darkness we all managed the crossing without mishap. Bhutawal reached, I stayed at the small Padmagarbha vihara in the midst of the market where one Theravāda Buddhist monk resided, at that time a Ven. Cunda.

I for my part have a definite memory of staying two or three days in Bhutawal, accepting a number of invitations to Buddhist houses and no doubt preaching there, but my diary states that the very next morning I began 'a day of four times up and three times down' (a local saying about the journey to Phalpa Tansen). Whichever was correct, I started out at dawn from the vihara, where I had been cautioned that while it was possible to reach Phalpa Tansen in one day, most people took two over the journey. In the rashness of my youth I decided to reach it in one.

While walking these Nepali tracks I tried to practise mindful awareness of the acts of walking and seeing. I found this practice kept my mind in the present without excursions into the past, the future, or into fantasies. This *vipassanā*-style practice not only protected me from walking over the edge of precipices, or indeed from stumbling, but produced a clear mind able to enjoy without grasping the wonders of the scenery. In this way my journey became a real pilgrimage, one not so much concerned with reaching an exterior goal, as with staying with the goal in my heart.

After the experience of four up and three down I finally reached Tansen at 7.30 in the evening. I was guided to the vihara – many Buddhists lived in this town – where I was welcomed by the resident monks, led by Ven. Shākyānanda, and was invited to sit down while someone prepared a cup of tea. I was asleep on my seat before it arrived!

I spent some time there, a fascinating place in those days still retaining much of its traditional architecture and culture. To a large extent this was because everything brought into Tansen came on the broad shoulders of porters, even the kerosene for lighting. One of these stocky hill-men carried four large tins of kerosene on a bamboo frame, an incredible load, over that 'road'. The town, which was constructed upon a hillside, had no vehicular roads: paths wound along the hillside crowded with traditional shops and houses, with other paths, made of cobbled steps, connecting them at right angles.

What was occupying my thoughts at the time? I find in my diary, written over five days which were spent resting, meeting people, teaching, and reflecting, two quite meticulously drawn diagrams, giving my views of that time on how far believers may proceed in the different religious traditions when they are measured against the threefold Buddhist description of the Path: morality, meditation, and wisdom. While this estimation of others' religion is not without *some* merit I now detect a good deal of Buddhist triumphalism in my classifications. No doubt every believer would tend to see their own tradition as 'supreme', but to draw neat diagrams justifying this attitude perhaps points to the fact that I was not then so confident as I believed I was of the Buddhist path. And in any case, what is all this concern with inferiority and superiority? It sounds a bit like conceit!

Diary entry for 20 April: 'I had a facetious thought to send Sangharakshita in Kalimpong a telegram, "Delayed by dana".' Flattened rice, puffed rice, biscuits, potato curry … all this and sundry other things had been kindly offered to me, overflowing my bowl, so that it had to be accommodated in a bag. I was assured that the way ahead was very hard and nothing could be got to eat. I felt sure that the latter was wrong, and actually both proved incorrect. I was also presented with so many rupees that I felt embarrassed. Certainly Newari Buddhists are great givers of dāna. I was also given a set of robes (which I could not carry) and a Burmese umbrella which proved its use in the coming days as a walking stick. Ven. Shākyānanda and six laymen accompanied me out of town – generously carrying my bowl and bag. After a time four continued with the monk, and later two – who walked with me the first four miles. What kindness! They requested me to stay for the three months of the Rains Retreat. How many places have there been where I should have liked to oblige the people by staying!

By about four in the afternoon I came to the village of Phullebadi, a village on a ridge of good height. I decided to stop the night here in an old lady's house. These houses on 'main roads' are a bit like inns; people come and go, drink plain tea and some sort of liquor, and eat some simple foods prepared over the fire. The next day I recorded having spent a rather uncomfortable night, though the inhabitants of my straw mat dined well – on me! Possibly they were bedbugs – more likely lice; whichever they were, they bit and bit again.

The journey that day was – interesting. I set off early, after a good quantity of rice, fish curry, and plain tea, when it was just light enough to see the road well. For many miles there was good going and I strode along, stopping only once for milky tea. The track then decided to climb over a mountain, while the local birds which were calling for rain induced the deva to pour down a fine soaker. At first there was no effect upon the track, but then it became slippery in patches, and finally the rocks turned into greased glass and the whole became a quagmire – not amusing on one-in-three gradients! Slowly and slippily I eased myself downwards, falling quite heavily once and damaging the lacquered bamboo top of my Burmese bowl. The umbrella from the same country proved its worth, however, both by keeping off the worst rain and acting as an alpenstock. In one place the vagaries of this 'road' – the main one between Tansen and Pokhara – included it becoming one with a stream bed full of slimy boulders. The rain stopped only after I had followed the path as it dropped into a valley, whereupon the sun came out and the track improved greatly.

I spent the next night on this journey at Phutliket, in a quiet room kindly offered by the Village Development Officer. On 22 April, waking stiff and feeling rather lifeless, I set off later than was desirable. The local Buddhists had told me, 'You have only to climb about 2,000 feet and then it is all downhill.' My recorded impression was, 'A good though exhausting route for mindfulness.' While resting a while in the shade of some bushes I ate, perhaps inadvisably, some rather sour but thirst-quenching yellow raspberry relatives. All around me the rocks and trees were covered with many ferns and orchids.

After reaching the top of the '2,000-foot' climb – it felt twice that much at least – I was quite done up, and sat a while to recuperate in a village blessed with a tea shop. I began to get serious pains in my stomach at this time. Though I continued trudging along, from time to time I had to sit awhile on mossy rocks, more to relieve my intestines than to rest my legs.

The track was now curving round a mountain; it was dug out of a very steep hillside, almost a precipice above and below it. It curved steadily to the left, and on its verges were startling but neat little clumps of sky fallen on to the earth, a species of gentian in full flower which for some reason flourished just there. I was so captivated by these beautiful flowers that for several minutes I did not raise my eyes to the view ahead. When I did so I came to an astonished halt. The awe of that moment has not left me after all these years. Before my eyes stretched range after range of hills disappearing into a blue haze. The deep blue sky was cloudless and within it hung strange white shapes – but not clouds surely? Then after a minute or two of stunned surprise I realized that these were mountains, a panorama of the Himalayan peaks.

I was so fortunate to have the rare experience of glimpsing this whole magnificent vista in such crystal air. With no one to disturb me and even my stomach quite forgotten, I stood and contemplated the vision for I do not know how long. Three mountains in particular could be seen from my vantage spot: Dhaulagiri, Matsyaputsli, and Annapurna.

The middle one is the most striking, more like a tiger's tooth than a fish's tail from where I stood. But from that time on the journey was slow, the sun was hot, and worse, my belly and guts full of abominable wind. Only frequent rests and hot tea secured me any relief. On one occasion a woman came from her house bearing a cup of tea after seeing me doubled up with stomach cramps. Such kindness!

At last Pokhara came into view and I wearily descended the track which plunged into the valley. Before finding the vihara there I bathed in the river, watched by a good gathering of children who may well have taken me, by my strange appearance, to have descended from the moon. At last light I was led to the vihara, which I had been told was only a small place but proved to be a large three-storey building. Anagārikā Dharmaśīlā, a nun in orange-pink robes, warmly welcomed me although she had not heard that I was about to arrive. (There was, outside the capital, no telephone system in Nepal then; communication with provincial centres was maintained by radio.) She was a Newari lady, of about fifty, with a refined face, courteous behaviour, and vigorous enthusiasm for Dharma.

Dharmaśīlā had established the vihara in the face of much opposition, as will be explained below, and it was, I found, a nicer place than the viharas of Bhutawal and Tansen, with everything well kept. In front of it was a well-ordered garden with hibiscus hedges and many flowers. I saw an elderberry flourishing there (probably its medical properties were well known), large white magnolias, locally called *rukkhakamala* or 'tree lotus', with lacquered green leaves all brownly tomentose below and growing upon a sizeable tree. The great white globes, distilling a powerful and slightly lemony scent, were often to be found on the vihara's shrine at that season of the year. There was also a diminutive magnolia relation which grew upon a rather nondescript evergreen bush. Three soft apple-green sepals enclosed the pure white flower of refined form, the whole being but an inch and a half across.

The ground floor of the vihara was a store-room, while the first floor contained the shrine-room with a guest bedroom where I slept. The second floor contained the kitchen and a sleeping area for the nun. The shrine-room showed real artistry and care, no doubt the touch of a woman from a cultured background. Two Buddha images adorned the shrine, one of alabaster from Burma showing the earth-touching gesture, the image decorated with a robe of local patterned silk cloth, the other a bronze Newari image with very fine expression and the hands in teaching-the-Dharma *mudrā*. Everything was kept spotless, with fresh flowers every day. The floor was red-clay-washed, while the walls had been given a colour wash. A good collection of pictures adorned the shrine-room, including pictures of Chinese bhikṣuṇīs.

I asked Dharmaśīlā how the Pokhara vihara was started. Through Radheshyam, my interpreter, she gave her life-story, which is well worth recording:

When she was thirteen she met the Nepali bhikṣu Mahādāna, and wishing to know what was the real Dharma, she asked him to instruct her. Until then she only had recourse to a mantra, given by her mother in exchange for 54 pice! Her family were nominally Buddhist but had no idea of what this really meant, so out of ignorance they forbade her to see the monk who, they said, was low caste. Still, she continued to seek his advice, to the extent of putting cushions in her bed and covering them with bedding – and so creeping out at night to listen to him, as to do so during the day was just not possible. Her brothers once caught her at one of the evening meetings and angrily asked her what her intentions were. They declared that if she kept company with this 'low caste man', she would not be able to eat with her own family, which was reckoned 'high caste'. Despite all this opposition, she kept the monk supplied with food, filching it from her family's kitchen – though the monk was not aware of this. Four years passed in this way before the family determined to marry her off and so put a stop to her 'wildness'. They took her to Bhutawal to separate her from the monk's influence and arranged for her to marry one Subha, but she refused to do so, giving them such good reasons for not marrying that no one could answer her. Subha's family determined, however, to force her into marriage and planned to kidnap her at the time of her early morning bath in the river. She was warned of this by friends, so she did not go, and fled the town one night soon after with her sister and a maidservant.

She went over the mountains to Pokhara, much afraid as there was no one to protect her. Another attempt was made to get her married so she fled again, and in the place where she went to stay many became her Dharma pupils. However, she was still fearful of her family and fled from there too, with her hair bound up under a scarf and wearing no ornaments so that nobody would know whether she was a woman or a man.

She had heard long before that a good teacher, U Chandramani Mahāthera, could be found in Kusinārā, and she determined to go to him. With courage and determination she went through jungles, sometimes having to hack out her own path. No food was available so she carried jaggery (solid palm sugar), dried rice, and some fruit. Once she arrived in the Terai, the plains area of Nepal, she was questioned by suspicious soldiers, whose commander, to her great good fortune, proved to be the son of one of her pupils. He gave her a ticket which took her by bus to Gorakhpur. Even after getting this far, her path was not easy as in those days Kusinārā was surrounded by jungles full of large and fierce animals. Eventually she reached Kusinārā and was able, through the compassion of U Chandramani, to get ordained as a nun and stay there with him as part of the community of Nepali Buddhist monks and nuns that he was training. After several years she returned to Nepal. At first there was much opposition from brahmins to her starting a vihara but she persisted – until it finally became a reality.

Later, I wondered whether there was much brahmin opposition to the Buddhist celebration of Wesak in the streets of Pokhara – though there was none during my stay. I do not doubt, though, that the redoubtable Dharmaśīlā would be quite capable of dealing with it had brahmins been so unwise as to protest.

Such persistence in the face of obstacles, such devotion to the noble Dharma, I found really moving, and when I reviewed my own temporary stomach discomforts, which continued for my whole time in Pokhara, they seemed insignificant in comparison. I had a number of engagements in town during my stay, including at the Multipurpose High School where I spoke on 'Why should we behave ourselves?' to about 300 boys and a few girls. There were lots of good questions afterwards so I could have continued for hours. I gave other talks to groups of devotees at the vihara, either spontaneously as they arrived or upon special occasions.

The greatest of these occasions was to be Wesak.[68] It seemed likely that I should be allowed to stay in Pokhara on medical grounds until at least the full moon on 19 May. I wondered if perhaps Wesak in Pokhara could be celebrated with more than the usual programme of talks at the vihara. My mind began planning and as various thoughts emerged I relayed them to Dharmaśīlā, who enthusiastically supported my proposals and contacted those whose assistance would be required. We planned, for instance, a meeting of Buddhists to consider various ideas about Wesak, but in fact no one arrived for such boring talk! We did, however, have a pleasant evening with the singing, in Newari, of Buddhist devotional songs, or gyānamālā, accompanied on a harmonium played by a fine young man, Prajñāratna, who also had a powerful yet subtle voice. A friend of his brought along two drums of different tones, one having a pottery base, the other wooden. These songs were to form part of our projected Wesak procession – sung in unison by many people.

Meanwhile, early in my visit I had walked out to the new aluminium-clad hospital to obtain a medical document that would certify that I was unwell and must therefore stay in Pokhara to recover. After I related my story and asked for a medical certificate, one was duly granted without any physical examination. The digestive troubles and constipation could not, apparently, be made into an excuse for staying in Pokhara, so I was made out to suffer, according to the medical officer, just the opposite, acute dysentery, and therefore needed time for recuperation! This bending of regulations amused me but I reflected that, after all, it was for the very good cause of helping with Wesak.

One of the sights around Pokhara was the Ratna Mandira, the Temple of Jewels, the provincial residence of the Nepali Maharaja. I have no notes of the actual 'palace' – it was probably an unremarkable bungalow, though I did notice the grounds. I paid a visit by jeep, accompanied by some Buddhist friends and an inspector of education who supposed, as many Hindus do, that he could tell Buddhists what they *should* believe. If the person is bumptious enough, he can hold forth on any topic in this way, with apparent authority. Just at the moment when I was sitting on an island in a lake, part of the beautiful scenery around the Mandir, it was jarring to hear his rather strident and tiresome voice holding forth upon the subject of *dhyāna* (deep meditative states). I had escaped the main party to (try to) sit peacefully at the water's edge occasionally jotting down some impressions.

This temple island was beautiful and well cared for, with old trees laden with orchids and ferns. Beneath them were swathes of long soft green grass. The new temple had well carved roof supports, doors, and windows, and pagoda-like roofs of beaten brass, crowned with a gold-plated stupa shaped like a bell. It shone, a jewel wrought by humans amidst the huge old trees, which were home to a kind of pigeon besides the gem-like epiphytes. It all gave an impression of peace. But then what did I notice? Some turkeys' wings were hung from a tree. Worse, there was a deeply cut wooden block and, worse still, there on the ground around it were pools of some brownish-red liquid. It was blood, the blood of animals sacrificed to the god there. This one, Hindus say, is satisfied by these bloody offerings, in fact he drinks the blood. Outside the temple all was clean and beautiful, but the inside was dirty, greasy, and blood-stained, and of course, fetid. A whited sepulchre indeed.

From some way off the school inspector's talk droned on uninterrupted – I had given up making any interpolations – on the subject of meditation, in such a place as this!

The subject of Hindus knowing Buddhism better than Buddhists obviously bothered me during my stay in Nepal. Diary entry 15 May:

> I find it amazing that Hindus are prepared to proclaim, often at great length, what the Buddha really taught. Mostly such expositions reveal only ignorance and more than a little conceit, combined of course with that peculiarly Hindu idea, that all religions are the same in essence – the same as Hinduism. How many weary times has this tired old nag been trotted out for me to pat. Alas for those profound metaphysicians, usually I order this discreditable view to be speedily re-stabled. A small booklet entitled 'Buddhism, a Glory of Hinduism' informed me of what the Buddha truly taught. It is remarkable that we Buddhists have been wrong these last 2,505 years, no doubt we should listen to these sagely Hindus for our better instruction. The booklet continues in this fashion, one I find contemptible, as it tries deliberately to mislead people as to what the Buddha Shakyamuni was ('God in disguise') and as to what he taught ('in every way agreeing with the Vedas'). The author, a brahmin pundit with a strong anti-Buddhist trend and a Gītā-preaching organization supported by the king, touches upon Mahāyāna but omits to mention the indigestible contents, for brahmins certainly, of the Pāli suttas. The author can more easily play around with the very subtle ideas of Mahāyāna to prove his point whereas the Pāli Canon does not at all lend itself to the All-is-Oneist interpretation. That this booklet should appear at all is sign of the strength of the Buddhist reawakening, as well as being an attempt to squash it.

Pokhara did, however, offer some sights of great natural beauty untainted by the sort of thing we encountered at the Ratna Mandir; the mountains, for instance – especially brilliant shimmering in the clear morning light above the town. On the other face of Matsyaputsli lies the famous place of pilgrimage, Muktichetra, six days' hard journey from here, climbing to about 15,000 feet. There one can see fire coming not only from the earth but also from the hot water spring. It is believed that a visit to this extraordinary place will guarantee *mukti* or liberation. But perhaps one should remember the Buddha's words already quoted above:

Many a refuge do they seek –
On hills, in woods, to sacred trees.

Though one may not go for Refuge to such places, still they may be good for retreats or occasional meditations. I myself spent a peaceful afternoon near the river. Usually rivers in India prove malodorous due to their use as latrines, but the Pokhara river dives into a deep and narrow gorge overhung by creepers and stunted trees. Before that the river divides into many channels with small clear islands of conglomerate rock resembling concrete. A shady tree kept the sun off me, insects quietly hummed, and all the while the waters roared, though in a muted way, far down in the gorge. It was a peaceful place for meditation.

Besides the natural 'concrete', the variety of rock around the town was surprising. I noticed it particularly when the sun shone upon the stone chunks and slabs of the road. Much of the stone was beautiful, and some – which exactly resembled mother-of-pearl – was most lovely when the sun brought out its patterns and colours. One day I went down towards the river in its gorge. A grassy lane led down with rocky steps here and there, past an ashram of *dharmaśālās* and *mandirs* scattered around in an ancient picturesque way, and then to the edge of the cliff. Here the path descended steeply, with steps cut into the rock. It could hardly have been more beautiful, with the cliff in places overhanging the path so that the long gracefully curling grass hung down to brush one's head. Below, the river was more awe-inspiring than pretty. The grey torrent rushed, roared, and foamed along in several channels meeting and dividing. It scoured the limiting banks of beige-grey sand and growled at the rocks – house-sized to pebbles – in its way.

At the bottom were firm banks of grey sand with all sorts and shapes of rocks here and there. I had hardly expected such a profusion of colours even after seeing the paths of Pokhara. There were green ones and orange, glistening black and white in stripes, ringed ones in soft greys and browns. At the end of every winter the river rises to ten times this height, and all these rocks large and small, as well as the 'concrete' cliffs, continue to be shaped and worn away.

At the entrance to the congesting gorge the river plunged into a rocky chasm 150 feet below ground level. I wondered what this awesome place would be like in the wet weather. The sides of the gorge, only twenty feet wide in places, were carved into concavities and sharp

1. Khantipālo as a novice monk in 1961

2. Dhardo Rimpoche in 1963

3. Khantipālo, Vivekananda, and Sangharakshita in front of the
Vasant Nature Cure Clinic Hospital, Ahmedabad, in 1961

4. Dudjom Rimpoche

5. The octagonal shrine-room in the garden of Sangharakshita's hermitage in Kalimpong

6. Khantipālo, Yogi Chen, and Sangharakshita working together on Yogi Chen's book

7. The Triyāna Vardhana Vihāra in the foothills of the Himalayas

8. The standing Buddha rupa given to
Sangharakshita by Lama Govinda

9. Sangharakshita seated in front of the
vihāra in Kalimpong, 1963

10. Sangharakshita's hermitage in Kalimpong

11. The Maha Bodhi Temple, Bodh Gaya

12. Khantipālo in Australia, 2001

13. Buddhist procession from the Pimpli district carrying a Buddha image to the Vihāra

projecting masses, and many of them would surely fall. At that time an enormous block had recently tumbled down and wedged itself above the water but at that height the river took no notice of it. Spring waters would soon eat it away. The river, grey in the valley, became darker as it receded into the gorge, tumbling upon its peculiar path. After a while it began to rain with large gentle spots, still further variegating the multi-coloured stones. So I returned through a world of grey and green. The waters, rocks, and sands were grey, so were the cliffs, though adorned here and there with small twisted trees in new leaf and waterfalls of the long grass. Above the gorge, olive-green fields blended to the grey-green of the surrounding hills, and these faded into grey mist and grey clouds.

Such natural beauty had few admirers, though, among the local inhabitants, who failed to see much to enjoy in their surroundings, taking it all for granted, it seems. Aesthetics seem underdeveloped in those people who live surrounded by abundant beauty. To give but one small example from my experience there: some boys brought a spray of magnolia with one large white bud near its base. I am sure that, had they not been prevented, they would have stuffed this into a vase and been quite content with the result. Though I have no training in flower arrangement, I took a shallow plate, two rocks – one round and one uprightly suggesting a mountain, some earth, and a clump of little wall fern – and made from this assortment what seemed to me a pleasing combination of colour and natural forms. I must admit that it did not occur to me that the magnolia mountain could be perceived differently, but it seemed pointed rocks had only one meaning for the locals – *Shiva-lingas* – and I was both amused and a little dismayed when I discovered this. So much for the conditioned nature of aesthetic perception.

Still, there was the beauty of these stones! They are not such as would be fashionable in an English rock garden, but a Chinese or Japanese garden master would surely find a use for them. While wandering around I picked up a green one with white flecks, a grey and white striped specimen, and a round flattened one with a rather faint but almost perfect white circle. These reflections upon beauty, while rousing my slumbering interest in gardening, set one generally to consider the subject of aesthetics and how all Buddhist traditions have valued living in beautiful places as an aid to Dharma practice. Is there not a thread running through all species of Dharma practice that *viveka* or solitude in forests, surrounded by boulders covered with orchids and

ferns, inspires great meditation? Are there not verses by ancient saints
of the Buddha's time praising caves and cliffs and the creatures who
live there? I then thought of Sangharakshita and how both of us
appreciated beauty. Where he lived there was the natural beauty of the
surrounding country as well as the created beauty of the shrine. The
appreciation of these was certainly one thing I had in common with
him. While appreciation of natural and created beauty is, in effect, the
seeing of the beautiful in changing things, there is also the deeper
aesthetic appreciation of the Dharma's beauty – a subject perhaps for
a whole book!

I felt a strong inclination to find a cave or hermitage and retire there
from the mad world, hoping no doubt to find some peace from the
yatterings of the mind crazy with greed, hatred, and delusion. Perhaps
this may only now be possible for our generation, as the future of the
world seems likely to be one unending suburb. Places far from the
haunts of humanity are essential for deep meditation. But of course
the verse of a Zen master should not be forgotten:

> Outside of thine own mind
> Where wilt thou find
> That bamboo hut
> Amid remotest mountains?[69]

After these meandering memories of Pokhara I must return to Wesak
and give an idea of the preparations for the full moon celebrations. I
decided to produce a large picture of the Wheel of Birth and Death for
Wesak. Drawn on strong Nepali paper and illustrated with the classic
twelve pictures on dependent origination, it included indication of
past, present, and future lives, and the three central animals representing greed, hatred, and delusion – all with good explanations in
Nepali. There was the verse 'Ye dharmā hetuprabhavā ...'[70] in Sanskrit
and Nepali, and the Buddha outside the wheel pointing the way out
between sensation and craving. It was mounted in the style of Tibetan
thangkas, and was to be carried in procession, but its purpose was
mostly to get some local understanding of its meaning.

Some days were entirely spent painting and drawing. I prepared a
most ferocious Māra holding and eating all the states of existence, so
much so that children were quite overawed by its devilish aspect! I also
drew Lord Buddha pointing out the 'Ye dharmā hetuprabhavā ...' verse
and only wished that I could draw his tranquillity as capably as Māra's
ferocity! This was no doubt not just a matter of artistic skill but also

dependent on my own mental and emotional condition. The Wheel of Birth and Death is perhaps the first complex picture in religious history to be used didactically, and is still reproduced in the Tibetan tradition. This particular painting was a co-operative effort, as I did the outlines and supplied the notes, while a local artist coloured in the pictures and Radheshyam translated and wrote in the explanations.

As the preparations really got under way, a carpenter made a 'vehicle', actually a palanquin, in which to carry the Buddha image in procession. Programmes for the event were printed and distributed. A band of students rehearsed the devotional songs called gyānamālā, literally 'garlands of wisdom'. There were of course difficulties due to local conditions: the Wheel of Birth and Death really needed some good strong colours, unobtainable in Nepal, and we needed good cloth to mount the picture and cloth to wrap the volumes of the Tripiṭaka that were to be carried in procession. We made do, as we had to, with what was available in local shops.

We printed leaflets detailing our Wesak programme and distributed them up and down town. Meanwhile children brought me a great variety of white and fragrant flowers. Besides the 'tree lotus' and the apple-green and white magnolia, another of their relatives appeared, the smallest but with the most powerful scent, almost pungent. Double white gardenias also appeared to add their fragrance to the shrine-room. When the saṁsāra-cakra was completed the drawings really were quite good, especially the lecherous look on the face of the man in one illustrating contact (the drawing shows a man and a woman enjoying sex) and the deluded greed of the character getting drunk in the depiction of craving. Perhaps my ability to illustrate contact and craving said something about my own desires!

A few days before Wesak itself I gave the first talk based on the resplendent Wheel, mostly on the three wholesome and unwholesome roots of greed, hatred, and delusion, and their opposites, generosity, loving-kindness, and wisdom. But my stomach was upside-down again and stomach pains continued to plague me until Wesak itself. Indeed, on the morning of Wesak I unfortunately had to cancel the early morning meditation programme.

But the vihara was beautifully decorated on the day, due to Dharma-śīlā's efforts, and after breakfast we began to receive a flood of tribute from the ladies of Pokhara. They brought flowers, incense, colour, rice, cloth, and – above all – quantities of fried foods decorated by edible 'birds' nests' of every imaginable colour. A small bowl, two to three inches in diameter, shaped like a monk's alms bowl, was dipped into the uncooked rice that they brought with them and, piled with grains and a coin or two on top, was offered to me. I received it and poured it into my alms bowl, the Burmese one which I had been given at my 'going forth' ceremony in England. Though it was quite big and these offering bowls, which I returned to the donors, were quite small, by the end of the morning my bowl was completely full. Meanwhile the donors prostrated and I organized the recitation of the Five Precepts (with short Nepali explanations) a few times and once recited the Eight Precepts for those who requested it. Seeing so many of these beautiful small bowls put me in mind of the standing Buddha image in Sangharakshita's Kalimpong hermitage, for its left hand, held horizontally, was empty. Could a bowl be made for it, I wondered?

After the first group of ladies had left, many schoolchildren came to the vihara in procession, led by a teacher who intoned *'Bhagavan Buddha, non avatāra'* which they all cheerfully repeated. This 'honour' for the Buddha means 'Lord Buddha, the ninth manifestation', in line with the Hindu doctrine of the ten avatāras of Vishnu. By means of this doctrine the Buddha can be included in the Hindu pantheon, while Dharma and Sangha can be ignored as they do not fit very well. By such procrustean means the Buddha is made to fit into Hindu theology, and at the same time he is demeaned as a mere deva, a mere aspect of the god Vishnu. As it seemed likely that some of the children enthusiastically chanting this slogan were from Buddhist families, when they had all crammed themselves into the shrine-room I gave a talk on 'What is Buddha?' At the end I suggested that they chant on their way back to school, *'Namo Buddhāya, namo Dharmāya, namo Sanghāya!'* This suggestion met with a positive response, so that I heard, as they disappeared towards their school, the well-chanted praise of the Three Jewels, slowly becoming fainter.

During the morning there were three relays of ladies so that, what with attending to them and to many other things, time proved short. There was still the Wheel picture to mount, and the defects of the rather crude carpentry of the Buddha's ceremonial car to be covered with coloured cloths. The picture was rather a pale imitation of the Tibetan model, though it was much admired and aroused plenty of curiosity. The palanquin we managed to finish by about one o'clock with its blue spire, yellow roof, and red pillars. It was an arresting sight, if not very subtle.

Shortly after this, at two o'clock sharp, the rain started, very early for Pokhara, so we had some hope that it might cease in time for the late afternoon procession. As nothing was then possible outside the vihara, we started a programme in the packed shrine-room. Two gyānamālās followed and then a recitation and explanation by me of three of the Buddha's glorious victories, as set forth in the Pāli poem of the Eight Auspicious Victories of the Buddha. The verses I used were the one on the elephant Nālagiri to emphasize his attainment of Buddhahood, the verse on Cinca, which made the ladies laugh, and the Saccaka verse, in the explanation of which I stressed the Buddha's great wisdom that could overcome all wrong views.

A great beast Nālagiri was, a mighty elephant
Consuming fiery brew became fierce as forest fire
Ferocious as the flaming disk that Vishnu hurls to kill,
Or fearsome as the thunderbolt which out of heaven strikes:
The Lord of Munis conquered him, He poured out friendliness.
By the power of that victory may I win all success!

Pretending to be pregnant she, the woman Cinca called,
Upon her belly tied with string a rounded piece of wood,
And then amidst the crowds who came to listen to the Lord
Accused him foully face to face, speaking what was false:
The Lord of Munis conquered her, equable and calm,
By the power of that victory may I win all success!

The wanderer called Saccaka though blinded to the Truth
When arguing would cunningly raise up his twisted views
As high as flaunts the victor's flag, although the truth was lost
And proud, he sought to win debate, to overcome the Lord.
The Lord of Munis conquered him by wisdom's shining lamps.
By the power of that victory may I win all success![71]

Then there followed another gyānamālā while the rain poured down outside, straight and heavy. After a cup of tea yet more guests arrived, including an old bearded brahmin, looking very patriarchal in his swami's robes, and a plumply political-looking man, together with some of the élite of Pokhara. I decided this time to give a talk with more Dharma in it and addressed them all on the qualities of a Buddha, stressing that he was not an avatāra but neither was he just a man. At its conclusion it was inevitable that the Swami would debate some of my conclusions as some cherished Hindu assumptions had been shaken by what I had said. He spoke with me first through an interpreter and to his arguments I made some strong points in reply, and of course this made him more excited, so much so that he took to addressing the guests himself. That was good for me, no doubt, showing that unlike the Lord of Munis I could not 'conquer him by wisdom's shining lamps'. I thought it best to leave him to it....

Meanwhile, the rain had abated, and as it was already an hour past the planned time for the procession, we decided to set off not later than six – providing it remained clear. Then began all the preparations, a somewhat disorganized but immensely cheerful bustle.

All this culminated in the chanting of the Three Refuges over a loudspeaker and the singing of an extremely fine gyānamālā which was to accompany us all through the town, called 'Sundaramurti, He of Wondrous Form'. (After all these years I can still remember the tune.) That completed, we set off: the Buddha image borne shoulder-high in its palanquin all adorned with flowers; the Wheel of Birth and Death with a red border and yellow covering cloth, all its yellow banners streaming out well; Buddhist flags enthusiastically waved by small boys; the books of the Tripiṭaka wrapped in coloured cloth reverently held on the heads of the faithful, two drums carried and beaten rhythmically by one young man; while our principal singer, Prajñā-ratna, had a harmonium slung around him; before the musicians were carried the microphone, battery, amplifier and loudspeaker; and all of this was accompanied by many people of varying ages – boys and girls, women and men – all trooping along singing the words, or humming if they did not know them. Umbrellas were conspicuous at the beginning, but apart from the enormous parasol of honour over the Lord Buddha, all the others were soon rolled up as the rain, seeing our determination, finally stopped.

As we passed each road junction, or group of trees, the procession stopped, the Refuges echoed all around and then we slowly proceeded with 'Sundaramurti'. The top end of the town had a small stupa by a well; here too we stopped and many Buddhists came from their houses to worship the Buddha with lights, incense, flowers, colour, and rice.

Soon after that, the procession reached Vindhavāsinī, where a small vihara with a married priest was situated. As many people as could get into the temple's courtyard squeezed themselves in, lights were placed all round a little stupa, some gyānamālās were sung, and I gave a short talk on the Buddha's way as the vehicle of great bliss – Mahāsukha-yāna. Many of the people did their puja to the image in the vihara, and so with an unceasing flow of song we came away. We slowly retraced our steps along the same main street of houses and shops, but with a difference, for it was now a lamp-lit procession over the wet stone-flagged paving. Every window of every house was crowded and rice was thrown by pious ladies, whose reverence was very affecting. The town stupa came into sight, and oh, it was beautiful indeed! All around and upon it were rings of little lights and we, respecting it in our traditional way, kept our right sides towards it. Whenever the street broadened it was possible to have a very fine view of the whole moving assembly, by this time several hundred people. The colours and the shadows were ever-changing; all impermanent but a particularly worthwhile bit of impermanence!

So we returned to the vihara, all sparkling with little lights and with everyone tired but very happy. People had expected our procession to be a failure, as such an expression of devotion had never been attempted before in Pokhara, but – despite the adverse weather conditions – it was a splendid success. I hoped that this tradition we had started would become a regular feature of Pokhara's Wesak celebrations (and I hope that it has gone from strength to strength up to the present time). A few gyānamālās and a puja of lights completed our day. It is one I remember with happiness and I hope that others still bring it to mind occasionally.

Just before I went to sleep it occurred to me to wonder what sort of Wesak Sangharakshita had enjoyed in Kalimpong. Was it a quiet one in the shrine-room with a few other people, or was it, and this more likely, a public celebration in the middle of Kalimpong with a large audience? There might have been Indian and Tibetan speakers too, and possibly a short Tibetan puja employing all the instruments of such rites. Thinking these thoughts and hoping that, in whatever form, it had been very successful, I drifted off to sleep wishing Sangharakshita well.

This picture I have painted of Pokhara, drawing closely from my diary, is of a Pokhara of fifty years ago. It had one main stone-flagged street lined with traditional brick and timber houses, many with carved windows and doors – a street which had an endearing way of narrowing and spreading irregularly and was built for foot and horse transport. No modern shops could be found, nor any motor transport. No tourists were seen around the town, nor was there anywhere for them to stay. This was the undeveloped Pokhara, picturesque and very photogenic, though of course I had no camera, nor did I see one during my stay. Though it looked beautiful and traditional, no doubt there were many aspects of life in Pokhara that entailed a good deal of suffering. However, I doubt that I would find the 'developed' Pokhara of the present time more agreeable – though no doubt it is a good deal more prosperous.

I had intended to walk to Kathmandu, a route that I was told would take me seven days. There were many ranges to cross, and people assured me that not only was it very difficult but there were no Buddhists to give me any food. However, I had heard such predictions before, and while I did not doubt the steepness and crookedness of the path I supposed that food would be available somehow. Perhaps my kind supporters meant there were no Newari Buddhists along my route. In any case, these were rather theoretical considerations due to my continuing belly troubles. Though I had looked forward to making the whole journey on foot, I reluctantly acknowledged that setting off for a seven-day hike with villages few and far between, and probably scarcer doctors, would not be wise. I therefore gratefully accepted the air ticket that the generous Dharmaśīlā and her supporters offered me.

At the airport I said goodbye to good friends, and to the energetic and very kind anagārikā,[72] regretfully parting from these fellow Buddhists with whom I had worked so closely. I last saw them from the plane window, still waving – until height, clouds, and mountain ranges obscured the view. I described the journey as 'three short hops', a rather laconic note for the dramatic nature of one of those intermediate landings. I forget now, or perhaps I never knew, the name of the place where our pilot's skill was surely tested to the limit. The thirty or so people on the old plane were informed that the pilot intended to land at such-and-such a place if the conditions were suitable. This meant that first the plane descended suddenly into a valley and flew low over the airfield – just a stretch of grass – to see whether it was too rain-sodden for landing. Apparently there was no radio connection with the ground. Having accomplished this manoeuvre we were faced with a terrifying wall of rock which, improbably, we just avoided by climbing very steeply. The pilot, satisfied that the field would bear the weight of his plane, then repeated the whole exercise. Top marks, I thought, to the plane's constructors and to the ingenuity of that pilot.

I stayed at Ānanda Kuṭi Vihāra, just outside the city, and on the day after I arrived I went for a walk through the quiet early morning woods, slowly and meditatively climbing a path composed of sets of three steps followed by short level stretches of stone flagging. It was peaceful and the path was well maintained. Gradually some small stupas came into sight through the trees and a good many houses in traditional style – which I suspected were viharas. Many were heavy with age and all bowed about like English timbered mansions. The richness of everything is too much to describe. The profusion of wood-carving, painting, and metalwork, the hundreds of stupas, or was it thousands, all with their little Buddha and Bodhisattva figures seated within niches in their four sides. Then as one comes round a corner, the great Svayambhu Caitya looks down upon you. Its all-seeing eyes are depicted on the four sides above the dome, the ascending golden rings represent the stages of the Bodhisattva's path, and the final and elaborate parasol and little 'flying stupa' borne above it combine to fill one with a mixture of awe and peace. The details of the shrines, temples, and monasteries would fill a large book.

Besides these impressions of the monuments, the scene was well animated by the worshippers. From so many shrines, large and small, the *prasad*[73] from the devas was distributed so that devotees departed with vermilion on their foreheads and rice in their hair, with a flower or two for good measure. Elsewhere there were praises of the Buddhas energetically and tunefully sung in Newari by a group of older men, while from another direction, where a somewhat Roman-style temple of the Gelugpas had been built, there came the throb and surging rhythms of a Tibetan puja. Circumambulating the stupa many people intoned their own puja, often revolving the prayer wheels in the stupa wall. Others honoured the stupas and their deities with crimson colour and rice offerings, while an old lady happily fed hordes of monkeys, large and small, who vigorously competed for her grain with equally numerous pigeons.

I left the Great Stupa by way of the famous five hundred steps, over which looms its great golden spire. An old Newari warned me to keep my right side to all the various groups of small stupas on the way down – little stone-flagged paths are provided for this purpose. I continued my circumambulation around Svayambhu Hill and so came back gradually to Ānanda Kuṭi Vihāra.

Apart from the gold and glitter of the main stupa and the temples on the hill, there are groups of small stupas everywhere, surrounded by the houses of Shakyas and Vajracharyas, or found amidst grass and trees. One such group shelters in a saddle of the hill. This is, according to the Svayambhu Purana, the place where Lord Buddha walked with his great disciples, including Ānanda. This I could believe from the peace there – green grass, ancient stupas, and silence. Here a little rectangular brick building attracted my attention. What was it? A small shelter, perhaps? But no; it turned out to be a repository for old manuscripts and worn-out paintings which could be pushed into the interior, already piled high, through holes in the wall. Such things must never be wantonly destroyed but should be allowed to moulder away slowly, being honoured the while by the innumerable varieties of stupa all around.

While wandering in the maze of pathways near the hilltop, it occurred to me that there must surely be a turning there, if one could but find it, moss-grown and fern-walled, past which most people walked unheeding; but should one turn down that inconspicuous path, one might suddenly turn a corner and come upon the jewel trees of a sacred land and there see Amitābha Buddha enthroned in compassionate majesty expounding sublime Dharma. Oh, but where was that path?

On the day of Ashtami (literally, 'eighth day', celebrating the half-moon days of the lunar calendar), Nucche Bahadur Shākya and I walked into the city. Every Ashtami there was a great gathering of Buddhists at different viharas in the city. This time it was held at Puṇyakīrti Vajradhātu Caitya Mahāvihāra.[74] There were about 500 people present, most of them Newari Buddhists. When we arrived, puja had just begun, led by a Newari Mahāthera, who I heard was a real Theravāda bulldog, a fact that could be believed from the determined set of his face. Afterwards, another monk gave an old-style talk on Dharma – elaborating the meaning of a verse from the *Dhammapada*. Then it was my turn. I thought that a talk on caste, its origins and evils, would not be out of place in this caste-ridden land. I gave quite a strong discourse listing the defects of caste, for which I suppose I would have been arrested and expelled from the country only a few years eariler.

In the middle of the courtyard stood a large combination stupa-temple elegantly adorned with carvings. The main shrine faced east, according to tradition. This courtyard, ringed by ancient buildings there were originally viharas for monks but now contained their married descendants, is entered only by a rather small gateway – making this Buddhist community quite separate from dwellers in houses along the street. Such large courtyards are charming, and the care with which these were maintained spoke well for the Dharma practised there. On this occasion hundreds of little Buddhist flags were flying in strings between the stupa-temple and the surrounding houses. Their walls also had Buddhist paintings, some of them scroll-paintings like Tibetan *thangkas* but some directly onto the plaster of the walls.

A good *thangka* representing, I think, the Three Jewels: Avalokiteśvara – the compassion of the Buddha, Prajñāpāramitā – the wisdom of the Dharma, and Je Tsongkhapa – the purity of the Sangha, hung from an open window. Below Avalokiteśvara sat a gold Mañjuśrī and a fierce standing blue deity, while below them was a Pure Land with its lake and lotus flowers. Beneath Prajñāpāramitā were White Tārā and Marīcī, while under Tsongkhapa were his two chief disciples. Numerous Buddhas adorned the infinite skies. From the iconography it seemed to have been painted by a highly-trained Tibetan artist of the Gelug school.

We sat only a yard or two away, the supposed guardians (against all the nonsensical Mahāyāna accretions), of the Pristine Dhamma. At least, I suppose that both the Nepali bhikkhus were such guardians. As for myself, I must have been suspect in their eyes as I had shown an interest in 'heretical' matters. Pen in hand I had been busy making notes on the *thangka*, so I may have been regarded as 'tainted'. I fear that this impression must have been confirmed after I told the senior monk, in answer to his question, that I had been staying in Kalimpong with Sangharakshita. 'Oh,' he said dismissively, 'he is a Mahāyānist.' While to my ears these were words of praise, the expression on the face of the monk who uttered them, and the way that they were said, were obviously disparaging. Unfortunately I had no time to ask the Venerable whether he knew anything of Mahāyāna or not.

Mahāyāna is said by its detractors to be a mass of 'later developments', though these words could indicate growth rather than the decay implied. Supporters of the 'pure Theravāda' in Nepal therefore looked down on what they considered to be degenerations of the Dharma, in fact on the majority of practices, festivals, and pujas that make up the Newari Buddhist tradition. One incident that day made me wonder how many accretions there are in the supposedly 'pure' Theravāda. (In any case, a *tradition* can never be 'pure'; the word can only be applied to those who practise.) We recited the protection suttas, that is, the Discourses on the Truly Auspicious (*Maṅgala*), on Jewels (*Ratana*), and on Loving-kindness (*Mettā*), with all the Sri Lankan formalities of thread, holy water, flowers, and so on. These discourses, originally Dharma teachings, were gabbled out so fast that I could not keep pace with them – neither could the listeners understand what was chanted in Pāli nor, one suspects, did those who chanted these words pay much attention to their meaning. So was this ceremony a manifestation of the 'pure' Dhamma? I wondered what the Buddha would have said of this strange performance? Where in the Pāli suttas of the Theravāda does one find mention of such a ritual? Could this be, horror of horrors, a later accretion? Of course, if one believes that the Pāli commentaries (written down about 1,000 years after the Buddha's Nirvāṇa) are of the same age as the ancient suttas then one could justify these proceedings. Surely, though, only the blind could adopt such a position, so one is left with the impression that this is a gross outgrowth of the Pāli tradition.

It occurred to me that in the face of such ignorance it would be a great advantage to be able to consult Sangharakshita. There was only one of him, though, while the situation in Nepal, India, and no doubt other places required the existence of multiple Sangharakshitas. And though it was said that famous Tibetan masters could after death manifest three or even five different incarnations of themselves, these numbers are small in the face of such entrenched ignorance. I comforted myself by the reflection that mass-produced masters would no doubt lead to poor quality – and a lowering of standards was the last thing the Buddhist world needed!

Around this time I explored with Buddhaghosa, a Burmese-trained Newari monk, the overwhelming splendours of Hiranyavarna Mahā-vihāra[75] and afterwards tried to obtain some *bodhighanta* – literally 'awakening-bells', small bells with metal bodhi leaves attached to the clappers – to hang under the eaves of Sangharakshita's Kalimpong vihara.

It was a few days after the Ashtami gathering that I first heard some extremely cheerful, lilting music played by farmers passing along the road towards a temple of Avalokiteśvara, the Bodhisattva of Compassion. They were playing bamboo flutes, little drums, and cymbals. It sounded so heart-lifting, both energetic and harmonious, that it seemed a perfect tune for the Lord of the Compassionate Gaze. I heard it again the next day as the flute-players approached where I was walking, so I walked behind them. The farmers, about a dozen of them, had flutes about two feet long decorated with black and white patterns, bell-toned cymbals, and drums. The music was played with variations in rhythm and many trills.

We all walked towards the chariot of Avalokiteśvara where in the early morning hundreds of people sit on the ground chanting,

drumming, and ringing cymbals. The air was filled with the characteristic sweetness of the local incense, while thousands of small lamps
burned brightly through the puja. When it concluded the farmers took
the *prasada* of the Lord of Compassion and returned to their homes or
workplaces, the while continuing through the streets of the bazaar
with their joyful, sparkling music – truly a sound to stir those sunk in
the round of birth and death to practise the Dharma.

As for the bells, Buddhaghosa and I managed to find two, one of
brass, the other of bronze, that were reasonably well finished. As they
lacked the bodhi leaves we had to have them attached elsewhere. It
was about this time that I discovered some more information about the
Ashtagriha and its reverberations in Nepal. During the recent scare the
Newari Buddhist priests were frightening people with predicted doom
just as much as the brahmins. Among the Buddhists here there were
pujas galore, and many Theravāda monks performed protection ceremonies for their anxious supporters.

The king of Nepal spent lakhs of rupees at the Hindu place of
sacrifice outside the capital, the famous temple of Pashupatinath, as
did prominent government ministers. When the people saw that even
the king was frightened (or was he just forced to do this by brahmins?)
the level of anxiety was raised considerably. The price of food and so
on began to climb as the shops closed, and Nepal looked as though it
would come to a complete standstill. The king had then to declare
publicly that nothing would happen (not out of healthy disbelief but
from expediency) and the mayor of Kathmandu went around making
speeches imploring people to carry on as normal. One bright ray of
light amid this gloom of ignorance was a well-educated monk,
Amritananda, who toured here and there repeatedly teaching that the
whole thing was just stupidity. Even so, a powerful amount of ghee
was burnt.... Now the brahmins are telling people, 'You see how
effective our pujas are! Nothing happened because of the power of our
homas and *yajnas*.'[76] All this in the name of religion but in fact preying
upon ignorance and superstition in order to extort money.

While most of my days in Kathmandu were spent in pilgrimage to
the profusion of viharas and stupas in the valley, giving Dharma talks
in various places, and writing a little book, *Awake, Buddhists of Nepal*
(What is a sleeping Buddhist? Why should one wake up? How awakening is to be achieved), I had one other concern, a lost passport. It was
not really that I had lost it but due to my extended stay in Pokhara, the
Nepali authorities had forwarded it to the Foreign Affairs Department

in Kathmandu and there, under some dusty pile of ledgers, it may still lie. In any case, I did not have it and neither, apparently, did the Nepali authorities. Without this document I could not re-enter India, as I had only a receipt to prove that such a document once existed. Therefore on 4 June I went to the British Embassy, where the staff were very kind and helpful. The second secretary there asked me where I had stayed in Pokhara, for she appeared to think that Europeans could stay only at the Mission Hospital. However, I had stayed at the Buddha-vihara, about which probably she knew nothing. 'Were you formerly in Malaysia?' she asked – evidently thinking of Sangharakshita. 'No,' I replied, 'he is another Buddhist monk.' Her features expressed some disturbance of equanimity that there could be *two* Englishmen so renegade, in her eyes, as to become Buddhist monks!

In the few days remaining before I left Nepal, I still had time to wander to quiet places and reflect with joy at the blissful feelings that I often experienced in Kathmandu and Patan. One evening I decided to climb over Svayambhu Hill instead of going round it, a warming climb – those five hundred steps, past the three great Buddhas veiled in darkness – until I reached the bronze vajra at the top. A few people were still making clockwise circumambulation[77] around the great stupa, which was partly illumined by an occasional electric light. Those dark corners beyond the rays of the lamps were deserted and more mysterious. The super-lifesize Buddha from Patan enshrined in the new Tibetan temple gazed out through its gates – splendid in tranquillity. As I descended from the stupa area to the quiet place 'where the Buddha walked' I made a short *pradakṣiṇa* diversion around some of the stupas. All was still but for some humming insects and the cry of a monkey, while above me the new moon sent silver rays through the tangled branches. Ah, meditation....

During my time in the Kathmandu valley I visited Patan, twenty minutes away in a small, bumpy, and densely packed bus, where I stayed in various viharas. Patan is much more obviously Buddhist than the capital, with dozens of viharas and stupas everywhere. One walk took us to 'Mahā Bouddh' (Bodhi Mandapa Mahāvihāra),[78] a 'replica' of the great temple at Bodh Gaya. In ancient times when such replicas were made, it was not so much a matter of reproducing precisely the shape of the Maha Bodhi but of conveying its general characteristics: a square base containing a shrine-room with the main tower rising above its centre, with at first-floor level four small corner towers and another shrine-room. The Patan 'replica' therefore has its own features which differ in many ways from the original. A beautiful and considerably smaller temple, it was built in the cramped courtyard of the vihara. If Maha Bodhi was ever as well cared for, painted, and provided with images as this Newari copy, then it must have been a wondrous sight. Most of the niches on the Maha Bodhi's towers are empty; by contrast every one here had a carved brick Buddha figure well painted. The main Buddha image was splendidly decorated with Newari skills and gave a very different impression from the austerely furnished shrine at Bodh Gaya.

On another visit I managed to get the gates unlocked and entered the shrine on the ground floor. The ornate figure there represented perhaps a *sambhogakāya* Buddha, though some caution is required as the ornamentation prevents certainty. A *pradakṣiṇa* passage led around the main shrine with openings to the exterior on the four sides. On each side there were Bodhisattvas with accompanying female figures, so that the ground floor actually represented a mandala, though I could not determine which one.

As the *pradakṣiṇa* passage was not built for six-foot people, I went around it doubled up and snaked my way up the stairs that had eighteen-inch risers and three-inch treads. These stairs are placed at the front corners of the temple as they are at Bodh Gaya, but of course they are proportionately smaller. In the shrine on the first floor there was seated a Tibetan-style Buddha in plain monastic robes that could be regarded as the *nirmāṇakāya*. It was somewhat difficult to make one's way around the outside of this story as the small side towers rose almost touching the main pile. But the ascent of this temple did not end here, however, for by even narrower stairs, better called ledges, one wriggled upwards through a steep passage to the third chamber, in the centre of which was a plain stupa unadorned with Buddha figures. Perhaps this represented the *dharmakāya*. From this chamber's windows one looked out over the roofs of surrounding houses.

It was altogether a splendid structure with its five aspiring towers balanced by strongly horizontal lines of Buddhas, rows of lotus petals, and cunningly arranged series of ledges. All the Buddhas were carefully painted, each sitting in a carved brick niche, a feature which by itself spoke of great patience and skill; all in all Mahā Bouddh is a jewel of Newari craftsmanship.

The last time I climbed up to Svayambhu I met, and fell into 'conversation' with, a young monk outside the Tibetan temple – though he didn't know English nor I Tibetan. We went together to the parapet and gazed out over Kathmandu. Srigha Vihāra and its stupa are not quite visible from Svayambhu, being surrounded by buildings, but Bodhnath – out in the countryside – is easily seen each evening, for then the golden spire of the stupa catches fire in the red rays of the setting sun.

I also visited some of the little viharas scattered on a small hill that lay to the south of Svayambhu. I had several times gone this way, but so far had not explored the religious buildings on that hilltop. I walked along a grassy path and under a small archway, and so into a little courtyard with a tub of flowering bushes and climbers in each corner. The place was very neat and clean and, remarkably, an evident interest was taken in its beautification. An oldish monk was in charge who, since he wore a yellow robe, I took to be fully ordained, a bhikṣu. Unlocking the shrine-room for me, he showed me the image of Maitreya Buddha. This figure and the smaller images surrounding it were all well cared for – one had the impression of genuine devotion from the shrine's neatness. This vihara was named after the coming Buddha, Maitrī Vihāra, while its founder, the smiling monk in charge, had been in the sangha for many years and was regarded as their Dharma-guru by many in the houses round about. Having complimented him upon his garden and his beautiful vihara, I went with him to Kindola Vihāra next door.

This was an older and larger structure where one or two families lived together with a few *anagārikās* (nuns). On the ground floor was the image of Śākyamuni in a well-tended shrine. It is significant that I was allowed into both this shrine-room and that at Maitrī Vihāra, where the monastic sangha was in charge, rather than the traditional Newari priests (*gubaju*). The walls were painted in Tibetan style but not exceptionally well. My kind host then showed me up to the first-floor shrine where there was a Thousand-Armed Avalokiteśvara, the Bodhisattva of Compassion. I thanked him and paid my respects to him in the traditional fashion. As I was about to depart, an old anagārika living there asked me to stay to tea, which I did. I then went to the nearby house of Nucche Bahadur whom I was meeting to make arrangements to go to Bodhnath; he also agreed to help me with money for the new passport, provided that I would supply the Buddhist school library with some Dharma books.

The next day I walked to Srigha Vihāra at 5.30 in the morning with Nucche Bahadur, carrying all my things: two small shoulder-bags and my monk's alms bowl. People were constantly surprised by the smallness of my baggage: what freedom not to be dependent on so many things!

We had just got into Kathmandu when it started to rain. A good steady monsoon rain, heavy at times, fell throughout breakfast but, by arrangement it seemed, stopped when we wished to set out. Very kindly, Nucche paid for a jeep which soon whisked us the six miles to Bodhnath. Walking would have been nice but the weather was wet and warm and there was little time. The jeep passed the hollow wherein gleamed Pashupatinath's golden roofs. I did not go to this royal temple as it is a place of animal sacrifice. It is also doubtful whether I should have been admitted as, being a Westerner, I had no caste; indeed I would have been counted among the *mleccha* or outcastes.

One first sees Bodhnath through a gateway, and the impression is of a structure much more massive than stupas elsewhere. This is because the actual stupa is mounted on three brick terraces. Above the dome, the eyes of wisdom gaze in all directions; above the eyes is the gold-en-stepped solid spire which catches so well the rays of the rising and setting sun.

The terraces proved to be rather inartistically paved with patched and sloping cement, and their walls contained no sculptures – rather disappointing when one thinks of Borobudur in Java. The terraces clearly represent the three *lokas* of sensual existence, refined form, and formless existence, while the stupa surmounting them all is the *lokuttara*, the beyond-all-worlds. Around the outside are prayer-wheels, each with a little Buddha figure painted behind it. The Buddhas and their wheels are usually in groups of five, but their order is frequently changed. While doing our *pradakṣiṇa* we saw the temple and house of the Chinea Lama, with nearby houses that are famous, or infamous, for drinking, gambling, and whoring, an interesting juxtaposition with the great pilgrimage place of the Bodhnath stupa.

We were invited to see a Gelugpa Gompa newly erected outside the circle of houses surrounding the stupa. All looked well-ordered inside and the walls of the temple were covered with fine murals. Some of the shrines had particularly intricate carving on the glass-fronted cabinets holding precious Buddha and Bodhisattva figures. The monks were very friendly, and one or two who knew some English invited me to stay there. I wished that I had known of its existence sooner so that I could have experienced life in such a gompa. But as I was just a tourist I had only a few hours in the area that day.

After a meal in a Vajracharya's house, I talked with the son of the household for about three hours! He was very interested to know more about the Dharma so, after a short teaching to the family as a whole, I told him and a few others the significance of the fine painting of the Wheel of Birth and Death hanging on their living-room wall. Thinking that four hours of Dharma was enough for one household, I went from there to the bus stop and so to Patan.

I found the senior monk there at the vihara, and after resting for a short time we went to the Buddhist brass-beater's shop. I had ordered a new top for my Burmese bowl, as the old one had broken on the journey to Pokhara. Replacing it was a fine strong brass top stamped with a crossed vajra in its centre. This was very kindly paid for by the senior monk as a present to me. I thought it would be a long-lasting remembrance of the Vale of Nepal and may possibly outlast a good many bowls.[79]

I bought another bowl around this time, a small silver one to fit the hand of Sangharakshita's standing Buddha image. A little over an inch in diameter, and a line of silver beading round its top, it was finely crafted by a silversmith in Patan.

It was raining on the day I left Nepal. The rain stopped, however, for a final puja, and the bus to the airport even managed to get through the submerged sections of the road. At the airport I saw more Europeans and Americans waiting for the delayed flight than I had seen during the whole of my three months in Nepal. 'Are you some kind of missionary?' a plump middle-aged lady asked me. I told her I was a Buddhist monk. 'And where do you come from, son?' she responded. 'England,' I replied. Evidently shocked by this, she asked, 'And, son, what happened to your Christianity?' I told her I had given that up some time ago. She assured me that I should 'Think again. Buddhism,' she emphasized, 'never did any good for people.' I thought it best to refrain from arguing with her about the respective merits of Buddhism and Christianity, though in those days I saw in the latter little merit indeed.

The short flight ended in cloudy Patna and I went immediately to the station and caught the South Bihar Express to Gaya. By the time I reached Bodh Gaya in a cycle-rickshaw blown quickly along by a tailwind, I had to wake the Thai monks, for it was midnight. A letter from Sangharakshita awaited me, the main news being that the Irish novice Jīvaka was dead. Jīvaka had not stayed long in Sarnath after I had seen him but had somehow smuggled himself into the sensitive border region of Ladakh – it was not open to tourism then – disguised as a Ladakhi Buddhist monk. He described all this in his only full-length book: *Inji Getsul: a British Monk in a Tibetan Monastery*, by which time he called himself Lobsang Jīvaka. There, probably, he hoped that the Ladakhis would give him the prize he sought – as confirmation perhaps of his manhood – full ordination as a monk, but they proved in no hurry to do so. In fact, he was treated as a Ladakhi novice and had to work hard at the menial tasks of the monastery. No doubt when he had proved his sincerity they would have considered ordination, but he did not spend long enough in Ladakh for this to happen. Indian security became aware that, in their restricted zone, there was a British national in Buddhist robes – who could be no other than a spy! He was speedily ejected from Ladakh and sadly died shortly after returning to the north Indian plains.

Though I could do little for poor Jīvaka, the Sri Lankan monks at Sarnath had asked Sangharakshita to take charge of his few effects, so this entailed a change of plans. I was to go to the Maha Bodhi Society vihara in Sarnath outside Benares to receive some of these effects. Though I was tired, I did try to catch the express (which took five hours), but missed it and went by the 1.45 passenger train: a horrible ten-hour journey. The train was fearfully crowded with marriage parties and hordes of women going for a dip in the Ganges. I found, as a result of this experience, the sentence in my diary, 'Resolved not to go third class again on this route,' a resolve I kept very well! I slept soundly on the roof of the *dharmaśālā* in Sarnath, using my outer robe as a sheet/mattress and my bag as a pillow.

In Sarnath, I gathered the (manual) typewriter left by Jīvaka as well as the high priest's blessing. I also bought some Buddhist books for the school in Kathmandu from among the Maha Bodhi Society's publications as well as settling Sangharakshita's account for his two booklets, *Is Buddhism for Monks Only?* and *Buddhism and Art*.

I returned to Gaya and next day went to Bodh Gaya to make my last puja – a splendid place to return to, if only for a few hours. After my puja at the bodhi tree, sitting contemplatively, I wrote the following poem, entitled 'On Leaving Buddha Gaya':

> *Leaving, one is always leaving!*
> *Melancholy music sounds*
> *In minor key from far away*
> *It serves us as reminder –*

That we are always leaving.
Leaving what we love
And leaving unloved too.
Leaving, going far away
From friends and parents,
Wives and children
From all we love
And from respected teachers.

Always leaving, leaving,
Leaving without end,
Leaving never ceasing
Leaving the impermanent.
So should we not consider
The leaving of this leaving?
That we may live
Without lamenting leaving?[80]

My last few tasks were to collect some robes for Sangharakshita from
the Maha Bodhi monks and assemble my luggage, quite different now
from the scanty bag and bowl in Nepal. The monks of Wat Thai had
grown some seedlings of the bodhi tree and offered one of these for
planting in the grounds of the Triyāna Vardhara Vihāra. To survive the
rigours of the journey I packed it very carefully.

On 15 June I finally arrived back in Kalimpong, travelling the last leg
by bus. I had the front seat, with the bodhi tree in the crowded back.
I looked round frequently to see whether it was still safe, or being sat
upon. We all arrived safely, including the tree, at Kalimpong, and there
I transferred to a taxi. In this vehicle the tree and I arrived at last at the
vihara. I first went into the shrine-room and bowed down thrice. While
I was doing this Sangharakshita came out of his room, and there in
front of the Buddha I was able to offer him the little silver bowl which
he smilingly took and placed in the hand of the standing Buddha. It
fitted perfectly! I then paid my respects to him and showed him the
bodhi tree and the 'awakening bells' for the vihara's eaves. He was
most pleased with this end to my pilgrimage.

Chapter Nine

KALIMPONG II

From the beginning all beings are Buddha,
Like water and ice,
without water no ice,
outside us no buddhas.
How near the truth
yet how far we seek,
like one in water crying 'I thirst!'
Like the son of a rich man wand'ring poor on this earth,
we endlessly circle the six worlds....
This earth where we stand is the Pure Lotus Land,
and this very body the body of buddha.

Hakuin, 'In Praise of Awakened Meditation'[81]

Literary activities were very prominent among those who lived at Triyāna Vardhana Vihāra. In this, no doubt, I was greatly influenced by Sangharakshita's example; in fact he encouraged me to write on the Dharma and to express my understanding of it in ways that might inspire others. My first small book – on the Eightfold Path – was never printed, though it was considered for publication. That was probably a good thing, but as I no longer have the manuscript I cannot say what errors or failings this introduction to the Dharma contained. I recall only that it was a rather radical view of the eight components of the Path and was slanted very much towards Indian readers of English-language books.

My next effort was, however, successful in reaching the public, most of them doubtless in Britain. Rider & Co. of London were persuaded by the very pro-Buddhist Gerald Yorke, a reader they employed, to publish in 1964 *Tolerance, a Study from Buddhist Sources*. From the point of view of the number of copies sold, it was not a success, nor if I look at it now – for I still retain a copy in my library – do I consider its method to be entirely satisfactory. For months I had scoured libraries and noted down quotations with some bearing on the subject. As well as these, I included some events and other sayings that I considered fitting, and with these 'bones' the book was strung together, its flesh being my connecting sentences and paragraphs. If I open it at random now, I am at once struck by the very wide-ranging collection of quotations, most of them Buddhist. On most pages there are at least two and sometimes as many as five short ones, and rarely are there pages with only my own reflections upon the subject. I am amazed that I managed to assemble such a vast range of quotations from Buddhist sources, which were at that time a mere dewdrop compared to the present sea of Dharma books. Altogether there are 175 quotations listed in the course of the work; while at the end follow additional references and two appendices, as though I did not really want to finish the book but had to pack in every scrap of material! Following the title page comes the following dedication:

> *My gratitude is deep indeed to my ācāriya, Venerable Buddharakkhita Thera*
> *of Bangalore, in whose quiet vihara this book was thought out, aided by*
> *numerous books from the library. A discussion with Ven. Saddhārakkhita*
> *Bhikkhu is gratefully remembered as this was really its conception. The*
> *period of gestation and actual birth have been greatly helped by Venerable*
> *Sangharakshita Sthavira's advice and his beautiful hermitage-vihara in*
> *Kalimpong.*

So while the quiet Bangalore vihara with its library was helpful, my teacher there only helped the writing of the book in a rather negative way: that is, the book was my expression of dissent against his teaching. This contrasts with the vihara in Kalimpong, beautiful and remote, where Sangharakshita's advice was valuable in a positive sense.

Tolerance strikes me now as quite a critical book in relation to the varieties of Buddhist thought then available to me. It is distinctly set against the view that Theravāda represents the one true Buddhism, as propounded to me by Buddharakkhita, for one, while presenting a very liberal view of all Buddhist traditions, in line with Sangharakshita's thought. It is not a work that is gentle with wrong views, and I can imagine that some who picked it up would have found its message hard to digest, even finding its flavour rather astringent.

Certainly God-believers are given short shrift, whether Christian, Muslim, or Hindu. I had then as little sympathy for those of muddled views as I do now, but in *Tolerance* perhaps I expressed this rather brashly. Not only have theist ideas been shaken up but I find from looking through those pages that Communists also come in for some pungent criticism. But then, to be fair, I also offered a sharp examination of Buddhist weaknesses. When I consider this work now, I wonder that it was ever published at all. I question what benefit there was in producing it, apart from my own education. Perhaps its readers benefited from the strong dose of right view it contains, though I have never heard from anyone who read it so cannot judge what effect it had upon them.[82] I find, though, that I can still be moved by the words found on pages 111–12 quoting an article, 'Buddhism in the Modern World, Cultural and Political Implications', by Sangharakshita:

> *Hardly less striking (than the close relationship between Buddhism, culture, civilization and education) is the almost invariable association of Buddhism with peace. The exceptions were not only extremely rare but of merely local importance. King Aniruddha of Burma made war upon the neighbouring kingdom of Thaton in order to seize a copy of the Tripiṭaka which the King of Thaton refused to have copied. This was, of course, not the most Buddhistic way of obtaining the precious documents.... Even the most industrious research has been unable to dig out from the two thousand five hundred years of Buddhist history, during which time it spread over more than a quarter of the land surface of the globe, as many as ten incidents of this kind. Not a single page of Buddhist history has ever been lurid with the light of inquisitorial fires, or darkened with the smoke of heretic or heathen cities ablaze, or red with the blood of the guiltless victims of religious hatred. Like the Bodhisattva Mañjuśrī, Buddhism wields only one sword, the Sword of Wisdom, and recognizes only one enemy – Ignorance. This is the testimony of history, and is not to be gainsaid.*

These stirring words, and others in the same strain, ring deeply sonorous bells in some remote regions of my mind. Dharma, non-harming, non-violence, no Buddhist wars,... these have always stirred and inspired me. Even as a young teenager in the middle of the Second World War I was very impressed by a history master, Charles Taylor, himself a Christian pacifist, who taught us Indian and Chinese history for a year.

Tolerance, which was actually typed by a supporter in Thailand, was completed, apart from a few Thai historical references, on the dining-

room table in Triyāna Vardhana Vihāra. Of course I discussed portions
of it with Sangharakshita, and he gave me some good advice about its
content and structure, suggesting a number of texts that would be
useful. Besides the article quoted above, I also used a portion of
Sangharakshita's inspiring article, 'The Nature of Buddhist Tolerance'.

After breakfast, Sangharakshita took up his literary work, or correspondence, in his room and I used the only other room in the main
building that had a table and chair. On days when the sun shone it was
pleasant to get up occasionally and stroll out into the garden relaxing
one's eyes, away from letters on paper, into the vast distances, heights,
and depths of the foothills. Sometimes Sangharakshita was also relaxing in the garden and on occasion we talked, but sometimes, being
immersed in what was being written, he with a manual typewriter, I
by longhand, we did not speak.[83] Another morning or afternoon would
pass and more pages accumulated. At other times, as during the
monsoon, going out for a stroll would be impossible. That rain! It
drummed upon the roof which though good and solid could not keep
us dry. Besides the rain the very atmosphere seemed composed more
of water than of air. Everything – our robes, the floor, table top, and
writing paper – was damp. It felt as though at any moment fungi
would erupt and creep over everything; in fact such things as robes
and even *thangkas* did start to go mouldy. We wrapped ourselves with
several layers of robes and under-jackets and continued, sometimes
shivering, to write and write.

One aspect my writing during that Rains was the contribution of a
number of articles and book reviews to the *Maha Bodhi Journal* of which
Sangharakshita was then editor. He often asked me to review books
sent to him by publishers. Some needed only a paragraph; others,
though, turned into review articles, such as the pages given to *Through
Death to Rebirth*, published by the Theosophical Press. This work
evoked a fairly sharp criticism from me, for while it was well written
the subject had been badly mangled from a Buddhist viewpoint.

I suppose the main part of *Tolerance* must have been finished fairly
early during my stay with Sangharakshita. If its writing had been
prolonged into the Rains I would have had no time for another literary
Dharma project. This new book engaged not only my attention but
also Sangharakshita's, not omitting to mention the most important
person, the author of this book, the Buddhist Yogi, Chen Chien-Ming.
We came to be known in this book produced by our collaboration as,
respectively, the writer, the listener, and the speaker. As the writer it

was my job to take notes, turn them into a connected English – though one which often reflected Mr Chen's Chinese background – question him on knotty points, and then produce the final text. Sangharakshita as the listener by no means maintained a complete silence, as he questioned Mr Chen and at other times discussed matters with me. And then the speaker, what shall I say of him?

An important part of my Buddhist education in Kalimpong was my introduction by Sangharakshita to some of the Buddhist teachers and practitioners then resident in the Kalimpong area. Most of them, of course, were Tibetan and our meetings with them will be described below. Mr Chen, though, did not appear to be a teacher. As readers can see from the photograph, Mr Chen was of short and stocky build and when I met him was perhaps in his forties. Even if he was older he gave the impression of vigour and good health. His face was generally cheerful, often adorned with a wide smile, but it could also manifest grief at others' sufferings. His own, I suppose, for he had experienced many changes in his life, were faced with equanimity. When he spoke Dharma it was with a tranquil but occasionally forceful seriousness. His sincerity, born of deep practice, did not preclude a certain impishness which could only be called eccentricity if one did not know him well. He was kind and generous to others but very content with his simple lifestyle as a hermit. He was immensely learned, as well as being a Dharma practitioner, and was accessible because his 'hermitage' was situated in the middle of Kalimpong and also because he spoke English in an understandable if peculiar manner. He was known locally, in fact, as an amiable eccentric, but also respected for his obvious devotion to practice. At the time when this book of his was written he had undertaken a three-year retreat vow not to leave the confines of his two small rooms. The larger room – whose walls were covered with *thangkas* and contained many shrines overflowing with offerings – was where he practised, while the smaller, rather dingy one, can be glimpsed through its window bars in the book's only photograph. In this room he received visitors and the work on his book was carried out.

Sangharakshita had met Mr Chen before my sojourn in Kalimpong and obviously respected him for both his learning and his practice. It must have been during the course of these meetings that it became obvious that the Chinese practitioner wished to communicate his vast store of Buddhist knowledge by writing books in English. He had already published several in Chinese, besides translating one or two into his brand of English – not always clear in meaning. Sangharakshita, who devoted his time to so many and various Buddhist works (by no means all of them to be seen with the eyes or heard with the ears), had no time to rewrite our Buddhist yogi's books, whereas it was my own good fortune to be able to help produce one of them. Besides his words, I added a little introduction to each chapter to give the reader some of the local flavour of Kalimpong at that time, as well as introducing Mr Chen to his audience.

During our meetings I would take notes, trying to preserve something of Mr Chen's original expressions and peculiar style. The next day, the subject being still fresh in our minds, these notes were converted into a rough draft and given to Sangharakshita for his comments and corrections. Then they were taken along to the next meeting with Mr Chen, who carefully amended them, resulting in a final manuscript that we hoped would be an accurate presentation of the Buddhas' teachings and Mr Chen's practical experience of them.

Obviously the production of this book required the outlay of a good deal of energy by all three of us. The author appeared to speak on his subject spontaneously and made only a few notes, though occasionally he produced and consulted a Chinese book. Most of the time, though, the Dharma flowed from his mouth, and yet readers will see that it is arranged very neatly with many sections and subheadings. This is not to say that the material is presented in a dry fashion, for quite apart from the interesting nature of this practical Dharma, it is liberally sprinkled with the author's own anecdotes as well as stories of others which illumine the subject.

As to our expenditure of energy, this involved a 2½-mile walk into town, 'nearly all downhill', as I am reminded by the introduction to chapter 2, and after the session with Mr Chen was over, the same walk back again – certainly an exercise that kept both of us fit! We usually arrived at Mr Chen's 'Five Leguminous Tree Hermitage' at half past four in the afternoon, and it was often only after three or four hours had passed that we set off on our return journey, sometimes in the dark. Since the slow weekly gathering of the material, a chapter at a time, began during the Rains and continued into the winter, on occasion we got liberally sprinkled.

Altogether the book has seventeen chapters plus three appendices, two of which were answers to questions raised by Sangharakshita and myself. As it was eventually produced in Kalimpong (in an edition of one thousand copies from the Mani Printing Works in 1967), it contains, besides the seventeen chapters, only two out of the three appendices

– Sangharakshita's and my own questions – the other being reproduced in one of Mr Chen's series of booklets. All told, this edition of
Buddhist Meditation – Systematic and Practical amounts to 450 pages of
thin yellowing Indian paper. If I calculate its production at one chapter
a week this would entail twenty weeks or perhaps more of fairly
intensive work; in other words, it covered the months June–December
of 1962. The conclusion of my Note to the Readers which serves as a
preface is dated the full moon day of December in the Buddhist Era
2989 (1962CE), while I was still at Triyāna Vardhana Vihāra.[84]

This Note was written at the end of the work upon the book. Though
it is hard to imagine that I finished the whole work in Kalimpong, the
major part of it must have been completed there. Some sections of the
book would have been difficult to type when I went to Thailand, and
it seems unlikely that I placed its completion in the hands of others.
Mr Chen added some small pieces here and there before publication –
they can be detected by his use of English – and eventually read the
proofs. The resulting book abounds in printing errors, and some pages
of my copy, which he so kindly sent to me, can hardly be read, so faint
is the printing. These defects, however, are surely the work of Mani
Printers, who no doubt had to produce the book within the budget of
Mr Chen's donor, a Mr Khoo Poh Kong of Malaysia.

The scope of Mr Chen's work is very extensive and the content of his
chapters inspiring because of both his deep learning and his experience. Though the content of this book cannot of course be reproduced
here, I have described it in some detail to show its range in the hope
that others will wish to read it.[85]

As visitors from another hermitage we did not observe his practice
of meditation, but the whole book is testimony to how well he had
practised. From his biographical fragments one could see his life as a
quest for knowledge from meditation teachers and a diligent practice
of what they taught. In an early chapter of the book Mr Chen lists the
ten advantages of meditation as detailed in the *Samādhirāja Sūtra*, also
known as the *Candrapradīpa*. I have listed them to demonsrate how far
our yogi has gone along the Path.

First, the body's bearing should be erect but relaxed while the facial
expression should be pleasant. Second, the mind should be humble
and full of loving-kindness. Third, such a person should have little
dukkha and less delusion. Fourth, the senses should be naturally
restrained. Fifth, one should be content even without food because
meditation leads one to enjoy divine food.[86] Sixth, one can renounce

all desires and attachments easily. Seventh, meditation always produces good results with no wasted time. Eighth, the defilements, or demons' net – as Mr Chen calls them – are destroyed. Ninth, one abides always in the knowledge of Buddhahood while one's surroundings become a Pure Land. Tenth, one is completely ready for Liberation.

I have no doubt that the first seven of these had already been experienced by our yogi, and that at the time we met him there was little remaining of the 'net of demons'. Also I believe that he was well on the way to naturally regarding his surroundings as those of a Buddha, while all that we experienced of Yogi Chen pointed to his ripeness for the ultimate freedom.

If then we turn to consider his practice of the Perfection of Wisdom there is much evidence from the book itself. For his 'wisdom through learning' and 'wisdom through thinking'[87] there is the learned content of the book and the way in which it is all ordered, an impressive feat. As for the 'wisdom gone beyond', our yogi makes occasional modest references to experiences indicating his personal knowledge of Prajñāpāramitā.

Though a reading of the whole book will confirm this, if particular confirmation is sought of Yogi Chen's erudition the meanings of the important Buddhist term *bodhicitta*, as outlined in his book, may be consulted. Perhaps one would like to know how Buddhist scholars have defined the word *nirvāṇa*. That, too, is included. Or again, chapter 6 presents a thorough examination of the three vehicles or *yānas*.

There are a number of diagrams and tables in the book, produced by Yogi Chen and partly commented upon in the text. Not all the information contained in these diagrams is explained in the text. Such omissions were inevitable if the book was not to be 4,500 pages instead of 450! There are also interesting tables summarizing particular subjects such as breathing, or the provocative comparison between the twelve allowable ascetic practices (*dhutanga*) and modern Western life.

These are all part of the emphasis on being systematic. Almost every chapter provides evidence of Mr Chen's systematization of the colossal amounts of information on different Buddhist meditation methods in each of the three *yānas*. At least part of the systematization that he presents is quoted from ancient or more modern Buddhist authors, while the rest is the work of our yogi himself.

The only photograph to appear in the book, of Mr Chen, Sangharakshita, and me, was taken on our visit to record the first part of chapter 13, a day which was on or around my thirtieth birthday. To celebrate this the speaker had arranged a little shrine of long-life deities – a painting of Amitāyus (the Buddha of Infinite Life), with another showing Amitāyus and White Tārā in *yab-yum*[88] with Vijayā shown projected from the heart of Tārā's wisdom-body. In front, fruit, flowers, and even a birthday cake were carefully arranged, and at the conclusion of this chapter Mr Chen gave Sangharakshita, myself, and the young Tibetan present (who turned away his head so we see only part of his body) biscuits, oranges, and cake. It is interesting to note – and perhaps a foresight of Yogi Chen – that the homage to this chapter is to the great siddha Padmasambhava together with his consort Yeshe Tsogyal in the form of herukas, as well as to the five great vajra herukas and finally to Adibuddha Samantabhadra. Did he see perhaps that one day I should have practices connected with some of these figures?

Yogi Chen gave me an elaborate drawing of the Dharma protector Wei-To, printed in China. His dedication to Wei-To is confirmed by several of his remarks. The card on which it is printed in sepia is now yellowed and its top and bottom frayed by thirty or more years in my puja book. The reverse contains a Chinese chant addressed to Wei-To. A picture of the deity dressed as an imperial commander is reproduced overleaf.

The book also covers the Vajrayāna generally and the third initiation in particular. Many Theravāda practitioners, such as Thais, associate deep Dharma practice with ascetic monks living in faraway caves and forest retreats. Monks like this who are strictly celibate become therefore the symbols of ultimate purity. In such a culture, references to sexual yoga, which Mr Chen had practised in Tibet – though, as he says, not very successfully (p.301) – would be thought quite improper, even a perversion of the Dharma. Our yogi nevertheless explains the place of these practices for lay *tāntrikas*, perhaps the first book in English to do so. As his explanations are based on his own experiences rather than quoting from translations of the Buddhist tantra, they make interesting reading, demolishing completely such notions as 'Buddhist *tāntrikas* just indulge themselves in lust, worse than average people'. As elsewhere in our yogi's book, each practice is shown to be based securely on previously practised aspects of Dharma, so vajra-love is closely allied to the ascetic and yogic life that few only will wish for, or have the opportunity to cultivate. Any connection with un-restrained indulgence – 'cigarettes and whisky and wild, wild women' – is utterly demolished.

韋馱大將軍

On re-reading some parts of the book, I am astonished that he presented to me then information that only now makes some sense. I recognize some of his explanations and practices as those actually taught by living Dzogchen masters, notably Namkhai Norbu Rimpoche. Our yogi's section on the Meditations of the Great Perfection is full of such material, particularly his account, given only in outline, of the Golden Instruction. This practice guarantees, but only with a guru's personal instruction, Full Enlightenment in seven days. It is a form of Toegyal practice, transliterated 'Torga' by Mr Chen. Such practices will no doubt lead to Awakening within such a short period (one may compare this to the promise at the end of the Pāli version of the *Foundations of Mindfulness Sutta* which also mentions seven days), but of course only if the practitioner is thoroughly prepared by first working through all the basic practices.

As he had practised even this highest form of Buddhist yoga, it was not surprising that his actions departed from the ordinary and were occasionally eccentric – if judged negatively – or spontaneous, if one took a more relaxed view. For instance, after discoursing about the advantages of meditation, he turned to touch upon the harmonization of the extremes – 'and began to play hopscotch around the room, hopping with great agility and balancing a tin on his outstretched hand....' His sudden action in this case felt perfectly integrated with his previous explanations. The same could be said of his impromptu theatre as he demonstrated the Holy Pride of Buddhahood and how this term can be misused by gurus who are either deluded by their partial attainments, or just crooks intent on deceiving people.

One of the appendices contains the answers to my questions, many of which are questions asked on behalf of readers for whom the book could be their introduction to Buddhist meditation, or indeed to the Dharma generally. I gave Mr Chen a list of twenty questions which he divided up under the scheme of the Five Sorrows: anger, doubt, pride, lust, and ignorance. My questions fell under the last three of these, and under these categories he decided to review them. Though I asked them on behalf of readers newly come to the Dharma, they reflected in part my own desire for clarification, for at the time of writing I had been in robes for only four years.

Sangharakshita's questions reflected his more mature knowledge of Dharma and interest in practice of the Vajrayāna. Yogi Chen chose to answer these questions under three headings: Problems of Philosophy, Problems of Tradition, and Problems of Practice. The last of the third group is still of great interest to practitioners, as he asked what sort of character a meditation teacher should have and how to tell a good teacher from a false one. Yogi Chen's reply, though brief, is very comprehensive. He lists the characteristics of a good Hīnayāna teacher (later I met some in Thailand who agreed with his description), those of a Mahāyāna master, and then the conditions marking a capable Vajrayāna guru, after which he lists the characteristics of a false guru and concludes with some considerations about one who combines knowledge of all the three *yānas*.

In the brief concluding chapter, our yogi gives his thanks to the writer and to the listener with words which, unfortunately, cannot be quoted here due to copyright restrictions. However, a précis can be given of his long and heartfelt thanks.

Mr Chen took a clockwork monkey holding dumb-bells from the top of a cupboard and wound it up. As it exercised he compared himself to the monkey performing tricks in a small circus, while Sangharakshita and myself were the human actors, one older and more experienced, one younger and with many works to do. Then he proposed a different analogy, comparing Sangharakshita the listener, silent upon his chair, to the Vajrayāna. The writer he compared, because of the amount of work involved in writing, typing, visiting him with queries, and the vigour with which it was performed, to the Mahāyāna. Again self-deprecating, Mr Chen compared himself to a boy pupil mostly playing about in the monastery grounds, to the Hīnayāna. Mr Chen then said that we had long distances to walk to and from his hermitage while he had nothing to do except talk! His words, he declaimed, did not come from a holy person but if the words were good then they should be practised rather than emphasizing any holiness in the author. He repeated that he had no realization (we understood these self-deprecatory remarks to be the good results of modesty developed through his training, as well as partly due to standards of politeness in his homeland), and that his words should be investigated to determine whether they were true or false.

Though Mr Chen's book was finished long after the Rains of 1962 had vanished, we now need to return to them to record a few incidents that took place then. One event that stands out in my mind was Sangharakshita's birthday, not because this was celebrated in the conventional Western way with a party, drinks, and cake, all of which I remember were noticeable by their absence. I am not sure now how I came to know the date of his birthday – perhaps he received a card or two from relatives or supporters and told me. One thing is certain, I did not know his birthday through comparing astrological signs, common enough in our society now but not likely to happen in our case. Neither Sangharakshita nor I had much confidence in destiny predicted from the stars, as readers will have gathered from the accounts of the Ashtagriha. However it was, I came to know that his birthday was in August. That particular day was, I recollect, a specially fine one with a warm sun making the garden attractive. In the afternoon I took a vase with water in it and descended the garden terraces to a patch of flowers – chrysanthemums were among them – cut some of them, and arranged them, as I thought, in a balanced fashion and then looked at this offering. Was there not something missing? I recalled our flower offering at the shrine in which the well-known Pāli verse from Sri Lanka was chanted:

> *The Buddha I revere with varied flowers,*
> *By this, my merit, may there be release;*
> *Even as these flowers fade away*
> *So will my body be destroyed.*

So I took a strangely shaped but quite dead piece of wood and rearranged the flowers around it. When I had achieved an interesting balance of form and colour I carefully carried the vase up to the dining room and presented the offering to Sangharakshita, wishing him long life and many birthdays yet to come when he would continue to turn the Wheel of Dharma. But, I pointed out, impermanence should not be forgotten and for this reason the piece of dead wood had been included. His face showed pleasure that I had remembered to make this birthday offering and a little surprise that the reference to the impermanent was included.

Though this annual event occurred only once while I was in Kalimpong, both Sangharakshita and I had a repeated experience which involved a close neighbour of ours. I have already remarked upon the splendid views from the veranda, the sort indeed which would vastly increase the property's value in the eyes of estate agents. In our eyes, though, the vast panorama of hills, valleys, and mountains reflected outwardly what was an inner vastness of the Buddha's path, especially of the Bodhisattva's practice towards Buddhahood. Though it would be an exaggeration to compare our experience of living at Triyāna Vardhana Vihāra with Nirvāṇa, yet it was like a glimpse of it. As the *Dhammapada* says:

If as a broken gong
Never you reverberate,
Quarrelling's not part of you:
That Nirvāṇa's reached.[89]

We had no quarrels at the vihara, in fact I do not remember a single harsh word passing between us in all those months. The days passed with Dharma practice, with the reception of visitors and the writing of books, combined with our own occasional forays into town. Around our 'little nirvāṇa', though, things were quite otherwise. As I remarked in the introduction to one or two chapters of Yogi Chen's work, the clouds of war were gathering, but apart from such major conflagrations brought about by the evil roots of greed, hatred, and delusion, we had another repeated experience of the conflicts of saṃsāra. This came in the form of an invitation to lunch in the house of an English-born neighbour who lived further up the hillside, in a house which shared the same views from its well-appointed windows as we perceived from ours. Though the views were the same, the experience of visiting that house was very different. It was as though, as Bodhi-sattvas out of compassion for the suffering world, we had put aside our nirvāṇa and descended into the maelstrom of sufferings. While we perceived a vision of beauty inspiring us to practise Dharma, our hostess saw mostly the dark sides of human life. The lunch, while excellent, was always accompanied by a thorough tour in words through the dark deeds of Kalimpong's bazaar and political life. We had to listen to all the juiciest bits of gossip and so got to know – our hostess presuming that we would be interested – of not only who was sleeping with whom, but what murders had been committed and what quarrels had broken out. She knew all the darkest financial dealings as well as the ramifications of political plots and their likely outcome. In fact, she delighted in retailing to us, our ears otherwise largely unsullied by such matters, every event spiced by greed, hatred, and delusion. No doubt it was good for us, living as we did in our little nirvāṇa near by, to hear some of this, to remember that others' view of the world was one of unending conflict. However, after an hour or two of this unrelieved by any news of the *good* that others were doing, it seemed as though our ears were being assaulted by a continuous stream of evil. Sangharakshita had always to excuse us from further exploring these byways of Kalimpong life by remarking that we had to return to our vihara because visitors were expected, or work had to be finished upon a book, or letters required an immediate reply....

The *Kazini*, as she was usually known, was married to a Sikkimese nobleman, Kazi Lhendup Dorje-Khangsarpa, who was a Buddhist. We saw him far less frequently than we listened to her. She had some interest in the Buddha-Dharma and liked to invite us to their splendid house set in an immaculately groomed lushly tropical garden. Not only were the surroundings beautiful but the house had furnishings of high quality. There was an expensively decorated shrine-room with some particularly fine *thangkas*. A number of servants attended this lady and her husband. One would think, therefore, after quickly surveying this scene, that the inhabitants of this paradise would be happy and content with their good fortune, and easily be able to live a life in which, as material considerations were so comfortable, the Dharma could be practised.

The same view but different mind! These excursions offered us a perfect illustration of how

> Dhammas are forerun by mind,
> Mind's their chief, mind-made are they.[90]

Or, as the great Nāgārjuna puts it:

> As a water-vessel is
> Variously perceived by beings:
> Though nectar to celestials
> For humans it's plain drinking water;
> While to the hungry ghosts it seems
> A putrid ooze of pus and blood,
> It is for water serpent-spirits
> And the fish, a world to live in,
> While space it seems to gods who dwell
> In the sphere of infinite space.
> So any percept, live or dead,
> Within the person or without,
> Differently is seen by beings
> According to their fruits of karma.[91]

Though on a previous page Sangharakshita and I are referred to as 'Bodhisattvas', I for one certainly felt myself to be a tiny 'baby *bosat*',[92] one whose feet were weak and who could only crawl on this magnificent path. Sangharakshita, while praising the Mahāyāna path of practice, never boasted of his attainments, in fact he was most reticent to discuss any spiritual awakenings he had experienced. Neither of us felt that our progress could be gauged by the ten Bodhisattva stages, while I had serious doubts about the Four Noble Levels of the Pāli texts. I believed even then that the latter were indications of experience rather than concrete 'attainments' and that the same symbolic value attached to the former. When such lists of spiritual stages were taken literally I had noticed that serious distortions of Dharma life and practice resulted. Before my eyes, only a few years prior to my residence in Kalimpong, was the dreadful example of Kapilavaddho, who believed he had 'got' Enlightenment and was an Arhant. Not only did his conceit demolish him as a teacher but others were also 'destroyed'. One of his monk-disciples decided that he could fly and leapt out of a third-storey window. And a group of his lay disciples who had seen various visions of Buddhas in their bodies were designated by him as Arhants. They were at that time in charge of the English Sangha Trust and were also the most miserable bunch of Arhants I have ever met. This experience made me very wary of anyone claiming attainments and I concluded, in line with all teachings of the Dharma, that those who had really experienced extraordinary spiritual growth were the very ones who said little about it, or who, like Yogi Chen, disparaged their own attainments as insignificant.

This is not to say that Kalimpong lacked teachers who had experienced the taste of Dharma. Both Sangharakshita and I were fortunate to have contact with some who knew this taste from personal experience. Mr Chen has already been mentioned in these pages. Now it is time to draw on my memories of Dhardo Rimpoche who, like Mr Chen, I met through Sangharakshita, though not so frequently.

When Sangharakshita and I met Dhardo Rimpoche it was always in the grounds of the school that he had established. When we came upon him he was usually in the middle of attending to several matters and one had the impression that all of them were accomplished well. He wore his monk's robes, often looking as though they were his 'working robes', and had cropped hair in the monk style. His face lit up with a smile upon seeing us and he would order someone to offer us tea, that is, the Tibetan variety with butter and salt, often accompanied by some Amdo bread. Though he had one or two monk-attendants staying with him, clearly his aim in Kalimpong was not to build another monastery as more conventional Gelug teachers did but to educate part of the next generation of Tibetans. Those who served him revered him deeply, as was obvious from their very respectful way of addressing him. Long hours of early morning and late evening ritual practice of the Dharma were balanced in him by his tireless activities for the benefit of others. Of Dhardo Rimpoche one could say with confidence: Here is a true Bodhisattva. Though he can only be introduced to you now with words on paper, I hope, from what is written of him here, that this claim will be fully substantiated.

For an incarnate lama of those days he had led an unusual life, though to be sure it began fairly conventionally. Born of a prosperous merchant family around 1926 in Dhartsendo, a centre of trade with China in far eastern Tibet, he was recognized as the incarnation of a previous Dhardo Rimpoche who had died some ten years earlier. Although in that past life Dhardo Rimpoche had started his religious path in a monastery of the Nyingmapas, the most ancient lineage of Tibetan Buddhist teachings, he had been invited while in Lhasa to pursue his studies in the great Gelugpa monastery of Drepung. His predecessor had thus been 'captured' by the reformed tradition of Gelug teachers and the lineage of which he was the twelfth was henceforth associated with Drepung and its traditions.

The Dhardo Rimpoche known to Sangharakshita and me was thus the thirteenth of his line, and while the earliest of them may have been Indian, succeeding incarnations of whom we know little had all been Tibetan, and probably lived all their lives within the frontiers of Tibet. The thirteenth Dhardo was destined to return to India, though his conventional upbringing as a student monk in Drepung showed little sign that this would occur. He was a particularly brilliant student and passed his geshe examinations with flying colours – in fact, in his year, he tied for first place with a Mongolian student in the exceedingly arduous oral examinations for the highest grade, the Lharampa level of geshe. This means, at least, that the possessor of such eminence will be vastly learned, though in Dhardo Rimpoche's case this was only apparent after some time and in the context of long discussions on the Dharma. Though such a living storehouse of Buddhist treasures, he concealed his learning modestly. Apart from passing examinations, which were always conducted orally, Rimpoche had of course been ordained first as a novice and later as a monk, and had undertaken the Bodhisattva's vows to save all beings, as well as receiving and practising many forms of Vajrayāna meditation teachings. It is difficult from a Western perspective to understand how these seemingly diverse aspects of Dharma could be integrated into a whole. 'Examinations' have for most people no connection with religious practice, still less with the purification of body, speech, and mind. A 'monk' sounds to Westerners like someone who retires from ordinary life and thereafter has no connection at all with this world. The nearest Westerners ordinarily approach to the Bodhisattva's vow is to take up social work of some kind and busy themselves – and perhaps experience 'burn-out' – with the well-being of the less fortunate members of human society. 'Meditation' again sounds reclusive and could even be taken negatively to imply escapism and indifference to the world's sufferings. In traditional Tibetan monastic education all these elements were integrated to form part of a syllabus of study and practice which had no less than the spiritual Awakening of a Buddha as its goal.

Dhardo Rimpoche's education from a young age round to his early manhood was thus conventional by Tibetan standards, though startling by Western ones. It may have seemed to him as a young man that his life would be spent in Tibet continuing with his studies and meditations, but this was not to be. The construction of a Tibetan temple at Bodh Gaya had been begun in the late 1940s, but few monks resided there and there was neither a well-trained teacher nor an abbot. The consequence of this was that those monks living there appropriated for themselves such income as the temple had and lived as they pleased. The Tibetan government determined to change this situation and appointed Dhardo Rimpoche as abbot, due to his success at teaching Dharma during a previous visit to India for medical reasons.

So in 1949, Rimpoche, with his mother, attendant, steward, servants, a fair-sized library, and other baggage, arrived in Bodh Gaya. His tenure of the Tibetan temple there was not easy, as the monks and their established leader resented Rimpoche's reforms, both those regarding finance and others relating to the strict practice of Dharma by the residents. However, Rimpoche prevailed in the long run, though he encountered considerable opposition. It was due to his efforts that the temple I saw twelve years later was so well established and its practices so well regulated. Rimpoche thought not only of the monks who lived there but also of the increasing number of Tibetan pilgrims visiting Bodh Gaya and Buddhism's other sacred sites in the winter season, the only time when they could bear the Indian climate. He constructed a pilgrims' shelter for them in the grounds of the temple, though the need even for this was contested by those short-sighted monks.

There were also conflicts with others in authority, or who thought they were in authority, at Bodh Gaya. Tibetan government officials in

India tried to make trouble for Rimpoche because his efforts to upgrade the temple bypassed them, or showed them in a poor light. They were also involved in a dispute over the brick staging for rows of lamps lighted for festivals near the bodhi tree. Anagārika Munindra, a Theravāda Buddhist from Chittagong, objected to these lamps, claiming the tree was being adversely affected by their heat. Though this matter was eventually settled when the staging was constructed, Rimpoche had to suffer in the meantime. All is not light and love, as some might suppose, at the great place of the Buddha's Awakening!

Buddhists in Kalimpong who had benefited from Rimpoche's first visit to India, requested him to teach there on a more permanent basis. When, at their invitation, he spent a while in Kalimpong he immediately became aware of a situation that required action. Due to the increase of Tibetan refugees fleeing persecution by the Chinese, many poor families could no longer support their children – who consequently became beggars or thieves and had no knowledge of their own culture or religion. The plight of these children, and the fact that a number of Christian missionary bodies hoped to use the situation to convert them, decided Rimpoche's mind: he would establish a residential school for such children, which would teach both traditional subjects – language, grammar, script, and the Dharma – as well as the necessary 'modern' subjects which should include English and Hindi.

My experience of this school began in the first months of 1962, for it was then that I wrote (together with a Buddhist nun, Amita Nisatta), a letter to the editor of the *Maha Bodhi Journal* contrasting the conditions at the Indo-Tibet Buddhist Cultural Institute (ITBCI) with those at a school run by the Plymouth Brethren. Parts of it are worth quoting. Of the former, I wrote:

> While staying in Kalimpong we were happy to see a Tibetan school efficiently run by an eminent 'incarnate lama' [Dhardo Rimpoche]. In an atmosphere of Tibetan culture, over two hundred pupils are studying under fourteen teachers. The children, some of them orphans, looked cheerful and most were well-dressed in Tibetan costume.... Contrast this with another school we saw, where instead of education in the rich tradition of Tibet, advantage is taken, by the Plymouth Brethren missionaries in charge, of the orphans taught there. The missionaries admitted to an emissary of the Tibet Society, London, that they were not interested in educating the children or in teaching them handicrafts; they wanted only to convert them to Christianity. So that they are able to convert others, the children are taught Tibetan, Nepali and

English.... Worst of all, many of the school and house walls display vile, anti-
Buddhist posters which were banned from public hoardings in Kalimpong by
the Deputy Commissioner, Darjeeling.... Why should this disgraceful
attempt at forced conversion of young children be allowed to continue?

At the time when I visited the school, often in the company of Sangharakshita, it was housed in the old Bhutan Palace, a building where the
thirteenth Dalai Lama had once stayed. Though originally a building
of distinction in traditional style, by the time I saw it, lacking repair for
many years, its condition was ramshackle. However, it served as
Rimpoche's dwelling and temple where he practised, with space
downstairs for classrooms and dormitories. If we arrived early enough
in the morning when school was about to begin, before we actually
saw the building, we *heard* its young students. All of them were chanting at the tops of their voices the mantra of Mañjuśrī, the bodhisattva
of wisdom: *'oṁ a ra pa cha na dhīḥ dhīḥ dhīḥ dhīḥ dhīḥ dhīḥ!'*[93]

Sangharakshita's friendship with Dhardo Rimpoche had ripened
over several years, though they came from very different backgrounds.
It began during the Indian Government's celebration of 2,500 years of
Buddhism in 1957,[94] when Sangharakshita, on bus journeys to many
historic and industrial sites, preferred to sit with Dhardo Rimpoche
rather than with other Theravāda monks. Sangharakshita came then
to appreciate the immense scholarship and kindness of Rimpoche,
while he in turn appreciated Sangharakshita's noble efforts to propagate the Buddha-Dharma in India, especially among the outcastes.
Since both resided near Kalimpong, Sangharakshita often visited
Dhardo Rimpoche to discuss some point of Dharma or the organization of a festival, while Rimpoche walked out of town to see Sangharakshita when he had some work to do for the school that involved
English language. In fact, the latter, possessing a manual English
typewriter, became the unofficial secretary for the ITBCI.

On one of Sangharakshita's visits to the school I remember him
explaining the elaborate and colourful silk banner, flown on special
occasions and designed by Rimpoche on the basis of Indian Buddhist
texts which he had studied in their Tibetan translation. This gave me
a glimpse of a quite different Hīnayāna world apart from the
Theravāda one with which I was acquainted. What a loss India had
sustained with its destruction, but what treasures there were contained in it for those willing to investigate. A passage in Dhardo
Rimpoche's biography explains this Dharma symbol.

*Here, two deer ... hold up the Buddha's 'Wheel of Truth'; above flies a banner
showing an eagle-lion, a fish-otter, and a crocodile-conch. These are the
hybrid animals representing the peace and harmony which prevailed when
the Buddha was alive. Topmost are three radiant jewels. A golden jewel
represents the Buddha, the exemplar of wisdom and compassion; a blue jewel
represents the Dharma, the teaching he imparted and the Truth he discovered;
and a red jewel represents the Sangha, the community of those who,
throughout time and across space, tread the Buddha's Path.*[95]

On another occasion of meeting Rimpoche, though Sangharakshita
has no recollection of this event, I requested an initiation into the
practice of Green Tārā. I do not now seem to have any details of this
practice, though the formal photograph of Rimpoche reproduced here
I connect with this initiation. As though to emphasize the impermanence of mind, of memory, I find in my ancient puja book a treasury
of chants copied from many sources, an account of a Green Tārā
practice given by 'Chatul (Bondless) Sangye (Buddha) Dorje (Vajra)
Rimpoche (Nying-ma-pa)', but no date is mentioned. I do not remember meeting this teacher in Kalimpong, but from the evidence of the
puja book I must have done so. This means that my belief that the
Green Tārā practice came from Dhardo Rimpoche may not be accurate....

One occasion on which Sangharakshita and I certainly met Rimpoche
was for the bestowal of Bodhisattva precepts. This occurred on 12
October, according to Sangharakshita.[96] The Bodhisattva ideal, the
dedication of this and future lives for the benefit and Awakening of all
beings, inspired both of us. It is not surprising that there are sets of
precepts to guide one on this path. Those who practised Awakening
themselves to the Arhant ideal as a monk (it was assumed that no one
living a household life would be able to attain this) wrote, or originally
chanted, their own list: the Prātimokṣa precepts. In accordance with
that ideal, the Awakening of oneself, no mention is made of salvation
for the ocean of suffering beings. Though Arhants were compassionate
and would no doubt help such human and other beings as they could,
they had to accomplish that in the life remaining to them, as after death
their state could not be determined, for they would neither return to
saṁsāra, cease to exist, both of these together, nor 'neither exist nor not
exist'. A Bodhisattva, though, is committed to work towards the Awakening of all living beings, no small task when their inconceivable
numbers on this planet alone are contemplated. As 'sentient beings'
includes such creatures in this tropical climate as ants, which are

everywhere – even on my desk – it is a dedication which will take innumerable lifetimes to accomplish. Sangharakshita and I felt that we should dedicate our lives to this noble goal and that this would be given a more concrete base by undertaking the Bodhisattva precepts.

No doubt the ceremony was in Tibetan, chanted by Dhardo Rimpoche, which may account for my lack of details of this event. Sangharakshita also writes: 'My mind, too, fails to provide any details of the day we took the Bodhisattva precepts from Dhardo Rimpoche, except that it was a very positive occasion, of which I retain a distinct *visual* impression.'[97] For myself, what remains of that event is the formal photograph of Dhardo Rimpoche that he gave me at that time and an English translation of the precepts that we were given. This translation was the result of a collaboration by our Tibetan teacher with Sangharakshita, and as the former knew little English and the latter little Tibetan, the medium of translation was Hindi.

The three yellowing sheets with all sixty-one Bodhisattva precepts on them were typed by Sangharakshita and given to me some time after the ceremony. They are entitled, 'The Bodhisattva Saṁvaraśīla (according to the Tradition of the Ven. Tsongkhapa) rendered into English in accordance with the Oral Explanations of The Ven. Dhardo Rimpoche (explanatory additions in brackets are derived from the Commentary of Tsongkhapa)'. All of them begin, in this translation, with 'It is a bad thing....' and are divided into eighteen Root Offences plus forty-six offences of less gravity. Like the Prātimokṣa precepts of monks and nuns they are quite a mixed bag, derived ultimately from various Mahāyāna sūtras, notably the *Bodhisattvabhūmi*. Some of them indeed are not especially Mahāyāna in flavour and could as easily be found in the Pāli suttas, such as for instance the precepts 'It is a bad thing to praise oneself and disparage others,' or 'to adhere to false views', while others in particular emphasize the Bodhisattva's attitude and practice: 'It is a bad thing to withhold the wealth of Dharma from others ... to disparage the Hīnayāna ... to give up the Bodhicitta....' Some of these precepts address the tension between the Arhant and Bodhisattva ideals emphasizing how important it is to choose the more compassionate way. Among the root precepts one finds, 'It is a bad thing to discourage others from striving after Buddhahood and encourage them to aim at inferior goals', and among the ordinary failings are included 'to be capable of practising the Bodhisattva ideal yet, abandoning it, to follow the Hīnayāna' and 'to think that one will lead oneself alone to Emancipation.'

Lest these precepts be regarded as another list of things not to be done in any circumstances, as indeed a monk or nun practising the Prātimokṣa rules must see them, one of the minor offences for a Bodhisattva reads 'It is a bad thing not to be prepared to break, out of compassion for others, the seven kinds of Vinaya rules.' This precept emphasizes that rules must not be regarded as applying in all times and places, as many Theravāda monks in our times insist they must be. Such insistence leads merely to a sterile and often arrogant morality which is the opposite of true practice of the Dharma. As the first category of 'the seven kinds of Vinaya rules' lists the four Defeats (sexual intercourse, stealing a valuable object, deliberately killing a human being, and boasting of attainments which have not been realized) for which a monk or nun can be expelled from the monastic sangha, breaking these 'out of compassion' could lead to serious consequences. However, the Bodhisattva should realize that rules cannot represent an absolute morality and should remain flexible, not indeed like the indulgence of ordinary people able to change their morals to suit their momentary desires, but rather the noble compassionate actions of a Bodhisattva. Just as some monks' insistence on keeping even the minutiae of the Vinaya rules leads only to aridity, so a rule like the one under consideration could lead, *where wisdom and compassion are lacking*, to mere selfish indulgence justified by a good deal of delusion. Māra has set traps everywhere!

My record of these precepts shows a good deal of study of the subject over quite a long period of time. In the margins I have made notes relating different precepts together, while additional explanations derived from one of Mr Chen's booklets have also been noted. I have recorded the Mahāyāna sūtras which he says are the sources of these precepts and noted occasions when they are duplicated – for instance, 'It is a bad thing to praise oneself and disparage others,' occurs as the first Root Offence *and* the thirty-second ordinary failing. Likewise 'to disparage the Hīnayāna' is both fourteenth Root and the twenty-seventh ordinary offence.

I have also compared them to the Chinese tradition of the Bodhisattva Śīla derived from the Mahāyāna *Brahmajāla Sūtra*, a record of which is contained in another book which I wrote out, with the help of my friend John Blofeld in Bangkok. This was after I received these Bodhisattva precepts from a senior Chinese monk, Acharn Yen Boon, in the late sixties. (I told this to no one at all; Thais would not understand as it was beyond their Buddhist tradition, while Western

Buddhists in Thailand were very committed, sometimes much too seriously, to attaining the Paths and Fruits of Theravāda practice.) The Bodhisattva ideal, so much praised by Sangharakshita and exemplified by his practice thus persisted when I was immersed in Theravāda, and years later, when I came to Australia, caused me to include the Bodhisattva's Four Great Vows in the *Namo Chanting Book* issued by Wat Buddha Dhamma:

> *Though the many beings are numberless,*
> *I vow to save them.*
> *Though greed, hatred, and delusion rise endlessly,*
> *I vow to cut them off.*
> *Though the Dharma is vast and fathomless,*
> *I vow to understand it.*
> *Though the Buddha's Way is beyond attainment,*
> *I vow to embody it fully.*[98]

Returning now to the precepts received from Dhardo Rimpoche, a reading of them does rather confirm the impression that Bodhisattvas in India were expected also to be monks or nuns, though in theory aspiration to Buddhahood need not be confined to monastic Buddhists. What will a lay person do when he or she reads, 'It is a bad thing to give up the Prātimokṣa,' since this code of rules applies only to Buddhists leading a monk's or nun's life? On the whole, though, they apply to all Buddhists whatever their lifestyle.

Sangharakshita notes of his novice and monk ordinations that his teachers spent no time after these ceremonies explaining the meaning of the precepts,[99] though as a novice he had committed himself to a group of ten and as a monk to no fewer than the 227 Pāṭimokkha precepts.[100] Dhardo Rimpoche by contrast not only gave the Bodhisattva ordination but explained in detail its sixty-four precepts, which enabled Sangharakshita to make the translation. Not only that, for Sangharakshita maintained contact with Dhardo Rimpoche, frequently meeting him while he stayed in India and remaining in correspondence with him after he returned to Britain. In many ways, indeed, our Tibetan teacher exemplified the Bodhisattva ideal; as his biographer recalled, 'only two things interested him: to keep alive Tibetan culture, and to render assistance to the poor.'[101] He was determined that the traditions of the Buddha-Dharma preserved for centuries in Tibet should not disappear. They should continue to be propagated in the new and often unfavourable circumstances of India.

Dhardo Rimpoche also features briefly in Mr Chen's book, where a visit of his to the Five Leguminous Tree Hermitage is recorded. Mr Chen with an opened heart full of faith received him with the triple prostration, and weeping tears of joy made offerings to him. After this, Dhardo Rimpoche chanted a short puja in Mr Chen's shrine-room, and when this was completed partook of light refreshments. It was a joyful occasion, a meeting of two apparently very different Dharma practitioners who made profound heart contact with each other. Sangharakshita had arranged this brief visit – Rimpoche excused himself from staying too long as there was much to be done – and both Sangharakshita and I were impressed with the courtesy each paid the other. Thinking how wonderful it would be if such harmony and tolerance existed among Western practitioners of the Dharma, we returned to our Abode Where the Three Vehicles Flourish.

This mind – I hesitate to call it 'mine' because of its extraordinary ability on the one hand to retell the stories of my past, while on the other to remember nothing – also recalls a visit to Dudjom Rimpoche, who lived in a house on the outskirts of Kalimpong, about half an hour's walk from the vihara. He was at that time the foremost Nyingma teacher in Kalimpong. I have for years related that my first initiations into Vajrayāna Buddhist practice were from Dhardo Rimpoche, from whom I received Green Tārā and from Dudjom Rimpoche who gave me White Tārā. As we have seen, the first now lacks evidence, and when I scan my old puja book all that it contains from Dudjom is the 'Combined Method of the Brahmā-vihāras and Recollection of Buddhas', with no mention of White Tārā. All I can find is the formal studio photograph of Dudjom Rimpoche reproduced in this book. Still, there is some part of the mind that is certain that in Kalimpong I had both these initiations from these venerable teachers, evidence or not.

I suppose at that time conditions were not conducive to my practice of Vajrayāna: I knew no Tibetan, while good interpreters of Dharma teachings from that tongue into English were hard to find. In addition, the flood of books on Tibetan Buddhist practice that we now enjoy were then quite absent. Also, a factor to be considered was my bias towards Pāli Buddhism – not indeed the whole of Theravāda as this narrative has made clear – a bias which was connected with my strong interests in history. At school, history had been almost the only subject in which I took an interest, so it was natural that I became most interested in the teachings that emphasized the historical Buddha and what had been recorded as his teachings. First, then, I had to immerse myself in a Theravāda Buddhist country (Thailand 1962–73), all the while keeping in touch with Mahāyāna and Vajrayāna interests, as my extensive library in Bangkok of Mahāyāna books, as well as my ordination into the Chinese Bodhisattva precepts, shows. Though my Mahāyāna library grew hugely at Wat Buddha Dhamma, the Australian retreat centre at which I was the resident teacher outside Sydney, the seeds planted so long ago in Kalimpong by Sangharakshita and two or three Tibetan tulkus only germinated as practical interest in Dzogchen with my first retreat with Namkhai Norbu Rimpoche in Conway, Massachusetts, in 1990. However, that is another story.

But not quite. On another level both Sangharakshita and I sought something hardly to be found in India at that time, that is, a sangha. Of course, both of us, nominally, were members of the Theravāda sangha of monks, but according to the Vinaya the two of us did not count as a sangha, at least four bhikkhus being required. Neither did I find the sense of sangha in Bangalore where Buddharakkhita played the role of a dominating guru and we his disciples had to mind our p's and q's. Nor was there a sense of sangha at Wat Thai in Bodh Gaya, where I was definitely an outsider; nor, to my surprise, did I ever discover this sense of community in all my years in Thailand. There the monks I made friends with were a few from the West and India, and one from Tibet. It seemed as though I did not fit anywhere for I never found a *sangha of friends practising Dharma*. Perhaps this was partly due to the hierarchical nature of Asian Buddhist sanghas, or perhaps to the culture gap which, wide enough in Bangkok, became an immense gulf among the forest monks of north-east Thailand, most of whom were village boys with little or no education.

Mr Chen may have foreseen that all would not be so easy for me when I went to Thailand. The book records: 'On one of our last meetings, Mr Chen added another obstacle (to the obstacles of Mercy —misunderstood compassion, Propriety—limitations of precepts, Small-enlightenment—accomplishment, teaching too many too soon).' After some talk on the writer's intention of going to Thailand to practise meditation where, he thought, conditions were more favourable, our yogi exclaimed: 'There is another obstacle which we have not talked about – the Obstacle of Avoiding Obstacles....'

With the Dzogchen Community at last I have found a sense of sangha – but at the time with which this book is concerned, only with Sangharakshita could I say honestly that I had found a Dharma friend.

Sangharakshita, after surveying the Western Buddhist scene when he returned to Britain and discovering the lack of friendliness between monks there, founded a tradition flowing naturally from his Buddhist experience, the Western Buddhist Order, in which special emphasis is placed on noble friendship. Not only should there be respect and love between teachers and pupils, as indeed one finds generally in Asian sanghas, but fellow practitioners should cultivate the path of friendliness towards each other. This emphasis is very much in agreement with the Buddha's recorded words correcting his disciple Ānanda, who said that, 'Half the religious life is good friendship, good companionship, good comradeship', by the remark, 'Do not say so, Ānanda, The whole of the religious life is good friendship, good companionship, good comradeship.'[102]

This book has nearly reached its end, but before the conclusion I should like to relate one incident in Kalimpong which moved me profoundly. This took place on the lonely road from Kalimpong out to the vihara. Earlier in the day I had gone to town to see Mr Chen over some points that were unclear in my notes of his last chapter. By the time I left his hermitage it was early evening, with the sort of translucence of air that often characterized those foothills. I walked steadily and contemplatively until I came to a wider than normal terrace below me, in fact a small field, with extensive views of valleys and ranges. There, a group of Tibetan refugee monks, Kagyu I believe, had established a makeshift tent monastery and were struggling to maintain the shattered traditions of their practice. As I reached them two of the monks seated in one of the tents began to play a melody upon a *gyaling*, a Tibetan woodwind instrument. I stopped to listen. Then upon a convenient rock at the roadside I sat down. The ever-changing melody flowed on, the music singing, as it were, of impermanence – not sad at all but just as it was, just as it always is.[103] This is how I heard it, sitting with a completely tranquil heart, the impermanence, the music, flowing through me – though it was not 'I' that heard it. I do not know how long I sat there unmoving, perhaps twenty minutes or so, but I do know what a marvellous experience this was. When the musicians finished and I rose slowly. It was already twilight and it seemed that I floated back to the vihara.

The final scene, quite asynchronous in a book that is mainly chronological, is set fittingly at Triyāna Vardhana Vihāra. This occasion was Shaka Dawa,[104] the Buddha Śākyamuni's Awakening Day according to the Tibetan calendar, falling in 1962 on the full moon, 18 June. As I left

India in December of the same year, or even January of the next, we are now backtracking to present an interesting climax, a scene to round off these writings properly.

Readers will remember that I brought to Kalimpong from Bodh Gaya a bodhi tree sapling grown by the monks of Wat Thai. It remains to tell how this tree was planted. In fact the planting took place on Shaka Dawa as part of the celebrations. A short notice in the *Maha Bodhi Journal* (July 1962) records the day's events. At that time, besides Sangharakshita and myself, two other monks were in residence at the vihara, one being Thich Thien Chau of Vietnam who studied at the New Nālandā College, the other Pāsādiko, a German monk also of scholarly inclinations. The first important event of the day was the planting of the bodhi tree. Of this the *Maha Bodhi* says, 'About two feet high, the tree appears to be a combination of three seedlings (symbolizing well the union of the three *yānas*, or again, the inseparable nature of the Three Jewels).' Sangharakshita wielded the spade with the vigour necessary to make an impression on the poor stony soil while I firmed the roots, filling in the hole and getting my hands into the dirt as I always loved to do. Auspicious chanting in Pāli and Vietnamese accompanied this ceremony. Shortly afterwards I recorded that the tree was growing well, and Sangharakshita has informed me 'it was flourishing when someone sent me a photograph of it a few years ago, by which time it had attained a height of 25–30 feet, despite the poverty of the soil.'[105]

In the specially decorated shrine-room we then performed a puja. Besides the four monks, Richard Robinson – an American scholar specializing in Chinese Buddhist studies – was present with his wife. We chanted the praises of the Three Jewels as usual, adding some specially auspicious items such as the *Ratana Sutta*. The last item of the puja was not from the Pāli tradition; in fact it was in Sanskrit and repeated no fewer than twenty-one times. The repetition of the original text of the *Heart Sūtra* that number of times would have taken the best part of an hour. My diary notes, perhaps regretfully: '108 (times) would have taken about five hours!'[106] As a fitting conclusion my record in the *Maha Bodhi* states, 'the mantra (was) repeated rhythmically and softly, melting at the puja's end into the silence.'

Here, then, is the *Heart of Perfect Wisdom Sūtra*, not indeed in Sanskrit as we chanted it on that day but in an English translation of mine that I still use:

*Arya Avalokiteśvara Bodhisattva doing deep Prajñāpāramitā perceived the
essenceless emptiness of all five aggregates.*
O Śāriputra, form is no other than emptiness, emptiness no other than form;
Form is precisely emptiness, emptiness precisely form.
Whatever is form, that is emptiness – whatever emptiness, that is form;
Sensation, perception, formations, and consciousness are also like this.
O Śāriputra, all dharmas are marked by emptiness –
Not born, not destroyed, not stained, not pure, neither lacking, nor complete.
Therefore Śāriputra, in emptiness is no form,
No sensation, no perception, no formations, no consciousness,
No eye, no ear, no nose, no tongue, no body, and no mind,
No forms, or sounds, or smells, or tastes, or touch, or dharmas at all,
No realm of eyes, until we come to no mind-consciousness realm,
No ignorance and no extinction of ignorance, until we come to
No old age and death and no cessation of old age and death;
No suffering, no cause, no cessation and no path,
No wisdom, no attainment, and no non-attainment.
Therefore Śāriputra, caused by non-attainment
Bodhisattvas by relying on Prajñāpāramitā have no obscurations of mind.
With no mental obscurations they fear not,
They have righted what is inverted and instantly attain Nirvāṇa.
Awakened Ones of the three times all,
By relying on Prajñāpāramitā awaken
To Perfect Unsurpassed Awakening.
Therefore know the Prajñāpāramitā is
The greatest mantra, the mantra of insight
The supreme mantra, the incomparable mantra
Which allays all suffering – true this is and not deceptive.
Therefore set forth the Prajñāpāramitā mantra
Set forth this mantra and proclaim –

Gate gate pāragate pārasaṁgate bodhi svāhā
Gate gate pāragate pārasaṁgate bodhi svāhā
Gate gate pāragate pārasaṁgate bodhi svāhā
Gate gate pāragate pārasaṁgate bodhi svāhā
Gate gate pāragate pārasaṁgate bodhi svāhā
Gate gate pāragate pārasaṁgate bodhi svāhā
Gate gate pāragate pārasaṁgate bodhi svāhā
Gate gate pāragate pārasaṁgate bodhi svāhā
Gate gate pāragate pārasaṁgate bodhi svāhā
Gate gate pāragate pārasaṁgate bodhi svāhā

Afterword

While I was with Sangharakshita in Kalimpong there was part of my mind that would have liked to remain, but another aspect that wanted to experience a country in which the Dharma was established. So while I regretted leaving Sangharakshita I could not help also looking forward to a different Buddhist world which I hoped would offer me both learning and meditation practice. Still, I knew that my view of Thailand would always be coloured by the instructions and practices that I had received from Sangharakshita, particularly the Bodhisattva's aspiration. This meant that privately I should always be a rather deviant Theravādin! From Sangharakshita I was also inspired to cultivate my abilities in writing and teaching, though the latter would take a back seat during my eleven years in Thailand. Lastly, due to him my dedication to meditation retreats was strengthened.

Upon leaving Sangharakshita I was a very different person from the one who had landed in India three years earlier. Due to his kindness I was given opportunities to learn and to practise the Dharma in many situations. Though it is hard to measure maturity, I certainly felt much more confident when I left India, having learned so much. It was only two weeks after leaving Sangharakshita in Kalimpong that I found myself plunging into the very different Buddhist world of Bangkok. How odd it was for me may be gauged from the fact that Thailand then had only two other Western monks, one from America and the other my first teacher, Paññāvaddho. I kept in touch with Sangharakshita in the first few months and remember sending him a letter in which, rather over-enthusiastically, I invited him to come to Thailand and experience both the seats of Buddhist learning in Bangkok as well as the simplicities of forest monastic life. After our correspondence lapsed

I read frequently of Sangharakshita's doings in the *Maha Bodhi* and later in Western Buddhist journals.

In Thailand I remained as a monk for eleven years based at Wat Bovoranives Vihāra in central Bangkok, though I took many opportunities for longer and shorter retreats in forest monasteries, caves, and isolated jungle huts. Forest life appealed to me, though the rigours of one meal a day and the lack of communication were very difficult. I slowly learned the Thai language, but this was not of much use in the forest wats (monasteries) of the north-east where Laotian was spoken.

Return trips to Bangkok were often necessitated by physical problems, but I made good use of my time there, translating from Pāli as well as writing some books on the Dharma. Notable among these was *Buddhism Explained*, still in print after thirty years; a collection of Dharma discourses called *Pointing to Dhamma*, formally delivered in the great temple of Wat Bovoranives; as well as my only book of poetry, entitled *The Dharma Flavour*. Translations apart from Pāli include a collection of short works from many hands, much of it Mahāyāna in flavour published as *Wisdom Gone Beyond*, and a three-volume Vinaya (monastic discipline) treatise, *Vinayamukha*, written in Thai in the nineteenth century. I found time also for a two-volume Life of the Buddha compiled from existing sources in Pāli, Sanskrit, Chinese, and Tibetan as well as editing three volumes of Ven. Ñāṇamoli's translation of the *Middle Length Discourses of the Buddha* brought out in Bangkok with the title *A Treasury of the Buddha's Words*. Smaller works were composed for the Buddhist Publication Society in Sri Lanka, on, for instance, the forest monk's life, a monk's almsround, and the practice of Dharma for householders. From time to time I travelled out of Thailand – to Malaysia, Indonesia, Laos, Vietnam, Burma, and once returned briefly to India – for various Dharma practices and activities.

While in Bangkok I gradually became to my abbot and preceptor, Venerable Sāsana Sobhana, a sort of secretary dealing with Westerners, both those who wished to get ordained as monks as well as visitors to the Wat. Had I stayed there without seeking rural retreats from time to time there was no doubt that I should have become part of the Thai Buddhist hierarchy, but I did not fit well into this and felt uncomfortable with monastic titles and remuneration.

There was another sense in which I did not fit perfectly into Thai Theravāda. My library in Bangkok bore witness to my interest in Mahāyāna. This extended beyond books through my very good friend John Blofeld who had lived in the China of the 1920s and 1930s and become a devoted Buddhist who was fluent in Chinese. After I had told him about the Bodhisattva precepts I had received from Dhardo Rimpoche, he suggested I might like to take the corresponding precepts in the Chinese *Brahmajāla Sūtra* tradition. This I did from the Venerable Yen Boon with John Blofeld kindly translating.

In 1973, after a bout of illness, my preceptor suggested to me that a change of climate would be beneficial and that I could accompany a senior Thai monk to Sydney to establish a Thai Buddhist temple primarily for the benefit of Thai students but also for interested Australians. This became Wat Buddharangsee, quartered in a fantastic turreted Victorian house in the inner suburb of Stanmore. It was quite a noisy place with the roar of both road and air transport, and I longed to find a quieter place. This took some five years to mature, but meanwhile I travelled on invitation to all the state capital cities where there were Buddhist groups and helped to found the Buddhist Society in Western Australia, while my one-night visit to Darwin was a seed which soon became the Buddhist Society of the Northern Territory. Invitations came not only from capitals but also from Nimbin in northern New South Wales – which has been described as the alternative capital of Oz – where I gave the first Buddhist meditation retreats in Australia. I enjoyed working with the hippies – I found their openness refreshing and a great contrast to the stodgy unquestioning attitude of many Australians.

In 1975–6 I had a year away from Australia when I accepted Venerable Nyanaponika's invitation to help him at the Buddhist Publication Society in Kandy. My year with him was spent in the Udawattekele Forest and some of my work for the Buddhist Publication Society attests to my continued interest in the Mahāyāna, even in such a bastion of Theravāda thought and practice. 'Wheel' publications that I produced around this time are evidence: *Sixty Songs of Milarepa, A Vesak Offering* (from the *Mahāvastu*), *The Buddha's Last Words* (a sūtra from Chinese) and *The Wheel of Birth and Death* (based on original Indian Sanskrit texts, but preserved by Tibetan artistic traditions).

One of my Nimbin students was Ilse Ledermann, who became a Buddhist after hearing me speak on the Four Noble Truths. She and her husband, Gert, had an organic farm at Obi-Obi near Nambour in southern Queensland and she invited me to stay there on a few occasions. Eventually Ilse decided that she wanted to practise the Dharma but relinquish her marriage so the farm was put up for sale. During a Rains Retreat at Wat Buddharangsee where Ilse stayed, she

offered to look for a quiet place for Dharma practice. I agreed to help
with the search so we began to advertise and inspect various properties. Near the beginning of this search, the estate agent who was listing
her property in Obi-Obi told her that he had on his books a place we
ought to see. It was within two hours of Sydney, entered through a
national park on ten miles of dirt road, and consisted of 220 acres, only
thirty of which were cleared, and had two houses. The price was also
very attractive: $35,000 for the lot! It sounded too good to be true.
When we inspected it, we agreed that it was both beautiful and
secluded but we had doubts whether the dirt road, the National Park's
locked gates, and the distance, would deter any except the most
determined. As other properties could not rival this one, we eventually
decided that Ilse should purchase it. In this way Wat Buddha Dhamma
was born, the place where I stayed for the next fourteen years. A lay
community slowly developed and houses were built in 'the village',
while at the other end a meditation hall and huts for retreatants were
constructed in the bush. A few novice monks and nuns were ordained,
while other people were 'exported' to various Buddhist countries there
to take up monastic sangha life. Many came there to meditate on the
regular meditation courses while even greater numbers of Asian
Buddhists visited and made generous offerings for the construction
and maintenance of the place.

Besides some more book writing I had in those days an enormous
correspondence with people all over the world, though due to all the
other things to be accomplished, they often had to wait for replies. A
series of letters, the first in 1990, strung out over a few years, came from
Dammika, a Buddhist in Sri Lanka, asking at first if she could become
a nun. Later, almost in another life, I was to meet her....

Ilse Ledermann, a year or two after the Wat's foundation, decided
that she wanted to be a nun and was ordained as Ayya Khema in Sri
Lanka. She eventually took full ordination in the Chinese sangha. She
died in 1998, after an international career of Dharma teaching. Before
that, her rather incomplete autobiography was published.

Towards the end of my time in the Wat I had begun to write a
full-scale examination of the monks' and nuns' rules (*Vinaya*), a fairly
massive tome which was eventually called *Moss on the Stones*. The
writing of this began a period of questioning whether the Buddha
himself actually was the author of these rules, now more useful for
bondage than liberation. In general, I came to the conclusion that he
was not and that the presently organized sanghas of monks (and nuns

where they exist) were not his vision for his disciples' spiritual lives, but rather an organization imposed by those who later followed him.

This investigation progressed concurrently with an interest in the Dzogchen teachings of Chogyal Namkhai Norbu, and in 1990 I went with a group of others to a retreat organized by his followers in Massachusetts. I went 'in mufti', not wearing the monk's robes but still recognizing myself as a monk. This retreat, a marvellous experience led by Namkhai Norbu Rimpoche, convinced me that I should practise the Dharma without a shaven head and special robes. It followed naturally that after a Yantra Yoga retreat (a Dzogchen form of yoga from Tibet) at Wat Buddha Dhamma in 1991, I decided to stop wearing robes and to write to my preceptor in Bangkok informing him that I was no longer a monk, as well asking for his blessing.

While I received many dozens of letters supporting my decision (and none opposing it), in the next few months there was some conflict with the trustees of the Wat which led me to conclude that I should no longer live at Wat Buddha Dhamma. Fortunately, I was most kindly offered hospitality by two Dzogchen practitioners in the Blue Mountains. Had it not been for their kindness I should have found it very difficult indeed to adjust to ordinary daily life.

After some months with them I moved to northern New South Wales and eventually found a house on the extensive property of Vajradhara Gompa outside Kyogle, a small country town. I lived there until I was able, in 1993, to visit my brother and his wife in Britain. During this visit I was able to meet one afternoon with Sangharakshita – after such a long time. Over a cup of tea we discussed many activities and exchanged much Dharma news.

When I had decided to visit my brother it also occurred to me to meet my so-far-unseen friend, Dammika, in Sri Lanka, with whom I had corresponded in my 'last life' as a monk. During the last year or so of our correspondence our letters had become less formal as she enquired about the reasons for my change of life and also showed an interest in Dzogchen. When at last I met her in Kandy I found the kalyāṇa mitra (noble friend) it seemed I had known in many lives, we related together so well that we got married and until the present time work together for the Dharma. This has culminated in the establishment in Cairns, a tropical city in north Queensland, of Bodhi Citta Buddhist Centre, a non-sectarian organization. As part of our programme we invite guest teachers who help to revolve the Wheel of Dharma in

Cairns. The most important of these so far has been Chogyal Namkhai Norbu who stayed here and taught Dzogchen in January 2000.

At present, Bodhi Citta Buddhist Centre does not have its own premises and though now accommodated in a spacious house high in the hills overlooking the northern suburbs and beaches, Trinity Inlet, and the distant Yarrabah Mountains, to continue its Dharma work it will need its own land and buildings. This will happen if causes and conditions are auspicious. In any case, there are still countless beings in the suffering wheel of birth and death with karmic affinities to the Dharma. May they all experience the three happinesses through its practice.

Sarva maṅgalaṁ

May all be auspicious!

NOTES AND REFERENCES

1 *Aṅguttara-Nikāya* v.57

2 There was of course the Pali Text Society, founded in 1881 to publish texts in roman script and English translations of the Pāli Tipiṭaka, but the officers of this learned society often were not Buddhist and did not espouse practice of the Dharma.

3 For more on Going for Refuge see, for example, Sangharakshita, *Going for Refuge*, Windhorse, Birmingham 1997.

4 Nālandā was destroyed by Muslim invaders in the 1230s CE. At the height of its influence it had a thousand teachers, mostly Buddhist monks, and ten times as many students. Some of its 'skyscrapers' towered thirteen stories and were capped by golden roofs. Teachers and pupils were put to the sword, and its library of Buddhist texts, torched by the invading barbarians, burned for three months.

5 A footnote seems required on the words 'Theravāda' (the Elders' Way) and 'Mahāyāna' (the Great Vehicle), often thought of as two rather conflicting versions of the Buddha's teachings. Theravāda, the kind of Buddhism found today in Sri Lanka, Burma, Thailand, Laos, and Cambodia, with outlying populations in Bangladesh, Vietnam, and southern China, proclaims itself the true word of the Buddha and criticizes others who recorded his message differently. Mahāyāna Buddhism, at present established in Nepal, Tibet, Bhutan, Mongolia, China, Vietnam, Korea, Japan, and Taiwan, acknowledges the traditions of Theravāda (which it knows as a species of Hīnayāna – the Lesser Vehicle) as well as possessing a vast body of its own scriptures and traditions. Conflict between these two is more apparent than real, though there is still a good deal of ignorance of those 'other Buddhists'. Fortunately, all Buddhists have been better at debates than wars! And practice of the Dharma is surprisingly similar in all traditions, though polemics would seem to place them far

apart. There is also Vajrayāna, the Adamantine Vehicle, based upon the Buddhist tantras which contain many meditation practices. These two or three vehicles are combined in, respectively, Chinese and Tibetan cultures.

6 Lama (*blama* in Tibetan); in Sanskrit, *ācārya*, a teacher. This title should not be used for the generality of monks, who were not qualified to teach.

7 Throughout this book I have called Sangharakshita by his Dharma name. As a junior monk I never addressed him thus, nor referred to him in this way. I always addressed him using the polite word 'Bhante' which means something like 'O Fortunate One'.

8 Sangharakshita, used to the ascetic simplicities of his Kalimpong vihara, remarked that he found the Thai monks' beds 'high and very wide', a fact that shocked him as he understood that monks in that country 'were strict observers of the Vinaya'. My later sojourn in Thailand found a few monks who strictly observed – a great number who were relaxed about – the Vinaya rules without committing any gross infractions, and a very small minority who fell down badly.

9 Aśoka reigned c.273–236 BCE.

10 See the story behind the establishment of the Vinaya rule forbidding the consumption of alcohol by monks and nuns, *pacittiya* 51, in the Vinaya translation, *Book of the Discipline*, part 2, pp.382f.

11 In Sanskrit, *ṛṣi*.

12 *Satthā-devamanussānaṁ.*

13 The best source for the life of Anagārika Dharmapāla, a great reviver of the Dharma both in Ceylon and in India, is Sangharakshita's 100-page sketch published by the Buddhist Publication Society, Kandy, Sri Lanka, as numbers 70–2 in the Wheel series, which is still in print. It has also been reprinted and enlarged as *Flame in Darkness*, Triratna Grantha Mala, Pune 1980.

14 For Ambedkar's life in detail see *Ambedkar and Buddhism*, Sangharakshita, Windhorse 1986, and for the conversion of his followers see in addition, Terry Pilchick, *Jai Bhim! Dispatches from a Peaceful Revolution*; Padmasuri, *But Little Dust: Life among the ex-Untouchable Buddhists of India*; and Sangharakshita's own account, *In the Sign of the Golden Wheel: Indian Memoirs of an English Buddhist*, all from Windhorse.

15 *Sanātana*: eternal, without beginning.

16 The Buddha's teachings/path/practice (Dharma), or the Buddha's Dispensation, including the ways in which it has been organized (*sāsana*).

17 *Brāhmaṇa, kṣatriya, vaiśya*, and *śūdra*.

18 'Dharma' is used here with a meaning significantly different from Buddhist usage. Hindus use it to mean 'caste duty'. The *Bhagavad Gītā*, a rather late Hindu scripture, centres upon a dialogue between the god Krishna and his charioteer Arjuna. The former advises the latter to fight as it is his royal 'dharma' to do, while the latter is reluctant to do so, reluctant to shed blood. The god's arguments are not convincing.

19 It is noteworthy that the doctrine of accumulating merit or *puṇya* – beneficial karma such as generosity, keeping the precepts, and cultivating the mind – would have been particularly attractive to the merchant caste. While the Buddha's discourses do contain the seeds of this doctrine, later Buddhist stories such as the Avadāna collections elaborate upon this theme.

20 More recently transliterated as Pune (pronounced Poona).

21 The four *brahma-vihāras* (Divine Abidings) are loving-kindness (*mettā*), compassion (*karuṇā*), joy at others' happiness (*muditā*), and equanimity (*upekkhā*).

22 The Vinaya. Though translated as 'discipline', this means literally 'what leads one out of suffering'.

23 *Dharmapālas* are powerful, non-human beings, converted to the Dharma by the Buddha and later Buddhist teachers, who made a vow to protect the Dharma and its practitioners. Of course, if these practitioners no longer practised correctly there was little the dharmapālas could do.

24 An account of this was written several years ago but never published.

25 Soka Gakkai (Nichiren Shoshu) could be cited as an example of a large fringe Buddhist group that formerly used forceful persuasion (*shaku-buku*) to induce Japanese to become members.

26 There are various forms in Pāli tradition for requesting the Refuges and Precepts, but all of them translate something like 'We/I request the Three Refuges together with the Five Precepts (from you).' Note also the verse in Pāli used in Thailand to request Dhamma teaching:

> The Brahma-god Sahampati, director of the worlds,
> Having hands in reverence, begged a very boon:
> 'Here there are beings, little dust in their eyes –
> From out of your compassion, pray teach the Dharma now.'

27 In most parts of northern India, people greet each other by saying 'namaste' and bowing with their palms together in front of the heart.

28 Now that I come to think about it, I cannot explain why these Mahar villagers were on good terms with their high-caste Maratha neighbours. Perhaps this was explained to me at the time.

29 *Dhammapada* verses 129–30, my translation, published in *Jewels within the Heart (Dhammapada)*, Silkworm Books, Chiang Mai, Thailand 1999.

30 *Lobha, dveṣa/dosa, moha.*

31 Accounts in the *Maha Bodhi Journal* show that Sangharakshita was accompanied by Vivekānanda and conducted numerous conversion ceremonies in Maharashtra in which no fewer than 25,000 people became Buddhists. He also addressed educated audiences in Poona before returning to Kalimpong on 19 May, having been away for more than seven months.

32 *Svetambara* ('white-clad') sect monks and nuns wear white cloth while *Digambara* monks – there are no nuns – are naked. *Digambara* literally means 'sky-clad'. These are the two most ancient Jain sects.

33 *Lābhasakkāra Saṁyutta, Saṁyutta-Nikāya* 17. This is a whole chapter of short suttas on the dangers of gains, honour, and fame.

34 Buddhadasa Bhikkhu, *Teaching Dhamma by Pictures*, Social Science Association Press of Thailand, Bangkok BE 2511/1968, pp.46–7. The picture shows three armed monks attacking the Buddha, but only one layman.

35 *The Rainbow Road*, Windhorse, Birmingham 1997.

36 I find, from my records, that I arrived in Bangalore on 20 April 1961.

37 'Kamalāñjali' was published in *Sangīti*, a slender volume of miscellaneous articles commemorating the Sixth Buddhist Council, in Burma in 1956.

38 The *Saṅgāyanas*, literally 'Chantings Together', are usually referred to as the Buddhist Councils.

39 *Vibhajjavāda*: 'The Way of Analysis', an alternative name for Theravāda, though other Buddhist sects also taught in this way.

40 The *khandhas* are the five 'aggregates': form, sensation, perception, formations, and consciousness.

41 This is examined in detail in my 'Moss on the Stones: Discipline for Buddhist monks and nuns', unpublished at the time of writing.

42 The *Maha Bodhi Journal* informs its readers that I received the *upasampadā* on 13 July. I prefer the evidence of my ordination booklet. This seems to be a minor case of the confusion of dates that bedevils Indian Buddhist history!

43 Known in Thai as Phra Phimontham. For more about Vimaladhamma, see Kamala Tiyanavich, *Forest Recollections*, ch.9, especially pages 226–31.

44 See Bernard Wasserstein, *The Secret Lives of Trebitsch Lincoln*, Penguin 1989. One of Lincoln's 'manifestations' was as the Buddhist monk Chao Kung

from May 1931 until his mysterious death in Shanghai in 1943. Tao Lo's photograph as a young woman appears in this book.

45 For example, a monk undertakes not to carry goat's wool for more than three leagues and should he do so the penalty of expiation (confession) with forfeiture falls upon him. The remote possibility of a monk today being given a load of goat's wool to tote through the streets of Sydney, London, or Bombay should raise a smile if not a laugh. This is *nissaggiya-pācittiya* 16, one of the 'principal training-rules in the pure life' (*ādi-brahmacārikāsikkhā*).

46 Though such punishment is meted out to young offenders in the Asian monasteries of many Buddhist traditions, it cannot be justified by referring to the Buddha's teaching.

47 *Udāna* 5.2.

48 The *Mettā Sutta, Sutta-Nipāta* 143–52. This is very frequently chanted by Buddhists.

49 *Dhammadāyāda Sutta, Majjhima-Nikāya* 3.

50 *Ratana Sutta, Sutta-Nipāta* 229.

51 The three vehicles for the journey to Awakening are the Small Vehicle (Hīnayāna), the Great Vehicle (Mahāyāna) and the Adamantine Vehicle (Vajrayāna). These may also be understood as persons or states of mind.

52 The *brahma-vihāras* or 'Divine Abidings' are loving-kindness, compassion, joy at others' happiness, and equanimity. *Buddhanussati* means recollection of the Buddha.

53 These three occur in Pāli commentaries: *pariyatti, patipatti, pativedha*.

54 This Buddha image later survived the journey from India, where it had been cared for by Dhardo Rimpoche after Sangharakshita left Kalimpong, to Britain where it now inspires people at Padmaloka, the Friends of the Western Buddhist Order's retreat centre in Norfolk.

55 A wooden fish is a Chinese Buddhist percussion instrument, made from a hollowed-out log with a longitudinal slit, which is struck with a padded drumstick.

56 These were *Dhammapada* verses 277–9, 183–5, 188–92, 194, 197–200, and 296–302.

57 Literally, 'Lesser and minor training rules', *Khuddakānukhuddaka sikkhāpada*. See F. S. Vajira, *Last Days of the Buddha*, Buddhist Publication Society, Kandy 1998, p.84, where the Buddha allowed their abrogation.

58 *Kālāma Sutta, Aṅguttara-Nikāya* iii.65. The famous passage from this short discourse reads: 'Enough of your doubt, enough of your uncertainty,

Kālāmas. In a doubtful matter uncertainty does arise, (therefore) do not (believe merely) by traditional religion, nor by spiritual lineage, nor by legendary historical law, nor by collections of scriptures, nor because of logic and reason, nor because of philosophical standpoint, nor by reasoned reflection, nor because of delight in speculation, nor by a teacher's personal competence, nor by devotion to our guru – but when you know for yourselves: "these dharmas (doctrines, practices) are unwholesome and blameworthy, censured by the wise, undertaken and practised they lead to harm and suffering," then you should renounce them.'

59 *Tattvasaṁgraha* 3588:

> *Tapāc chedāc ca nikaṣāt*
> *suvarnam iva paṇḍitaiḥ*
> *Parīksya bhikṣavo grahyam*
> *madvaco na tu gauravat.*

60 'Guru' means, literally, one who is 'weighty', whose words carry weight.

61 This is verse 3 of the *Poṭṭhapāda Sutta, Dīgha-Nikāya* 9. The list is repeated in several other Pāli suttas.

62 *Dukkha*: the existential suffering of the body and mind of a separate being who conceives of itself as 'I am'.

63 For example, *Kevaddha Sutta, Dīgha-Nikāya* 11, and the *Brahmanimantanika Sutta, Majjhima-Nikāya* 49.

64 From a Buddhist tirade in verse directed against the Vedas, brahmins, and their sacrifices including the *homa*, on which more below. See *Bhūridatta Jātaka* no.543. Probably I quoted the old translation in Jātaka Stories vol.6, which is rhymed and easy to learn. It is, however, a paraphrase rather than a translation. The rendering given here is mine. In these verses, 'unjust', 'unrighteous', and 'wrong' all translate *adhamma*, literally, 'what is not the Dharma'.

65 Sanskrit *aṣṭa* or eight (the seven traditional 'planets', including sun and moon, plus the 'south node' of the moon). *Gṛha* means house or zodiacal sign.

66 *Jātaka* 49. The whole verse reads in my translation:

> *Wasting time with constellations*
> *Fortune passes the fool,*
> *Fortune itself the constellation;*
> *What indeed will the stars do?*

67 For Sangharakshita's account of this journey see *The Rainbow Road*, pp.413ff, Windhorse, Birmingham 1997.

68 Wesak, Vesak, Visākha, and Vaiśākha are all variant spellings of this festival, named after the astrological sign within which the full moon falls on that lunar month. We shall use Wesak throughout.

69 Untraced at time of publication.

70 *Whatever events arising from causes,*
The Tathāgata has told the cause of them,
And of their cessation too,
The Great Monk teaches thus.
(*Vinaya, Mahāvagga* i.23.)

71 Verses 3, 5, & 6. This is my translation, or rather paraphrase, made while I was in Thailand. The verses are anonymous and were perhaps composed in Sri Lanka.

72 'Homeless one', a term used in Nepal to refer to nuns.

73 *Prasad:* Food and other offerings to the Buddhas, Bodhisattvas, and gods, which after puja is returned to devotees, a custom shared by Buddhists and Hindus.

74 The name could be translated as 'The Great Abode of the Adamantine Relic Stupa of Meritorious Fame'.

75 'The Great Abode of Golden Hue.'

76 Fire sacrifice rituals.

77 *Pradakṣiṇa:* literally, 'keeping the right side towards', a traditional way of showing respect still practised in all Buddhist traditions.

78 'The Great Abode of Awakening's Temple.'

79 It certainly outlasted the bowl, which rusted through in Bangkok where perhaps that lid still survives.

80 Published privately in Thailand, and later by Mahamakut Press in a collection of poems, *The Dharma Flavour,* 2508/1965 and 2512/1969.

81 Roshi Philip Kapleau, *Zen: Dawn in the West,* Rider, London 1987, pp.182–3.

82 It did receive a short though glowing review in the pages of *The Middle Way,* journal of the Buddhist Society (in London), volume 39, no.1, May 1964, which ended with the words, 'This is a wonderful book which will inspire anyone who reads it with the Dhamma of tolerance.'

83 At this time Sangharakshita was writing articles on Buddhism for the *Oriya Encyclopædia,* which were eventually revised and published as *The Three Jewels* and *The Eternal Legacy.*

84 I assume that this date, if not a printing error, is a traditional Chinese or Tibetan calculation of the Buddhist Era. According to Theravāda tradition,

1962 would have been be BE2505 or thereabouts, but Western scholars, disputing the accuracy of the Sinhalese computation of time in the *Mahāvaṁsa*, the Great Chronicle of Sri Lanka, prefer a date for the Great Final Nirvāṇa of the Buddha about sixty years closer to the Common Era.

85 *Buddhist Meditation: Systematic and Practical*, was reprinted in America after Yogi Chen moved there. Free copies are available from Dr Yutang Lin, 705 Midcrest Way, El Cerrito, CA94530, USA. Some of the text is available at www. yogichen.org

86 *Dhammapada* 200:

> *We for whom there's nought*
> *Live indeed so happily,*
> *Feeders on joy we'll be*
> *Like resplendent gods.*

87 *Śruta-mayī-prajñā* and *cinta-mayī-prajñā*.

88 *Yab-yum* (Tibetan): literally 'father-mother', deities shown in sexual embrace, the mother representing wisdom (*prajñā*) and the father *upāya* or skilful means, which includes compassion (*karuṇā*).

89 *Dhammapada* 134.

90 *Dhammapada* 1.

91 I have not found the source of this quotation, though it appears in all editions of my *Buddhism Explained*.

92 *Bosat* is a Sinhalese contraction of Bodhisattva.

93 The word *dhīḥ* in Pāli and Sanskrit actually means 'wisdom', while the syllables following *oṁ* are the first five of a syllabary derived from the Buddhist tantras. With its distinctive Indic script it is still much employed in China for magical and protective matters.

94 This calculation depends on the history contained in the *Mahāvaṁsa*, the Great Epic of Sri Lanka. There is good reason to suppose that somewhere in its account sixty years have crept in so that instead of calculating the Buddhist era by adding 543 to CE we should add 483. This would give us the (approximate) date of the Buddha's Final Nirvāṇa. 2002 would therefore be BE 2485 and the 2,500 years celebrations have yet to come!

95 Suvajra, *The Wheel and the Diamond: The Life of Dhardo Tulku*, Windhorse, Glasgow 1991.

96 Sangharakshita, *The History of My Going for Refuge*, Windhorse, Glasgow 1988, pp.71–2.

97 Personal correspondence.

98 Translated from the Japanese by Robert Aitken Roshi.

99 The breaking of any of the first five of the novices' Ten Precepts by deliberately killing, taking what is not given, sexual contact, false speech, or the taking of intoxicants to confuse the mind, are generally reckoned to be reasons for disrobing a novice. Four of the 227 when broken entail the expulsion of a monk from the Sangha. These Four Defeats have been mentioned previously (p.159).

100 *The History of My Going for Refuge*, p.72.

101 *The Wheel and the Diamond*, p.123.

102 *Saṁyutta-Nikāya* v.2.

103 I have since heard this piece, played on the same instruments, on a CD together with a number of other Tibetan pieces. I recognized it at once.

104 Shaka Dawa is the Tibetan equivalent of the main event celebrated at Wesak, the Perfect Unsurpassed Awakening. Theravāda traditions add Prince Siddhartha's birth and the Great Final Nirvāṇa, though Mahāyāna traditions celebrate each of these on separate days.

105 Personal communication.

106 Sangharakshita did in fact suggest to me that at some time we did chant it 108 times, though neither he nor I have any clear recollection of doing so.

Further Reading

Chen, C.M. *Buddhist Meditation – Systematic and Practical*, published privately. See Note 85, p.180

Khantipālo, *Jewels Within the Heart (Dhammapada)*, Silkworm Books, Chiang Mai, Thailand 1999

Padmasuri, *But Little Dust: Life among the ex-Untouchable Buddhists of India*, Windhorse, Birmingham 1997

Terry Pilchick, *Jai Bhim! Dispatches from a Peaceful Revolution*, Windhorse, Glasgow 1988

Sangharakshita, *Facing Mount Kanchenjunga*, Windhorse, Glasgow 1991

Sangharakshita, *The History of My Going for Refuge*, Windhorse, Glasgow 1988

Sangharakshita, *In the Sign of the Golden Wheel*, Windhorse, Birmingham 1996

Sangharakshita, *The Rainbow Road*, Windhorse, Birmingham 1997

Suvajra, *The Wheel and the Diamond: The Life of Dhardo Tulku*, Windhorse, Glasgow 1991

INDEX

The windhorse symbolizes the energy of the Enlightened mind carrying the truth of the Buddha's teachings to all corners of the world. On its back the windhorse bears three jewels: a brilliant gold jewel represents the Buddha, the ideal of Enlightenment, a sparkling blue jewel represents the teachings of the Buddha, the Dharma, and a glowing red jewel, the community of the Buddha's enlightened followers, the Sangha. Windhorse Publications, through the medium of books, similarly takes these three jewels out to the world.

Windhorse Publications is a Buddhist publishing house, staffed by practising Buddhists. We place great emphasis on producing books of high quality, accessible and relevant to those interested in Buddhism at whatever level. Drawing on the whole range of the Buddhist tradition, Windhorse books include translations of traditional texts, commentaries, books that make links with Western culture and ways of life, biographies of Buddhists, and manuals on meditation.

As a charitable institution we welcome donations to help us continue our work. We also welcome manuscripts on aspects of Buddhism or meditation. For orders and catalogues contact

WINDHORSE PUBLICATIONS	WINDHORSE BOOKS	WEATHERHILL INC
11 PARK ROAD	P O BOX 574	41 MONROE TURNPIKE
BIRMINGHAM	NEWTOWN	TRUMBULL
B13 8AB	NSW 2042	CT 06611
UK	AUSTRALIA	USA

Windhorse Publications is an arm of the Friends of the Western Buddhist Order, which has more than sixty centres on five continents. Through these centres, members of the Western Buddhist Order offer regular programmes of events for the general public and for more experienced students. These include meditation classes, public talks, study on Buddhist themes and texts, and 'bodywork' classes such as t'ai chi, yoga, and massage. The FWBO also runs several retreat centres and the Karuna Trust, a fund-raising charity that supports social welfare projects in the slums and villages of India.

Many FWBO centres have residential spiritual communities and ethical businesses associated with them. Arts activities are encouraged too, as is the development of strong bonds of friendship between people who share the same ideals. In this way the FWBO is developing a unique approach to Buddhism, not simply as a set of techniques, less still as an exotic cultural interest, but as a creatively directed way of life for people living in the modern world.

If you would like more information about the FWBO visit the website at www.fwbo.org or write to

LONDON BUDDHIST CENTRE
51 ROMAN ROAD
LONDON
E2 OHU
UK

ARYALOKA
HEARTWOOD CIRCLE
NEWMARKET
NEW HAMPSHIRE
NH 03857
USA

ALSO FROM WINDHORSE

SANGHARAKSHITA

AMBEDKAR AND BUDDHISM

The remarkable and stirring story of Dr Bhimrao Ramji Ambedkar, lawyer, politician, and educationalist, who, in 1956, started the most important social revolution occurring in India today: the conversion from Hinduism to Buddhism of millions of Indians wishing to escape the degradation of the caste system.

Sangharakshita knew Ambedkar personally, and has himself played an important part in the 'Mass Conversion Movement' that Ambedkar set in motion. In this book he explores the historical, religious, and social background to that movement, and assesses the considerable contribution made by Ambedkar to the spiritual tradition in which he placed his trust.

192 pages
ISBN 0 904766 28 4
£7.99/$15.95

TERRY PILCHICK (NAGABODHI)

JAI BHIM!
DISPATCHES FROM A PEACEFUL REVOLUTION

In the 1940s and 50s, Bhimrao Ramji Ambedkar – champion of India's 60 million 'Untouchables' – could have launched a violent struggle for freedom. Instead he asked his people to find dignity, strength, and prosperity by converting to Buddhism.

There are now millions of new Buddhists in India; they still meet and part with the words, 'Jai Bhim!' – 'Victory to Bhimrao Ambedkar'.

Travelling around the Buddhist localities, meeting and living with Ambedkar's modern followers, Terry Pilchick gained an intimate impression of the unique revolution they are building. In a colourful, moving account, he allows us to witness the revolution for ourselves.

256 pages
ISBN 0 904766 36 5
£5.95

SARA HAGEL (EDITOR)

DHARDO RIMPOCHE: A CELEBRATION

This book is a celebration of the life and work of Dhardo Rimpoche, one of
Sangharakshita's main teachers.

Dhardo Rimpoche was revered in his own lifetime as a living Bodhisattva. These
reminiscences from his disciples in the East, and his adopted disciples in the West,
reveal again and again his perfection of the qualities of selflessness, generosity,
kindness, and mindfulness.

128 pages with black & white photos
ISBN 1 899579 26 5
£9.99/$19.95

SANGHARAKSHITA

THE RAINBOW ROAD:
FROM TOOTING BROADWAY TO KALIMPONG
MEMOIRS OF AN ENGLISH BUDDHIST

At the age of sixteen, Dennis Lingwood discovered that he was – and always had
been – a Buddhist. This realization was to act as the motive force behind a life in
which Lingwood, now better known as Sangharakshita, has played a major part in
the introduction of Buddhism to the West.

The Rainbow Road traces Sangharakshita's development from a childhood
characterized by his insatiable appetite for books to his homeless wandering across
India and eventual ordination as a Buddhist monk. It takes us from the streets of
wartime London to the dusty villages, ashrams, and mountain caves of India. Full of
fascinating characters and keen insights, *The Rainbow Road* is as finely observed – and
as entertaining – as a first-rate travel book. More than that, it is a remarkable and
refreshingly candid record of a journey of spiritual exploration.

496 pages, with photographs
ISBN 0 904766 94 2
£16.99/$33.95

SANGHARAKSHITA

FACING MOUNT KANCHENJUNGA:
AN ENGLISH BUDDHIST IN THE EASTERN HIMALAYAS

In 1950 Kalimpong was a lively trading town where India runs into Nepal, Bhutan, Sikkim, and Tibet. Like a magnet, it attracted a bewildering array of guests and settlers: ex-colonials, Christian missionaries, princes in exile, pioneer Buddhologists, incarnate lamas from the Land of Snows – and Sangharakshita, the young English monk who was trying to establish a Buddhist movement for local youngsters.

In a delightful volume of memoirs, glowing with affection and humour, the author shares the incidents, encounters, and insights of his early years in Kalimpong.

Behind the events we witness the transformation of a rather eccentric young man into a unique and confident individual, completely at home in his adopted world, and increasingly effective as an interpreter of Buddhism for a new age.

512 pages, with photographs
ISBN 0 904766 52 7
£13.99/$27.95

SANGHARAKSHITA

IN THE SIGN OF THE GOLDEN WHEEL:
INDIAN MEMOIRS OF AN ENGLISH BUDDHIST

This engaging volume of memoirs recounts the unique experiences of an English Buddhist monk working in the mid-1950s to revive Buddhism in the land of its birth.

We follow Sangharakshita in his quest – from his hermitage in Kalimpong in the Himalayas to collaboration with a film star in Bombay, a visit from the Dalai Lama, and involvement in the spectacular festivals to celebrate 2,500 years of Buddhism.

Brimming with life and colour, this book is a notable addition to the canon of travel literature as we follow the spiritual adventures of an unorthodox and extraordinary Englishman.

384 pages, with photographs
ISBN 1 899579 14 1
£14.99/$29.95